# EDUCATION IN ANCIENT INDIA

# EDUCATION
# IN ANCIENT INDIA

A.S. ALTEKAR

Education in Ancient India



ISBN:978-81-8205-518-6



Reprinted 2014 in India by
Isha Books
B-69, New Gupta Colony
Near DDA Market
Delhi-110009
First Published in 1934

*Printed at*: Chawla Offset, Delhi

TO

PANDIT

MADAN MOHAN MALAVIYA

THE FOUNDER AND MAKER

OF

THE BENARES HINDU UNIVERSITY

WITH

REVERENCE AND AFFECTION

## CONTENTS

# PREFACE

In the following pages an attempt has been made to give an authentic, impartial and realistic picture of Education in Ancient India, its theories and ideals, rituals and institutions, courses and curricula and merits and defects. The account is based upon a first-hand study of all the material available,—religious books, literary works, epigraphical evidence, sculptural and archæological data, and accounts of foreign travellers and historians. Evidence from these diverse sources has been properly evaluated, no partiality being shown or undue importance being attached to any one of them. Every care has been taken to check and verify the conclusions based on the data from one of the above sources by considering what other sources have to say on the points concerned. References to original sources have been given in all cases, and original passages also have been quoted in the more important ones. This, it is hoped, will facilitate further independent enquiry on the part of the reader.

Ancient India covers a period of more than 2,000 years and educational methods, ideals and institutions could not remain unchanged through this long period. In this book the reader will find an effort made to show how changed ideals and circumstances were affecting the growth and evolution of education from age to age. Unfortunately it was not possible to do this in every case owing to the scantiness of the material available for the purpose. The book traces the history of Education in India upto about 1200 A. D. In many places, however, a brief account has been given of the state of affairs down to the advent of the British rule. Wherever possible, a comparison is sought to be made with the state of affairs prevailing in the West to enable the reader to get a proper perspective in the matter.

The book seeks to give a succinct yet comprehensive account of all the aspects of education in Ancient India. No important item or aspect has been left out. The subject matter is presented in a way which should be attractive both to the research student and the general reader. If the former thinks that the book throws considerable new light on several important points, and the latter finds that it gives a readable and realistic account of the Educational System in Ancient India, the author will feel amply compensated for his labour of love.

Benares Hindu University, A. S. ALTEKAR.
1-1-1934.

## ABBREVIATIONS AND TRANSLITERATION.

### ABBREVIATIONS.

| | |
|---|---|
| A. D. S. | Āpastamba Dharma Sūtra |
| A. G. S. | Āpastamba Gṛihya Sūtra |
| Ait. Ar. | Aitareya Āraṇyaka |
| Alberuni, | Sachau, Alberuni's India |
| Ap. Dh. S. | Āpastamba Dharma Sūtra |
| As. Gr. S. | Aśvalāyana Gṛihya Sūtra |
| A. S. R. | Archæological Survey of India, Annual Reports, New Series. |
| A. S. W. I. | Archæological Survey of Western India Reports |
| A. V. | Atharvaveda |
| Bau. D. S. | Baudhāyana Dharma Sūtra |
| Bau. Gr. S. | Baudhāyana Gṛihya Sūtra |
| Beal, Life. | Life of Hiuen Tsiang |
| Bh. Gr. S. | Bhāradvāja Gṛihya Sūtra |
| Br. Up. | Bṛihadāraṇyaka Upanishad |
| Ch. Up. | Chhāndogya Upanishad |
| Dr. Gr. S. | Drāhyāyaṇa Gṛihya Sūtra |
| E. C. | Epigraphia Carnatica |
| E. I. | Epigraphia Indica |
| Elliot, History | Elliot's History of India, as told by its historians, Vols. 1—2, London 1870. |
| Geschichte. | Geschichte der Indischen Literttur by Winternitz |

| | |
|---|---|
| Go. Br. | Gopatha Brāhmaṇa |
| Go. Gr. S. | Gobhila Gṛihya Sūtra |
| Gr. S. | Gṛihya Sūtra |
| Hi. Gr. S. | Hiraṇyakeśi Gṛihya Sūtra |
| I. A. | Indian Antiquary |
| I. M. P. | Inscriptions from Madras Presidency |
| I-tsing | Record of the Western World by I-tsing, edited by Takakusu |
| J. A. S. B. | Journal of the Asiatic Society of Bengal |
| J. B. B. R. A. S. | Journal of the Bombay Branch of the Royal Asiatic Society |
| J. B. O. R. S. | Journal of the Bihar and Orissa Research Society |
| Jai. Gr. S. | Jaimini Gṛihya Sūtra |
| Jai. Up. Br. | Jaimini Upanishad Brāhmaṇa |
| Kh. Gr. S. | Khādira Gṛihya Sūtra |
| Kū. P. | Kūrma Purāṇa |
| K. S. | Kāṭhaka Saṁhitā |
| K. Up. | Kaṭhopanishad |
| Mā. Gr. S. | Mānava Gṛihya Sūtra |
| M. A. S. I. | Memoirs of the Archæological Survery of India |
| MBH. | Mahābhārata |
| Mil. Pan. | Milinda Pañha |
| M. N. | Majjhima Nikāya |
| M. S. | Maitrayaṇīya Saṁhitā |
| Mu. Up. | Muṇḍakopanishad |
| Pā. Gr. S. | Pāraskara Gṛihya Sūtra |

| | |
|---|---|
| Par. Mā. | Mādhava's commentary on Parāśara Smṛiti |
| Pr. Up. | Praśnopanishad |
| R. V. | Ṛigveda |
| Sachau, | Alberuni's India, edited by Sachau |
| Śānti P. | Śānti Parvan of the Mahābhārata |
| Śat. Br. | Śatapatha Brāhmaṇa |
| S. B. E. | Sacred Books of the East Series. |
| SCS. | Smṛitichandrikā, Sanskāra Kāṇḍa |
| S. I. E. R. | Annual Reports of South Indian Epigraphy |
| Tai. Ār. | Taittirīya Āraṇyaka |
| Tai. Br. | Taittirīya Brāhmaṇa |
| T. S. | Taittirīya Saṁhitā |
| Tai. Up. | Taittirīya Upanishad |
| V. D. S. | Vasishṭha Dharma Sūtra |
| Va. Gr. S. | Vārāha Gṛihya Sūtra |
| V. G. S. | " " " |
| Vāj. Saṁ. | Vājasaneya Saṁhitā |
| Vi. Dh. S. | Vishṇu Dharma Sūtra or Vishṇu Smṛiti |
| VMS. | Vīramitrodaya, Sanskāra-prakāśa |
| Watters, | Watters, on Yuan Chwang's Travels |
| Yāj. | Yājñavalkya-smṛiti. |

## TRANSLITERATION.

Sanskrit, Prakrit and Pali words are transliterated according to the following scheme.

Current words like Brahmana, Smriti or Vaishya and modern names like Sivaji and Paithan are written usually without diacritical marks.

| | | | | | | | |
|---|---|---|---|---|---|---|---|
| अ | a | आ | ā | इ | i | ई | ī |
| उ | u | ऊ | ū | ऋ | ṛi | ए | e |
| ऐ | ai | ओ | o | औ | au | अं | aṁ |
| अः | aḥ | क् | k | ख् | kh | ग् | g |
| घ् | gh | ङ् | ṅ | च् | ch | छ् | chh |
| ज् | j | झ् | jh | ञ् | ñ | ट् | ṭ |
| ठ् | ṭh | ड् | ḍ | ढ् | ḍh | ण् | ṇ |
| त् | t | थ् | th | द् | d | ध् | dh |
| न् | n | प् | p | फ् | ph | ब् | b |
| भ् | bh | म् | m | य् | y | र् | r |
| ल् | l | व् | v | श् | ś | ष् | sh |
| स् | s | ह् | h | ळ् | ḷ | क्ष् | ksh |
| ज्ञ् | jñ | | | | | | |

## ERRATA

| Page | Line | Read | For |
|---|---|---|---|
| 9 | 21 | to | o |
| 20 | 8 & 9 | Read foot-note No. 2, p. 21 as authority for this statement. | |
| 21 | 5 | ceremony[3] | ceremony[2] |
| 21 | 23 | Read this note along with foot-note No. 2, p. 20 | |
| 100 | 20 | his teachers | teachers. |
| 109 | 1 | is | in |
| 111 | 14 | to spend | to spent |
| 112 | 14 | weak | week |
| 122 | 6 | becoming | become |
| 137 | 13 | sought | saught |
| 155 | 4 | calibre | cali re |
| 250 | 6 | Eurypedes | Eurepedes |
| 252 | 16 | schools | school |
| 309 | 4 | Trichinopoly | Trichanopoly |

In a few places, some diacritical marks have been left out; the reader can easily supply them.

## BOOKS BY THE SAME AUTHOR

A History of Important Ancient Towns and Cities in Gujrat and Kathiawar; reprinted from the *Indian Antiquary*, 1924-5.

A History of the Village Communities in Western India. Oxford University Press, Bombay, 1927.

Rashtrakutas and their Times; Oriental Book Supplying Agency, Poona, 1934.

# ANCIENT INDIAN EDUCATION

## CHAPTER FIRST

### EDUCATIONAL RITUALS

Religion has deeply saturated Hindu life in almost all its phases and the sphere of education is no exception. Rituals connected with the student's life are many, and several aspects of educational theory and practice will become clear to us if we study their nature and features. It is therefore proposed to devote the opening chapter to a critical survey and rationalistic interpretation of the rituals connected with education.

### VIDYĀRAMBHA SANSKĀRA[1]

*Vidyārambha Sanskāra*, which is described by some authorities also as *Aksharasvīkaraṇam*[2], was performed, as the name itself would suggest, at the commencement of primary education. Fifth year, which is now usually regarded as suitable for the beginning of education, was the time prescribed for it. If the ritual had to

[1] The original authorities for the information given in this section are the following :—*Vīramitrodaya*, *Sanskāraprakāsa*, pp. 321 ff ; Aparārka on *Yājñavalkya-smṛiti*, I,13 ; *Smṛitichandrikā*, *Sanskārakāṇḍa*, pp. 67 ff ; *Sanskāra-ratna-mālā* of Gopīnathabhaṭṭa.

[2] E. g. by Gopīnāthabhaṭṭa.

be postponed on account of unavoidable causes, it had to be performed at least before the *Upanayana.*[1] An auspicious day in the *Uttarāyaṇa* (January to July) was to be selected for the purpose. The ritual was a simple one, requiring the young boy to worship Sarasvatī and Vināyaka along with the tutelary deities and the Sūtrakāras of his family. Some authorities prescribe a Homa, but it is probable that it may not have been universally performed. The worship of the deities was followed by that of the Guru or the primary teacher, and the boy was then handed over to him. The teacher used to make the boy write on rice all the alphabet with the help of a specially manufactured golden or silver pen. Suitable presents made to the teacher and the Brāhmaṇas invited for the ceremony marked the termination of the ritual.

Vidyārambha is thus the earliest Sanskāra in the student's life, but it does not, like *Upanayana,* go back to hoary antiquity. The authorities, which prescribe and describe this ritual, are as late as the second millennium of the Christian era.[2] It appears indeed

[1]Cf. द्वितीयजन्मनः पूर्वमारभेताक्षरान्सुधीः । Bṛihaspati quoted in *Vīramitrodaya.*

[2]Viśvāmitra, Bṛihaspati, Mārkaṇḍeya etc., who are quoted by these authorities, cannot be much earlier, as would be clear from the astronomical details mentioned by them. Such details make their appearance only after the 7th or the 8th century A. D.

very strange that the earlier works like the Gṛihya-sūtras and the Dharma-sūtras, which have laid down rituals for such relatively insignificant occasions like *Gṛiha-nishkramaṇa* (when the child is first taken out from the house) and *Anna-prāśana* (when it is first given food) should have failed to associate the commencement of the primary education with a religious ceremony. The reason, however, is not far to seek. Although the Gṛihya-sūtras, which describe these rituals, were composed *c.* 600-200 B. C., the ceremonies described therein go back to a period several centuries earlier. At least such is the case with *Upanayana*, which is referred to both in the Rigveda and the Atharvaveda. At that early time when *Upanayana* was already recognised as a Sanskāra, there was no necessity to prescribe a further Sanskāra like *Aksharasvīkaraṇa* (Learning of the alphabet) for the simple reason that the alphabet was then probably unknown.[1] *Upanayana* then marked the

---

[1]The view of Dr. Bühler and others that the alphabet was unknown in India before *c.* 800 B. C. has now to be abandoned in view of the Indus Valley discoveries. There is clear cultural evidence to show that the art of writing was known in the later Saṁhitā period (c. 1600-1200 B. C.); see Ojha, *Prāchīna-lipi-mālā*, pp. 1-16. There is no evidence to show that the art of writing was known in the early Vedic period (c. 2500-2000 B. C.). The Aryans were probably ignorant of that art when they entered India, and it may be eventually proved that they learnt it from the 'Indus people.'

commencement, not of secondary education as in later times, but of primary education. Vedic Sanskrit was then the spoken language and both the alphabet and grammar were yet to be evolved. The education of children, therefore, naturally commenced with the memorising of the sacred hymns, which were the most valued possession of the Aryans and constituted almost their entire literature. Under these circumstances, *Upanayana*, which was prescribed at the beginning of the Vedic studies, could be the only ritual to be performed at the commencement of education.

In course of time Vedic Sanskrit ceased to be the spoken language, the sciences of exegis and grammar were developed, and the art of writing was invented or became known. Even the memorising of the Vedic hymns required some previous elementary education. *Upanayana* could therefore no longer mark the beginning of education and a different ritual called *Vidyārambha* began to be recommended for the commencement of primary education. This must have taken place at a fairly early date; the fact that the ritual is recommended only by very late authorities is probably to be explained by the circumstance that it was for a long time combined with *Chaula* or tonsure ceremony. The *Arthaśāstra* states that the education of the prince ought to commence at the time of the *Chaula* ritual.[1] In the *Raghuvanśa*[2] we find prince Raghu learning his alphabet

[1] Cf. वृत्तचौलकर्मा लिपिं संख्यानं चोपयुञ्जीत । I, 2.

[2] III, 28.

after his *Chaula-karma.* We learn from the *Uttara-Rāma-charit* that Vālmīki commenced the education of Kuśa and Lava after their *Chaula-karma,* and that the two brothers had mastered a number of sciences when they began their Vedic studies after their *Upanayana* at the age of eleven.[1] This combination of Chaula with the commencement of the primary education was facilitated by the fact that the time for the ritual, 4th to the 7th year, was suitable also for the commencement of the primary education. The number and nature of the locks of hair to be kcpt at the time of the tonsure ceremony had close connection with the Vedic sages with whom the family was believed to be connected[2]; this may also have suggested the idea that the celebration of the *Chaula-karma Sanskāra* should be the occasion of the commencement of primary education.

## UPANAYANA SANSKĀRA.

*Upanayana,* whose rendering into English as 'Thread Ceremony' hardly conveys its original purpose, is the only ritual whose connection with education is at present well known to the intelligent section of the

[1] Cf. निवृत्तचौलकर्मणोश्च तयोस्त्रयीवर्जमितरास्तिस्रो विद्याः सावधानेन मनसा परिनिष्ठापिताः। Act II.

[2] Cf. यथर्षि शिखां निदधाति। *A. G. S.*, XVI, 6; दक्षिणतः कपर्दा वसिष्ठानां उभयतोऽत्रिभार्गवकाश्यपानां पञ्चचूडा आङ्गिरसाम्। *V. G. S.*, section 4.

Hindu community. As already observed, the ritual is of hoary antiquity. The Brahmachārin, or the student who has performed his Upanayana, is mentioned in one passage of the Rigveda[1]; another passage of the same book seems to refer to a youth who had just performed his Upanayana.[2] But the nature of the ritual and of the items associated with it in the Rigvedic age is practically unknown to us. In two hymns of the Atharvaveda, however, we have a detailed description of the Brahmachārin.[3] *Brahmacharya* was at that time regarded as a period of strenuous study and rigorous exertions, when the youths and maidens of the community studied the sacred texts and prepared themselves for their duties in after life.[4] If a king rules his kingdom well or a maiden succeeds in getting a good match, it was the natural consequence of the Brahmacharya discipline and training.[5] Spiritual consequences of Upanayana and Brahmacharya were, however, more important than the temporal advantages.

---

[1] X, 109,5.

[2] III, 8, 4 and 5.

[3] VI, 138 and XI, 5.

[4] *Bráhma* originally meant prayer; the original meaning of *Brahmacharya* was thus the period of study of the sacred prayers or the Vedic Mantras. Since chastity was usually observed in this period, the term came to acquire the secondary sense of a period of chastity as well.

[5] ब्रह्मचर्येण तपसा राजा राष्ट्रं विरक्षति। XI, 5-17 ब्रह्मचर्येण कन्या युवानं विन्दते पतिम्। *Ibid*, 18.

The immortality of gods and Indra's prëeminence among them were both due to the efficacy of Brahmacharya.[1] Even cosmic functions like the upholding of the heaven and the earth were attributed by an *arthavāda* to the mysterious spiritual efficacy of Brahmacharya[2].

The Brahmachārin of the Atharvaveda period resembled his later day successor in several respects. He used to keep matted hair, wear a girdle, don a deer skin and offer sacred dried twigs to the sacrificial fire. He used to subsist on begging. Details about the student's life, more or less similar to those described in later Smṛitis, are to be seen in several passages of the Brāhmaṇa literature also.[3]

Later authorities describe Upanayana as an occasion when the student is brought into contact with his preceptor, Vedas, deities and disciplined life[4]. Originally, however, the term must have denoted the student's approach to the teacher for the purpose of

---

[1] ब्रह्मचर्येण तपसा देवा मृत्युमपाघ्नत। इन्द्रो ह ब्रह्मचर्येण देवेभ्यः स्वराभवत्। *Ibid*, 19.

[2] Cf. स दाधार पृथिवीं दिवं च। *A. V.*, XI, 5, 1.

[3] *Tai. S.*, VI, 3, 10, 5; *Śat. Br.*, XI, 5, 4: (here we have a detailed description of Upanayana); *Go. Br.*, I. 2, 1-8 (here we have several interesting reasons for the different rules of Brahmacharya).

[4] Cf. गुरोर्व्रतानां वेदस्य यमस्य नियमस्य च। देवतानां समीपं वा येनासौ नीयते द्विजः॥ तदुपानयनं प्रोक्तं...। "अभियुक्ताः" quoted in *VMS.*, p. 334.

education. Logically, therefore, it would follow that the ritual should be performed every time the student approached a new teacher. Evidence is available to show that such was actually the case, though occasionally some teachers like Aśvapati would voluntarily dispense with the formality[1]. Nay, we have instances on record of married men going through the formality of Upanayana when approaching renowned teachers for the completion of their education[2]. In early times the ritual seems to have been also repeated when a student commenced the study of a different branch of Veda, but later writers discouraged this practice.[3]

A ceremony, which was so often repeated in the student life, could naturally not have been a complicated one. In that far off age when the Vedic hymns were transmitted from generation to generation in the families of the sages, the father himself was the Guru. This is proved by the parable of gods, men and demons

---

[1] *Ch. Up.*, V, 11, 7. It may be noted, however, that the Brāhmaṇa teachers of the Kshatriya king had come prepared for the formality of Upanayana, though they were grown up scholars of established reputation. Cf. ते समित्पाणयः पूर्वाह्णे प्रतिचक्रमिरे तान्हानुपनीयैवैतदुवाच ।

[2] *Br. Up.*, VI, 2, 4.

[3] Consult the authorities on this point quoted in *VMS.* p. 337 and p. 543.

spending their Brahmacharya period under the guidance of their father Prajāpati, who was their Guru.[1] In Upanishadic times we find Śvetaketu's Guru was his father Aruṇi; when the son goes to the learned assembly of the Pañchālas at the end of his education, the members enquire whether his father himself had trained him.[2] Even 17th century authorities like Mitramiśra admit that the best Guru at the Upanayana is the father himself; an outsider was to be invited when the father was dead or incompetent.[3] Upanayana ceremony being thus domestic in origin, was naturally a simple one. The student had simply to approach his teacher with sacred fuel in his hand to indicate his willingness to serve him and his sacred fires.[4] At one period an oral request on the part of the student and a verbal acceptance on the part of the teacher were regarded as quite sufficient to constitute a valid Upanayana.[5]

For several centuries Upanayana was not regarded as a Sanskāra compulsory for all the members of the first three castes. Aruṇi's exhortation o his son Śvetaketu that he ought to pass through Brahmacharya, because members of his family did not claim Brahmana-

---

[1] *Br. Up.*, V. 2, 1.

[2] *Ibid*, VI, 2, 1 ; *Ch. Up.*, V. 3.

[3] तस्मात्पित्राद्यभाव एव आचार्यः कर्तव्य इति स्थितिः । *op. cit.*

[4] *Ch. Up.*, IV. 5, 5 ; V, 11, 7 ; *Mu. Up.*, 1, 2, 12.

[5] Cf. वाचा ह स्मैव पूर्वमुपयन्ति । *Br. Up.*, VI, 2, 7.

hood merely by birth,[1] would show that for a long time Upanayana was confined only to priestly or literary families. It was subsequently extended to the whole of the Brahmana class and then to all the Aryans We should not forget that the *Aśrama* theory, making Upanayana compulsory, became popular only in later times. Upanayana was no doubt regarded as a second birth as early as the time of the Atharvaveda[2], but that honour was for a long time conceded to the sacrificial Dikshā also[3]. In early times the term *Vrātya*, which in later days denoted a person who had not performed his Upanayana, used to designate a person who was not offering Soma sacrifice or keeping the sacred fires[4]. No irrevocable change in status resulted as a result of non-performance of Upanayana. Later Smritis[5] no doubt assert that a person becomes a *Vrātya* and consequently unfit for social and matrimonial dealings, if he does not perform his Upanayana before the time prescribed for his particular caste. But the

---

[1] *Ch. Up.* VI, 1, 1.

[2] Cf. आचार्यो उपनयमानो ब्रह्मचारिणं कृणुते गर्भमन्तः ।
तं रात्रीस्तिस्र उदरे बिभर्ति तं जातं द्रष्टुमभिसंयन्ति देवाः ॥
*A. V.*, XI, 5, 3.

[3] Cf. अजातो ह वै तावत्पुरुषो यावन्न यजते । *Sat. Br.*, II, 3, 4; *Jai. U. Br.*, III, 3, 1; Manu, II, 169.

[4] यस्य पिता पितामहो वा न सोमं पिबेत्स व्रात्यः । "श्रुत्यंतर" quoted in *Par. Mā.* at I, 1, p. 165.

[5] E. g. Manu, II, 39, Yāj., I, 37–8.

view of the earlier authorities was different and they were prepared to readmit a person to the Aryan fold, even if his three ancestors had failed to perform Upanayana altogether[1]. It is therefore quite clear that Upanayana in early times was not regarded as a Sanskāra compulsory for all the Dvijas. Nay, it was regarded rather as a privilege which gave a passport for entry into the sacred library of the race. Vicious, wicked or incompetent persons were naturally excluded from the honour and privilege of Upanayana[2].

In course of time, however, the ritual came to be regarded as compulsory for all, primarily on account of the extraordinarily great importance that came to be attached to the study and preservation of the Vedas. It was felt that the Sanskāra itself may transform the objectionable features in the character of undesirable persons. The mass of the sacred literature was increasing enormously with the growing number of the *Brāhmaṇas*, *Upanishads* and the *Sūtras*, and it had to be transmitted to the next generation only orally. There was some chance of the preservation of this vast sacred literature, only if the services of the whole community

---

[1] *Pā. Gr.*, II, 5; Āpastamba quoted by *VMS.*, p. 353

[2] अशूद्राणामदुष्टकर्मणामुपायनम्। *Āp. Gr.*, I, 1, 5.

विद्या ह वै ब्राह्मणमाजगाम गोपाय मां शेवधिष्टेऽहमस्मि।
असूयकायानृजवेऽयताय न मा ब्रूया वीर्यवतीतथा स्याम्॥

*Nirukta*, II, 4, 1.

were conscripted for the purpose. The best way to secure the cooperation of the whole Aryan society for the preservation of the sacred tradition was to represent Upanayana as a compulsory Sanskāra (*Śārīra-Sanskāra*), the non-performance of which would disqualify a person from contracting a valid marriage. This new theory was easily accepted by society, because the notion was already current since early times that Upanayana marked a second birth. It may be observed in passing that Buddhism also regarded the admission into the Order as a second birth of the individual. When the robber Angulimala was admitted into the Order, he exclaimed, 'Verily I have obtained an Aryan birth'.[1]

A natural consequence of the new theory that made Upanayana compulsory for all was to make the society progressively oblivious of the real nature of Upanayana. Forgetful of the fact that the ritual marked the beginning of the Vedic education, society began to tolerate, nay prescribe, Upanayana even in those cases where Vedic studies were inherently impossible. This accounts for the strange phenomenon of a number of authorities advocating the doctrine that Upanayana ought to be performed even in the case of the dumb, deaf and the blind.[2] The difficulty created by the impossibility of

---

[1]Cf. अरियाय जातिया जातो । *M.N.*, II. p. 103 ; *Therigāthā*, No. 17.

[2]Consult Baudhāyana and *Brahmapurāṇa* quoted in *VMS.* p. 361.

a dumb or deaf person reciting the Vedic Mantras was got over by the ingenious expedient that the Mantras might be recited by the teacher on behalf of the student.[1] Some thinkers like Śankha Likhita dissented from this strange view,[2] but the majority of the Nibandha-writers felt that this absurd position had to be accepted if the marriage of a dumb or deaf person were to be rendered possible. For, how could such a person be married if he had not previously performed Upanayana and become eligible for social and matrimonial intercourse with the regenerate classes ?

Another natural consequence of Upanayana being regarded as a *bodily Sanskāra* rather than as an *educational ritual* was the custom to perform it when the body happened to be defiled. A number of authorities[3] prescribe a fresh Upanayana as a penance if the body were defiled by the drinking of wine or eating of onions or similar sins. What a great difference! In early times the ritual was performed anew when a fresh course was taken or a new teacher selected by the student; now it was repeated when the body happened to defiled.

---

[1] Cf. बटुपठनीयानां......मन्त्राणां आचार्यं प्रत्येव पाठो विधीयते । *Ibid.*

[2] Cf. नोन्मत्तमूकान्संस्कुर्यात् । quoted in *VMS.*, p. 406.

[3] Cf. Śātātapa, Paiṭhīnasi, Yama, etc., quoted in *VMS.*, p. 545–7.

But perhaps the strangest consequence of the growing ignorance of the real nature of Upanayana and of the extraordinary sanctity attached to it is to be seen from a 14th century Karnataka inscription hailing from Malavalli.[1] This document discloses to us the existence of a pious Brahmana, who performed the Upanayana ceremony of the four Aśvattha trees planted by him at the four corners of a garden that he had dedicated to a temple. Aśvattha was no doubt a very sacred tree; but its sanctity could certainly be enhanced by the performance of the Upanayana Sanskāra. So deep had become the faith in the purificatory power of Upanayana and so dense the ignorance of its original nature.

While noting these strange consequences of the new theory that Upanayana was a compulsory bodily Sanskāra, we should not be oblivious to one very important and salutary result following from it. The theory made some amount of Vedic knowledge compulsory for all the Aryan community.[2] From about 800 B.C. it was not possible to be initiated into Vedic studies without a preliminary grounding in primary education. When Upanayana was made a compulsory Sanskāra for the three higher castes, literacy naturally became almost universal among them. It is to be

---

[1] *E. C.*, III, Malavalli No. 23, dated 1358 A. D,

[2] The prevalence of Vedic studies among women will be discussed in Chap. VII.

regretted that the theory that there exist no Kshatriyas and Vaishyas in the Kali age should have gained ground in society in the latter half of the first millenium of the Christian era, causing the discountinuance of Upanayana and helping the spread of illiteracy among two very important and useful classes in the society.

The extension of Upanayana to the dumb and the deaf indeed appears as strange. But the ritual came to be regarded as possessing a cultural significance as well, hence it was the idea of some thinkers that no section of the society should be excluded from the ceremony.

Most of our authorities prefer that the Upanayana of the Brahmana, Kshatriya and Vaishya should be performed in the 8th, 11th, and 12th years respectively. Several writers have expressed surprise that later years should have been prescribed for the Kshatriyas and the Vaishyas.[1] These classes no doubt did not continue their Vedic education as long as the Brahmanas, but then it is argued that their Vedic education should have commenced simultaneously with the Brahmanas but terminated earlier. Rev. F. E. Keay and Prof. S. K. Das have attributed the earlier Upanayana age for the Brahmana to the desire to emphasise his intellectual superiority.[2] It would, however, appear

---

[1] Keay, *Ancient Indian Education*, p. 29;
Das, *The Educational system of the Ancient Hindus*, p. 72.

[2] *Ibid.*

that there was no desire to emphasise any intellectual superiority, for the selection of the 8th, 11th and 12th years seems to be more or less accidental. It was due to the simple circumstance that the letters in each line of the first Vedic Mantra taught to Brahmana, Kshatriya and Vaishya boys happened to be 8, 11, and 12 respectively.[1] That there is no special sanctity attached to these particular years would be clear from the wide option given in this matter by early writers like Baudhāyana, who recommend for Upanayana any year between 8 and 16 and are in favour of the latest year, namely the 16th.[2] Several writers on the other hand have expressed the view that the 5th, 7th or the 9th year was particularly suitable for the purpose[3] in the case of Brahmana students.

This wide divergence about the suitable time for Upanayana is due to the fact that the conception and nature of Upanayana were changing from age to age.

---

[1] Cf. ब्राह्मणादिवर्णसम्बन्धिनां छन्दसां पादाक्षरसंख्येरब्दैरुपनयनस्य विधेः मुख्यासंभवे......। मेधातिथि on मनु II. 38.

गायत्र्याः पादेऽष्टाक्षराणि भवन्ति तेन ब्राह्मणस्याष्टमे वर्षे उपनयनम् ।
त्रिष्टुभः पाद एकादशाक्षराणि भवन्ति तेन क्षत्रियस्यैकादशे वर्षे उपनयनम् ।
जगत्याःपादे द्वादशाक्षराणि भवन्ति तेन वैश्यस्य द्वादशे वर्षे उपनयनम् ।

*VMS.*, p. 344.

[2] Cf. अष्टमे आयुष्कामं नवमे तेजस्कामं······त्रयोदशे मेधाकामं चतुर्दशे पुष्टिकामं······षोडशे सर्वकामम् । *Bau. Gr. S.*, II, 5, 5.

[3] *Gau. Dh. S.*, I, 1, 7; *Mān. Gr. S.*, I, 22, 1. *Vār. Gr. S.*, 6.

We have seen already that in early times it marked the beginning of primary education ; it was therefore quite natural that the thinkers of the age should have given preference for an early age like the 5th, the 7th or the 9th year. A child of 5 or 6 could not recite with proper accent and pronunciation even the Sāvitrī verse, hence the practice of the early age to postpone its teaching to a date about a year later than the time of the Sanskāra.[1] In priestly families where the father himself was usually the teacher, an early age did not cause any inconvenience, for the boy had not to migrate to a different locality or family for his education. In course of time, however, Upanayana became the occasion for the commencement of what may be conveniently described as secondary education, and then an early age like the 5th or the 7th year was found to be impracticable. Priestly families found the 8th year as a suitable one for their purpose, for the primary education could be finished and the secondary education commenced at about this time. Non-priestly families found the 8th year inconvenient, for they had to send their sons outside their families for their Vedic education. Circumstances differed widely in different localities and families, and Smṛiti writers thought it prudent to give a wide option in the matter. They therefore permit

---

[1] Cf. तां ह स्मैतां पुरा संवत्सरे अन्वाहुः संवत्सरसंमिता वै गर्भाः ।

*Sat. Br.*, XI.

The reason for postponing the teaching of the Gāyatrī Mantra given in this passage is fanciful and unhistorical.

the performance of Upanayana at any time between the age of 8 and 16. When Upanayana was followed by a departure to the preceptor's place or house, it was performed at an advanced age. Thus, for instance, we find Śvetaketu performing his Upanayana and departing for his teacher's house when he was 12.[1] Most of the Jātaka scholars were either 16 or had attained the age of discretion, when they used to leave their homes for higher education at Takshaśilā at their preceptors' houses.[2] We find the same to be the case in the stories of *Kathā-sarit-sāgara*, where scholars are to be seen proceeding to Valabhi for higher education at the age of 16.[3] When exactly the Vedic or higher education should commence was left to the convenience of the parties. It was, however, felt that it would be preferable to begin it before the age of 12, for the powers of mind that were required for the Vedic studies had to be trained at an early age. Commencement of the Vedic studies after the age of 16 was definitely discouraged, for it was rightly apprehended that a boy who commences his serious studies at such an advanced age would find them too tedious, his mind having become already susceptible to sensuous attractions.[4]

---

[1] *Ch. Up.*, VI., 1, 2.

[2] See Jātakas Nos. 50, 51, 55, 151, 181, 252, etc.

[3] XXXII, 42-3.

[4] नातिषोडशवर्षमुपनयीत प्रसृष्टवृषणो ह्येष वृषलीभूतो भवति ।

*Jai. Gr. S.*, I. 12

*P. T. O.*

An educationalist will find the survey of the Upanayana ritual very interesting and instructive. The ritual opens with a breakfast which precedes even the bath; on this occasion it is the custom in many parts of the country for the boy to share food with his mother in the same dish. A breakfast before bath is unusual in Hindu Sanskāras, and its occurrence at the Upanayana was probably intended to indicate that the earlier life of unregulated childhood had come to an end and that serious and disciplined life was now to follow. Breakfast was followed by a shave,—an invariable element in most of the Hindu *Vratas* and Sanskāras. The boy was then given a bath and offered a *Kaupīna*.[1] This was to remind him that Upanayana commenced a new epoch in his life from which dignity, decorum and self-respect could never be separated. A girdle (*Mekhalā*) was tied round his waist as a support for *Kaupīna*. It was made of a triple cord, the symbolism

---

(*Continued from the last page*)

The readiness of Mitramiśra (a 17th century writer) to permit Upanayana upto the age of 24, 33, and 36, in the case of the different castes is due to the exigencies of the times, when several non-Brahmins like king Shivaji were performing the ritual when reminded about it, or when it became absolutely necessary to perform it.

[1] *Kaupīna* denotes the small strip of cloth used by children to cover their private parts. *Kaupīna* was discontinued at about the age of 12 when the boy was reqnired to wear the full dhoti. Cf. Aśvalayana quoted in *VMS*., p. 432.

being intended to foster the belief in the scholar that he was being continuously encircled by the three Vedas[1]. The verses recited at the occasion of tying the girdle informed the boy that his belt was a daughter of Faith (Śraddhā) and a sister of the sages, possesed the power of protecting his purity and chastity and would keep him away from evil[2]. Hindu ideas of decorum required that when engaged in religious duties the upper part of the body should be covered with a piece of cloth. On the occasion of Upanayana the young scholar was therefore offered an upper garment. Our records go back to hoary antiquity and enable us to know that the glistening deerskin was the earliest 'piece of cloth' offered on such occasions. The *Gopatha Brāhmaṇa* informs the youth that the lovely deerskin is symbolical of *Brahmavarchasam* or spiritual and intellectual preëminence and its constant use ought to urge him to attain reputation as a youth of character and scholarship[3]. When spinning and weaving became

---

[1]Cf. त्रैवेद्‌त्रयेणावृतोऽहमिति मन्येत स द्विजः । अश्वलायन in *VMS.*, p. 432.

[2]Cf. श्रद्धाया दुहिता तपसोऽधिजाता स्वसा ऋषीणां भूतकृतां बभूव । *A. V.*, VI. 133. 4 ऋतस्य गोप्त्री तपसश्चरित्री घ्नती रक्षः सहमाना अरातीः । सा मा समन्तं अभिपर्येहि भद्रे धर्तारस्ते सुभगे मा रिषाम ।।
*Vā. Gr. S.*, 5.

The last verse occurs in most of the Gr. Sūtras with slight variations.

[3]1, 2, 1–8.

common, a real piece of cloth was offered to the boy on this occasion, and the *Āpastamba and Baudhāyana Gṛihyasūtras* require that the piece of cloth to be offered to the boy should have been spun and woven in his own house just before the ceremony[3]. A survey of the Gṛihya-sūtras, which describe the Upanayana ritual in detail, shows that investiture with the Sacred Thread did not form part of the Upanayana ritual. The upper garment that was offered to the boy was in lieu of the sacred thread or rather its predecessor. This will be shown in the appendix A, where the whole history of the Sacred Thread and its significance will be discussed in details.

Invested with the girdle and clothed in *Kaupīna* and the upper garment, the boy was taken to the sacred fire, one the earliest Indo-European deities known so far. He was asked to offer a *Samidh* (a piece of sacred fuel) to the gleaming fire and the Mantras recited on the occasion prayed that God Fire should be auspicious to the young scholar and endow him with brilliance, intelligence and vigour,[4] so that his scholarship and strength should grow up like the resplendent flame of

---

[1] अजिनं वासो वा दक्षिणत उपवीय । *Tai. A.*, II, 1.

[2] Cf. स्नानं दानं जपं होमं स्वाध्यायं पितृतर्पणम् । नैकवस्त्रो द्विजः कुर्याच्छ्राद्धभोजनसत्क्रियाः ।

*Yogayājñavalkya in SCS.*, p. 299.

[3] Cf. वासः सद्यःकृत्तोतं । *Bau. Gr.*, II. 5. 11.

[4] Cf. अयं त इध्म आत्मा जातवेदस्तेन वर्द्धस्व चेन्द्धि वर्धय चास्मान् ।

*Bh. Gr. S.*, I, 5.

fire. In order to intensify his reverence for religion the boy was then presented to a number of Vedic deities like Bhaga, Yama, Aryamā and Savitṛi. The last mentioned god was charged with the special duty of protecting the Brahmachārin from harm, disease and death.[1] When this presentation was over, the Guru assured his pupil that he was thenceforward under divine protection;[2] fortified by that consciousness the student should push forth his studies without any apprehensions.

The next element in the ritual is a symbolical one; the boy was asked to stand on a stone and enjoined to be steadfast in the pursuit of his studies.[3] Firm determination and singleness of purpose are most essential for a successful educational career and the necessity of cultivating them was emphasised on the scholar's mind by the *Aśmārohaṇa* element in the ritual.

The scholar was then brought before his teacher, who asked him whose Brahmachārin he was. The young boy naturally replied to the preceptor that he was the latter's disciple. The preceptor then used to correct him and asked him to note that he was the pupil of gods Indra and Agni, the most popular and powerful

---

[1] Cf. देव सवितरेष ते ब्रह्मचारी स मा मृत । *Aś. Gr. S.*, I, 20, 6.

[2] *Sat. Br.*, XI, 5, 4, 3.

[3] *Mā. Gr. S.*, I, 22, 12. Stone was also symbolical of strength; B*h*. *Gr. S.*, I, 8 held that the significance of the ritual was to make the boy invulnerable.

among the Vedic deities.[1] When formally taking charge of the pupil by seizing his right hand, the teacher used to announce that he was doing so with the command and concurrence of God Savitṛi.[2] The teacher then touched the heart of his pupil and prayed that there should be a perpetual and perfect accord between them.[3] All this was intended to emphasise that the relations between the teacher and the pupil were sacred and not mercenary and progress in education was possible only if there was complete harmony, sympathy and whole-hearted communion between the teacher and the taught. After taking formal charge of the pupil, the teacher used to teach him the famous Sāvitṛī Mantra, more popularly known at present as Gāyatṛī from its metre. This Mantra, which the boy was to recite daily at the time of his prayer, runs as follows:—

तत्सवितुर्वरेण्यं भर्गो देवस्य धीमहि । धियो यो नः प्रचोदयात् ।

'We meditate upon the excellent brilliance of God Sun ; may he stimulate our intellect'.

The prayer is simple and significant and quite appropriate for the student.[4]

---

[1] Cf. कस्य त्वं ब्रह्मचार्यसि । भवत इत्युच्यमाने इन्द्रस्य ब्रह्मचार्यसि अग्निराचार्यस्तव अहमाचार्यस्तव । *Pā. Gr. S.*, II, 3.

[2] *Aś. Gr. S.*, I, 20, 4.

[3] *Hi. Gr. S.*, I, 5, 11.

[4] Later writers like Bṛihat-Parāśara, IV, 75-77 see quite fanciful and mysterious meanings in this simple Mantra.

*P. T. O.*

According to traditional classification, Gāyatrī is the proper metre for the Brahmana, Trishṭubh for the Kshatriya and Jagatī for the Vaishya. So the daily prayer to the sun to be offered by the Kshatriya and Vaishya students was to be in their own appropriate metres. Tradition, however, is not unanimous as to which precise Trishṭubh and Jagatī verses were to be used by the Kshatriya and Vaishya boys for their daily prayer.[1] The divergence in tradition noted below in the foot-note may have bee ı perhaps due to Upanayana

---

*(Continued from the last page)*

Cf. तत्प्रकृतिः स स्वांतं विकारो बुद्धिरेव च। तुरित्येतदहंकारं वशब्दं विद्धि पापहम् ॥ रेस्पर्शं तु णि रूपं च थं रसं गंधमत्र भम्। गों श्रोत्र दे त्वचं वै व चक्षुः स्य रसता तथा ॥ धी नासा च म वाचा च हि हस्तौ धि च पादद्वयम्। यो उपस्थ मुखं योऽन्यो नः खं प्रकारमारुतम् ॥ चो तेजो द् जलं यात्क्ष्मा गायत्र्यास्तत्त्वचिंतनम्। So also about the significance of the *Vyāhṛiti* letters, *Kūrma-purāṇa, uttarārdha*, 14, 53 and *Ādi-Purāṇa*, Adi., 53. 54-5 maintain that they denote Pradhāna, Purusha and Kāla or Vishṇu, Brahmā and Mahesha or Satva, Rajas and Tamas respectively. Cf. प्रधानं पुरुषः कालो विष्णुर्ब्रह्मा महेश्वरः। सत्वं रजस्तमस्तिस्रः क्रमाद् व्याहृतयः स्मृताः।

[1] According to Medhātithi (Manu, II, 38), the Sāvitṛī Mantra for the Kshatriya is to be *R. V.*, I, 35, 2, :—

आ कृष्णेन रजसा वर्तमानो निवेशयन्नमृतं मर्त्यं च।
हिरण्येन सविता रथेन देवो याति भुवनानि पश्यन् ॥

According to Nārāyaṇa, the commentator on *Śānkhyāyana Gr. S.*, II, 5, the Kshatriya Mantra should be *R. V.*, I, 35, 9, :—

*P. T. O.*

not being quite common in these classes. It is possible, however, that it may also be due to different usages of different localities or families.

The boy was then given a staff (*daṇḍa*). The student is really a traveller out on a long road leading to the realm of knowledge. Staff was the traveller's symbol and when accepting it, the boy prayed that with divine grace he may reach the goal of his arduous

---

(*Continued from the last page*)

हिरण्यपाणिः सविता विचर्षणिरुभे द्यावापृथिवी अंतरीयते ।
अयामीवां बाधते वेति सूर्यमभि कृष्णेन रजसा द्यामृणोति ॥

As to the Mantra for the Vaishya, Medhātithi (on Manu, II, 38) and Śātātapa (quoted in *VMS.*, p. 430) and Laugākshi (quoted by Aparārka on Yāj., I, 15) hold that it should be *R. V.*, V, 81, 2, :—

विश्वा रूपाणि प्रतिमुंचते कविः प्रासावीद्भद्रं द्विपदे चतुष्पदे ।
वि नाकमख्यत्सविता वरेण्योऽनु प्रयाणमुषसो विराजति ॥

*Aś. Gr. S.*, III, 7 and *Vā. Gr. S.*, 6, however, prefer that it should be *R. V.*, V, 81, 1, :—

युंजते मन उत युंजते धियः विप्रा विप्रस्य बृहतो विपश्चितः ।
वि होत्रा दधे वयुनाविदेक इन्मही देवस्य सवितुः परिष्टुतिः ॥

Nārāyaṇa, however, recommends *R. V.*, IV, 40, 5, :—

हंसः शुचिषद्वसुरंतरिक्षसद्धोता वेदिषदतिथिर्दुरोणसत् ।
नृषद्वरसदृतसद्व्योमसदब्जा गोजा ऋतजा अद्रिजा ऋतम् ॥

It may be added that in some localities, the same Mantra was taught to the boys of all the castes. *Pa. Gr. S.*, II. 3. 10 refers to this custom.

journey.[1] One authority, however, holds that the significance of the staff was to remind the scholar that he was to be henceforward a watchman, armed with a staff, and charged with the duty of guarding the Vedas.[2] Another authority points out that the staff could also serve the purpose of making the student self-confident and self-reliant when he was out in the forest to collect the sacred fuel, or travelling in darkness or entering an unknown tank or river.[3]

Then followed *bhikshācharaṇa* or begging. The begging on the first day was more or less a formal and ceremonial affair, the boy being required to beg of such persons only who would not refuse his request. The boy would therefore approach first of all his mother and then his other relatives and friends. Begging of daily food to maintain himself was intended to be a permanent feature of the student's life; how far such was actually the case will be discussed in Chapter III.

Three days after Upanayana, *Medhājanana* ritual was usually performed with a view to invoke divine help in the sharpening of the intellect, memory and grasping power of the young scholar.[4] This marked the termination of the Upanayana ceremony.

---

[1] *Mā. Gr. S.*, I, 22, 11.

[2] *Vā. Gr. S.*, 6.

[3] *Aparārka on Yāj.*, I, 29.

[4] *Bh. Gr. S.*, I, 10.

At the time when the significance of the Upanayana ritual and Mantras was perfectly grasped, a very powerful impression must have been produced on the mind of all the parties interested in the ritual. The ritual heralded the beginning of a new epoch in the student's life, characterised by dignity, decorum and discipline. The scholar was to regard himself a. a self-reliant traveller bound for the realm of knowledge; the journey was to be long and arduous, but if there was singleness of purpose, devotion to studies and perfect accord between him and his teachers, he would surely reach his goal. For, divine help and co-operation were enlisted on his behalf; even death could not touch him if he followed the rules of his order properly.[1] His personality will develop like that of Indra, his intelligence will glow up like the refulgent flame of God Fire, and he will find nothing relating to his literary goal impossible if he worked with faith, assiduousness and determination. What better ideas can be conveyed to a young scholar at the beginning of his higher education ?

## RITUALS IN BRAHMACHARYA PERIOD.

In his student life the scholar had to perform two types of rituals, (i) annual ones and (ii) special ones. To the former group belonged *Upākarma* or *Śrāvaṇī* and *Utsarjana* and to the latter, several rituals like *Mahā-*

[1] *Śat. Br.*, XI, 2, 6 ; *Bau. D. S.*, I, 3.

*namanī, Āśvamedhika* etc., which were laid down at the commencement of special courses.

### UPĀKARMA OR ŚRĀVAṆĪ AND UTSARJANA.

Annual sessions of schools and colleges in ancient India began at the commencement of the rainy season after sowing operations were over and corps had begun to sprout up.[1] The succeeding four months formed a period of relative leisure and were therefore thought to be well suited for the annual educational session. Upākarma or Śrāvaṇī was a ritual performed by teachers and students at the beginning of the annual college or school session.[2]

---

[1] The full moon days of Ashādha, Śrāvaṇa and Bhādrapada are mentioned by different authorities as appropriate days for the Upākarma. (Cf. *Bau. Gr. S.*, III, 1, 2-3; *Kh. Gr. S.*, III, 2, 14; *Hi. Gr. S.*, II, 18, 1). Rainy season is receding back every century and it commences in different months in different provinces of India. Hence this divergence about the appropriate season for Upākarma.

[2] Upākarma is an abbreviation of *Chandasām upākarma* and literally means the storing or studying of the Vedas. It therefore denotes the ritual performed at the commencement of the annual session when the students assembed to prosecute further studies. Śrāvaṇī is a relatively modern name for the ritual. In early times it denoted the Nāga worship ritual performed on the full moon day of Śrāvaṇa; when this ritual went out of vogue, the name was transferred, to the *Chandasām Upākarma* ritual, because that too was usually performed on the same day.

To the modern mind, which is accustomed to associate Śrāvaṇī with the replacement of the sacred thread, the above explanation of the ritual may appear fanciful and untrue, but there are several passages occuring in the sacred texts to support it. *Aśvalāyana Gṛihya sūtra*, while describing Śrāvaṇī, observes that the ceremony is to be performed by the teacher along with the students.[1] *Baudhāyana Gṛihya sūtra* states that the Upākarma is to be performed when students are reassembled, and that at the time of Utsarjana the teacher should go outside the village along with the pupils.[2] Khādira prescribes that the teacher should recite aloud the *sāvitrī mantra* to his pupils as he does at Upanayana.[3] Pāraskara testifies to the still more significant belief that a teacher would get as many students as would be the number of sesasums that he would be offering as oblations in the Upākarma Homa[4]. Vārāha lays down a Mantra at Upākarma for a teacher, who is desirous to have many students at his school or college.[5] Jaimini requires the teacher to give a feast to his students on the day of Upākarma.[6]

---

[1] अध्येष्यमाणः अध्याप्यैरन्वारब्धः……… । 3. 4. 10.

[2] समारब्धेष्वन्तेवासिषु…उपाकर्म कुर्वीत। III. 1. 3. सहान्तेवासिभिः ग्रामादभिनिष्क्रम्य……उत्सर्जनविधिः । *Ibid.*

[3] शिष्याणां सावित्र्यनुवचनं यथोपनयने । III. 2. 18 and 19.

[4] स यावन्तं गणमिच्छेत्तावन्तस्तिलानाकूर्षफलेन जुहुयात् II. 10

[5] अन्तेवासिनां योगमिच्छन्नथ जपति… । *Va. Gr. S.*, 7

[6] सब्रह्मचारिणश्च उपसमेतान्भोजयेदाचार्यः I. 14.

These and similar statements that occur in the texts describing Śrāvaṇī make it abundantly clear that the ritual was originally performed at the beginning of educational session when the teachers and the pupils began their annual labours.

If such was the nature of Śrāvaṇī in the beginning, it may be naturally enquired as to how it came to be performed by the whole society, and why it was not confined only to students and teachers. The sacred texts themselves, as we have seen above, do not prescribe Śrāvaṇī for all. Harihara, the commentator of *Pāraskara Gṛihya Sūtra*, expressly observes that none but a teacher, who is duly keeping the sacred fire, is authorised to perform or preside over an Upākarma. He adds that the popular practice of all participating in Upākarma is based entirely on custom.[1]

The causes that led to the extension of Upākarma to all persons who had performed their Upanayana are not far to seek; they attest to the laudable desire of popularising and extending post-college education. Most of us are very familiar with the present unfortunate state of affairs when a vast majority of the students lose their study habits and forget most of what they had learnt when at the schools and colleges. Educationists in ancient India were confronted with a similar

---

[1] अतोऽध्यापयतोऽपि निरग्नेः साग्नेरपि अनध्यापयतो नाधिकारः। यत्तु लोके ब्रह्मचारिणं पुरस्कृत्य उपाकर्म प्रवर्तते लौकिकाग्नौ तस्याचारं विहाय न मूलं दृश्यते। At *Pā. Gr. S.*, II. 10

situation, and with a view to remedy the evil, they began to advocate that even when students had taken their degrees and entered into the struggle of life, they ought to devote a part of the year for revising their studies and adding to their knowledge they had acquired during their Brahmacharya. Śvetaketu, who is known to have initiated several other reforms, was apparently the first to advocate that even after marriage, a person should spend two months at his preceptor's. He pointed out that his own prëeminence in learning was due to his having followed this rule, and he urged all to do the same.

This departure proposed by Śvetaketu was not popular in the beginning and we find Āpastamba unwilling to subscribe to the new theory.[1] Its utility and necessity however began to be felt in course of time. Branches of knowledge were rapidly multiplying, and it was the duty of the Brahmanas to cope with them. Education could not be finished during Brahmacharya, and if its scope were not extended to the post-marriage period, the most price-less possession that a generation can possess, was likely to slip away. Śvetaketu's view that a part of the year ought to be reserved for keeping up and adding to our knowledge began to be felt as

---

[1] निवेशे वृत्ते संवत्सरे द्वौ द्वौ मासौ समाहितः आचार्यकुले वसेद्भूयः श्रुतमिच्छन्निति श्वेतकेतुः। एतेन ह्यहं योगेन भूयः पूर्वस्माच्छ्रुतमकरव-मिति। तच्छास्त्रैर्विप्रतिषिद्धम्। निवेशे हि वृत्ते नैयामिकानि श्रूयन्ते। A. D. S., I. 1. 2. 12.

eminently reasonable. Śvetaketu had advocated an annual exodus of two months to the house of the preceptor. This was bound to be felt very inconvenient by men engaged in active pursuits of life. But surely a graduate can stay at home and devote the monsoon time for the revision of what had been learnt, and for the prosecution of further studies.

This compromise is responsible for the extension of Upākarma or Śrāvaṇī to the whole society. That even married men were expected to study in this period, so that their learning should cease to be 'stale,' (*Yātayāmatānirāsārtham*) would be clear when we remember that during the period intervening between Upākarma and Utsarjana, Brahmacharya was prescribed even for married men, who were further forbidden meat-eating, shaving &c.[1] These rules were superfluous for Brahmachāris; they had to be enjoined because even married men were expected to perform Śrāvaṇī and spend the monsoon in study.

When we have realised that Upākarma was a simple religious ritual performed by the teachers and the students at the beginning of the annual college session, and by others at the beginning of monsoon when the annual period of rivision of earlier studies commenced, we can very well understand the significance of its various details. Study in the beginning

[1]Cf. न मांसमश्नीयान्न श्राद्धम् । न लोमानि संहारयेत् । न स्त्रियमुपेयादृतौ जायामुपेयात् । J. Gr. S., Upâkarma section.

meant the Vedic study and the various branches of the Veda have slightly varying details in this ritual. But the central idea is common to all, viz., on such an occasion, Vedic and sacrificial deities should be offered respectful oblations, presiding deities over intellect, memory, and imagination should be propitiated and tribute of gratefulness should be paid to the intellectual giants of the past who have enriched national literature. Thus according to *Aśvalāyana Grihya Sūtra* the Rigvedins are to offer oblations to Śāvitrī, Śraddhā, Medhā, Prajñā, Dhāraṇā and to various seers (or authors) of the Vedas. After this the first and last stanzas of the ten books of the Rigveda, which was to be the main topic of study, were recited and oblations of curds and *saktu* were offered to the sacrificial fire. The Yajurvedins naturally offered first oblations to sacrificial deities, for Yajurveda was intimately connected with sacrifice, and then invoked the blessings of the deities of *Saṁhitā* and the authors of its various sections. And then came the turn of the Ṛigveda, the Yajurveda, the Sāmaveda, the Atharvaveda and Itihāsa and Purāṇa to receive the respectful tribute of the living generation.[1] Famous scholars who had enriched Yajurvedic school were also not forgotten on the day, for grateful homage was paid to Kṛishṇa Dvaipāyana, Vaishampāyana, Tittiri, (the author of the Kṛishṇa Yajurveda) Ātreya, the author of the *Padapāṭha* of the Yajurveda, Kauṇḍinya the *Vṛittikāra*, Baudhāyana the *Pravachanakāra*,

[1] *Bau. Gr. S.*, III. 1.

3

Āpastamba, the *Sūtrakāra*, and to Satyāshādha, Hiraṇṇyakeśin, Vājasaneya, Yājñavalkya, Bhāradvāja, and Agniveśya. All these were celebrated scholars and authors of the Yajurvedic school and by paying them tribute on the opening day of the college, students were reminded of the deep debt of gratitude they owed to the literary celebrities of the past, and were asked to emulate their example. What better course can be devised for sharpening the ardour of young scholars ? The ritual of the Sāmavedins is based on similar lines ; it naturally invokes the memory of its own doctors like Jaimini, Tālavakāra, Rāṇāyani, Bhāguri etc.

If such is the nature of Upākarma, it may be asked, 'what about the renewal of the sacred thread which is now regarded as the very essence of Upākarma ?' Renewal of the sacred thread was so minor an element of the ceremony, that most of the Gṛihyasūtras do not refer to it at all. At the time of most of the *Vratas* and Sanskāras, fresh *Yajñopavītas*, *Ajinas*, *Daṇḍas* etc. were to be worn by the students, and Upākarma was no exception. By a strange irony of fate, the most insignificant element of the ritual has now assumed an altogether disproportionate importance and its real nature and significance is forgotten altogether !

It will be thus seen that Upākarma or Śrāvaṇī ritual had a high educational value. Under the guise of paying tribute to the celebrities of the past, it aroused ambition in the minds of young scholars. They commenced their annual labour with zest and vigour, hoping one day to equal the ancients by their own achievements. When the ceremony was in later times extended to the householders as well, it reminded them of their duty to be up-to-date in their own branches of learning. It is a pity that modern education systems have not got any ceremony of similar nature and import.

## Utsarjana Ritual.

The annual education session closed with the Utsarjana ceremony. It was performed in the months of Pausha or Māgha (January—February). The term of Vedic studies thus extended over about five or six months only. Such a small session was sufficient when the curriculum consisted of the study of the Veda only; later on when more branches of learning like grammar, phonology, logic, philosophy, etc. were included in the course, the duration of the annual term was also increased as will be shown in Chapter III.

Utsarjana ceremony is more or less modelled on the Upākarma ritual. Before parting for their homes, students used to offer their tribute of respect to the same deities and celebrities which were given that honour at the beginning of the annual session. At present we do not perform the ritual at the proper time, but try to atone for this failure by performing it on the day of the Śrāvaṇī, just before that ritual. This of course is due to our monumental ignorance of the real purpose of both the rituals. The modern practice, however, is at least

500 years old. Mitramiśra, a 17th century writer, quotes two or three anonymous writers to support the modern practice of performing both the ceremonies on the day of Upākarma.[1]

## MONOR VRATAS DURING BRAHMACHARYA.

Our authorities prescribe several Vratas or religious observances for the Brahmachārin during his Brahmacharya. Some of these lasted over a few days only, while others extended over a period of several months. These observances were usually prescribed at the commencement of the study of particular portions or rituals of the Vedic literature. Thus Āśvamedhika Vrata lasted during the study of the Aśvamedha ritual, Rahasya or Upanishad Vrata during the study of the Upanishads, Vrātika Vrata during the study of the Āraṇyakas, and so on.[2] Some Vratas like the Mahānāmika were believed to invest the Brahmachārin with mystic powers like commanding the rainfall. Most of these Vratas were probably observed in priestly families, which alone normally used to specialise in all the Vedic branches and rituals. In course of time as non-Vedic literature grew in extent and importance and came to be studied extensively by the Brahmana

---

[1] Cf. पुष्ये तूत्सर्जनं कुर्यादुपाकर्मदिनेऽथवा । खादिरगृह्य
उत्सर्जनं पौषमासे उपाकर्मदिनेऽथवा । स्मृतिसमुच्चय & स्मृत्यंतर
Quoted in *VMS.*, pp. 540, 543.

[2] See *Mā. Gr.S.*, I, 23, 14-20; *Vā. Gr. S.*, 8; *Jai. Gr. S.*, I, 16; Chandrakānta's commentary on *Go. Gr. S.*, III, 1, 28.

community, these Vratas became less and less popular. Hence it is that they are not mentioned in majority of the Gṛihya-sūtras and are altogether passed over by the Dharma-sūtras and Smṛities.

## GODĀNA VRATA.

At the age of 16 when usually the beard makes its appearance, the Brahmachārin used to perform the Godāna-vrata on the occasion of the first shaving of the beard.[1] The procedure and Mantras prescribed for this ritual are more or less similar to those laid down for the Chaula or tonsure ceremony, the only difference being that the beard was to be shaved instead of the head.[2]

When by about the beginning of the Christian era marriages of boys and girls began to be performed at an early age, Godāna ceremony began to be considered as marking the end of the Brahmacharya period. *Bhāradvāja* and *Vārāha Gṛihyasūtras*, which seem to belong to about this period, refer to the view entertained by a section of the society that Vedic studies should terminate at sixteen with the Godāna ceremony.[3] According to the scheme of the prince's

---

[1] *Aś. Gr. S.*, I, 18, 1-2; *Āp. Gr. S.*, XVI, 1-2, *Mā. Gr. S.*, I, 21, 13-14.

[2] *Bau. Gr. S.*, III, 2, 52.

[3] Cf. आगोदानकर्मणः (ब्रह्मचर्यम्) इत्येके। *Bh. G. S.*, 1. 9.; see also *Va. Gr. S.*, 9.

education, as outlined by Kauṭilya, he was to finish his studies at 16 and marry immediately after the Godāna ritual. Medieval commentators like Śrīnivāsa, accustomed to child marriages, argued that the termination of Vedic studies at 16 did not collide with the Sastric injunction that they ought to extend over 12 years, for Upanayana could be performed in the 5th year to permit a 12 years Vedic course.[1] As has been shown above, Godāna ceremony had originally nothing to do with the termination of the Vedic studies. For the latter occasion the ritual of *Samāvartana* was prescribed and it was altogether different from Godāna. In later times the two rituals were confounded with each other owing to the prevalence of early marriages. The confusion was facilitated by the circumstance of shaving forming an important element in both the Godāna and *Samāvartana* rituals.

## SAMĀVARTANA OR SNĀNA.

Samāvartana or Snāna ceremony was performed at the end of the Brahmacharya period to mark the termination of the education course. Originally the ceremony was performed only in the case of those scholars, who had finished the entire course and

---

1. Cf. ब्रह्मचर्यान्ते एतत्कर्म । पञ्चमे चोपनयने तदादि द्वादश वर्षाणि ब्रह्मचर्यं तन्मध्ये चानुकल्पाश्रयेण महानाम्नीसमासौ मेधाविना च अध्येतव्यजातस्य सर्वस्याप्यध्ययने अर्थादिदं षोडशवर्षे भविष्यति इति मुख्याभिप्रायेण इदं षोडश इत्युक्तम् । पक्षान्तरे यथा कथंचिद् ब्रह्मचर्यावसाने एवेदं कुर्यात् ।
On *Jai. Gr. S.*, I. 18.

performed all the Vratas; some were in favour of excluding those who had merely committed the Vedas to memory but were unable to expound their meaning.[1] In course of time, however, the original nature and purport of the ceremony were forgotten and it came to be regarded as a bodily (*Śārīra*) Sanskāra, to be performed necessarily in all cases, irrespective of the consideration as to whether any educational course was followed by the person or not. In early times it was performed when the education of the youth was over; marriage usually followed, but by no means immediately. In later times the theory gained ground that a person should not remain without an Āśrama even for a single moment; if a Snātaka was not immediately married, he would be spending some days when he would be neither a Brahmachārin nor a Gṛihastha or a householder. Medieval writers like Mitramiśra began to advocate that the Samāvartana should be performed only when the marriage of the youth was already settled.[2] This of couse was not the original idea. The ritual was intended to correspond in a great degree to the modern convocation function. Only those who have passed their examination are at present admitted to the convocation; only those who had finished their education were in ancient times honoured with the privilege of Samavartana or Snāna.

---

[1] Cf. अन्यो वेदपाठी । न तस्य स्नानम् । *Mā. Gr. S.*, I, 2, 3.

[2] *VMS.* p. 575.

Onr authorities prescribe no definite age for this Sanskāra. Duration of the student life varied with different courses and students, as will be shown in Chapter III; and so no definite time could be prescrided for this ritual.

Samāvartana ceremony is as simple as it is significant. An auspicious day was selected and the Brahmachārin was required to shut himself up in a room throughout the morning. This appears to be a queer procedure, but Bhāradvāja attributes it to the desire to save the sun the humiliation of being confronted with a superior lustre.[1] For, says this writer, the sun can shine only with the lustre he borrows from the Snātakas who have completed their education. What better compliment can be conceived for education ?

The student came out of his room at the midday, cleansed his mouth and shaved his head and beard. He then relinquished his girdle (*mekhalā*), deer-skin, (*Ajina*), etc., which were the insignia of the student's order. The period of stern discipline was now over and the teacher himself, who had sternly refused him the use of a number of luxuries, now came forward to offer them to him. The Guru was himself to give him a bath in fragrant water.[2] The bath was followed

---

[1] Cf. एतदहःस्नातानां ह वा एष एतत्तेजसा तपति तस्मादेनमेतदहर्नाभितपेत्। II, 1. 8.

[2] *Go. Gr. S.*, III, 4, 11: *Kh. Gr. S.*, III, 1, 9.

by an offer of new clothes. Ornaments, garland, collyrium, turban, umbrella and shoes, the use of which was a taboo to him in the Brahmacharya period, were now to be formally and officially offered to him by his teacher with the recitation of proper Mantras. It was expected that the guardians, who were well off, would furnish a double set of the above articles, one for the teacher and the other for his ward.[1] A Homa followed and the hope was expressed that the Snātaka would get plenty of students to teach.[2] The teacher then offered him *Madhuparka*,[3] an honour reserved for the very select few like the king, Guru, and son-in-law.

Dressed in his new dress, the student would proceed to the assembly of the learned men of the locality in a chariot or on an elephant.[4] He was there formally introduced as a competent scholar by his teacher. Returning home he would bid farewell to his teacher after paying him such honorarium (*gurudakshiṇā*) as he could afford.

A critical survey of the Samāvartana ritual will show how high was the respect in which scholars who had completed their education were held by society

---

[1] *Aś. Gr. S.* III, 8.

[2] *Bau. Gr. S.*, II, 6.

[3] *Madhuparka* denotes an offering of ghee, honey, etc. presented by the householder to a respectable guest on his arrival home.

[4] *Dr. Gr. S.*, III, 1, 26; *Āp. Gr. S.* I, 11, 5.

in ancient India. A *Brāhmaṇa* passage quoted in Grihya Sūtra asserts that the Snātaka is a powerful personality.[1]

## Rituals in Useful Education.

When we consider the great hold which religion possesses over the Hindu mind, it is natural to expect some rituals in useful and professional education also. Unfortunately none of our source books has been written by Kshattriya or Vaishya men of letters, who were out to explain in detail their scheme of professional education. Brahmana writers do not naturally evince much interest in the problems connected with useful education in which they were not as keenly interested as they were in Vedic and literary education. As a consequence we possess very scanty information about the rituals connected with useful and professional education.

## Ayurvedic Upanayana.

Upanayana ritual used to be performed in early times, as we have seen already,[2] every time a student approached a new teacher or commenced a new course. It was primarily intended for Vedic education, but very soon its principle was extended to useful education also. The earliest extant writers on Āyurveda, Charaka and Susruta, lay down a special Upanayana ceremony for

---

[1] Cf. महद्वै एतद् भूतं यः स्नातकः ।

[2] See *ante*, p. 8.

students seeking admission to the medical course. The medical profession was not like the Vedic scholarship an exclusive monopoly, in theory or practice, of any particular caste; so Suśruta holds that a Kshatriya or a Vaishya physician also can play the role of the Guru for boys of his own caste.[1] It is quite probable that even Brahmana boys may have been initiated by non-Brahmana medical teachers, though our texts do not attest to this practice. The surgical school of Suśruta was in favour of the admission of even Śūdra boys, though formal Upanayana with the recitation of the Mantras was prohibited in their case.[2] It is quite probable that Kshatriya and Śūdra surgeons may have been, by tradition and environment, better adepts in the use of the knife than their Brahmana and Vaishya compeers.[3]

Ayurvedic Upanayana was a short ritual modelled largely upon the Vedic prototype. An auspicious day was selected for thep urpose. *Darbha*, *Samidhs*, (sacred fuel) flowers etc. were collected, an altar was specially prepared, and oblations of ghee and honey were offered to various deities and sages, first by the teacher and then by the student. Naturally Dhan-

---

1 Sūtra-sthāna, II, 5.

2 *Ibid.*

3 Such minor surgical operations as were performed before the introduction of the modern surgery were usually attempted by barbers.

vantari, Aśvins, Indra, Prajāpati and the Sūtrakāras, intimately connected with the development of the medical science, occupied the place of honour in this sacrifice. Both the teacher and the student circumambulated the fire on the altar. Brahmanas and celebrated physicians were then worshipped by the pupil. Then in the presence of the sacred fire the Guru charged the student to follow the well known rules of the student life and refrain from lust, anger, covetousness, laziness, pride, untruth and cruelty.[1] The student was specially required to be always industrious and engaged in the pursuit of fresh knowledge. He ought to have faith in his teacher who was required to teach him all that he knew.

### Dhanurvedic Upanayana

We have no early authentic account of the religious rituals performed at the commencement of Dhanurveda or military education. *Dhanurveda-saṁhitā* of Vasishṭha, a fairly late work, informs us[2] that the ritual was to be performed on an auspicious day at the beginning of the militay education. The student, who was required to observe a fast on that day, used to offer oblations to gods at the outset. Brahmanas were then fed and presents were offered to the teacher. The most important part of the ritual was the offering of a weapon to the youth along with the recitation of a

---

[1] Suśruta, Sūtra-sthāna, chap. 2.

[2] I, 4-23.

Vedic Mantra.[1] Military training was no monopoly of the Kshatriyas in early times, and Vasishṭha therefore lays down that a Brahmana was to be invested with a bow, the Kshatriya with a sword the Vaishya with a lance and the Śūdra with a mace. The Guru, who could initiate the youths, was himself expected to be an expert in the use of seven weapons, viz., the bow, the disc, the sword, the spear, the mace, the arms and the *khārikārā.*

How for this Dhanurvedic Upanayana was common among the Kshatriyas or those classes of the community, who received the military training, we do not know. The ritual is not mentioned by any early authority, and the epic heroes are not stated to have performed it. The Mantras recited at the time of offering the weapon to the student has no connection with the occasion, as shown in the foot-note below. It is therefore very doubtful whether the ritual was in general vogue. Probably it was a later invention and confined to a small section of the Kshatriya community.

---

[1] The Mantra laid down by Vasishṭha is Kāṭhaka, XVI, 16,

काण्डात्काण्डं प्ररोहन्ती परुषस्परुषस्परि ।
एवा नो दूर्वे प्रतनु सहस्रेण शतेन च॥
या शतेन प्ररोहसि सहस्रेण विरोहसि ।
तस्मै ते देवीष्टके विधेम हविषा वयम् ॥

The stanza, however, refers to Dūrvā grass and has no connection with the bow or arrow.

## CHHURIKĀ-BANDHA CEREMONY.

*Chhurikā-bandha* ceremony corresponds to Brahmanical Samāvartana and was performed at the end of the military training. The central and essential part of the ritual was, as the name itself would suggest, the investiture of the budding hero with a dagger in token of his having completed his military training.[1] This ceremony is mentioned by Nārada alone, but it was fairly common in Rajputana among Rajput families at the beginning of the 19th century, and was known as *kharg-bandāi* (tying of the sword), which is the vernacular rendering of the *chhurikā-bandha* of Nārada. This ceremony, which was performed before the marriage, may have been common in higher aristocratic families.

---

[1] Cf. छुरिकाबन्धनं वक्ष्ये नृपाणां प्राक्करग्रहात् ।
विवाहोक्तेषु मासेषु शुक्लपक्षेप्यनस्तगे ॥
छुरिकाबंधनं कार्यं अर्चयित्वामरान्पितृन् ।
अर्चयेच्छुरिकां नित्यं देवतानां च संनिधौ ॥
व्रतलग्ने च बध्नीयात्कट्यां लक्षणसंयुताम् ।

नारद in *VMS.*, p. 580.

## CHAPTER II.

### THE TEACHER AND THE STUDENT.

The success and the achievements of an educational system depend to a large extent on the ideals that animate the teacher and the student, the nature of the relationship that exists between the two, and the type of life they lead. In this chapter it is proposed to discuss the main problems connected with the teacher and the student and their mutual relations.

### THE IMPORTANCE OF THE TEACHER.

Perhaps nowhere else in the world has greater importance been attached to the teacher than in India. Such has been the case since the earliest times. No person on the earth deserves greater reverence than the teacher, not even the father or the mother.[1] To our parents we no doubt owe our physical birth, but to our teacher our spiritual one. The idea that the Guru or the teacher is the spiritual father, which is quite common in the Smṛiti literature, occurs as

---

[1] There are contradictory passages in the Dharmaśāstra literature about the relative greatness of the father, the mother and the teaeher, but the balance of evidence is in favour of the view that the teacher deserves the greatest reverence.

early as the Atharvaveda,[1] and the *Baudhāyana Dharma-sūtra* declares that a Śrotriya or scholar, who teaches pupils, cannot be deemed to be issueless.[2] It was the function of the teacher to lead the scholar from the darkness of ignorance to the light of knowledge;[3] the lamp of learning is concealed under a cover, the teacher removes it and lets out the light.[4] His importance therefore cannot be exaggerated; he is in fact indespensable. This is graphically illustrated by the story of Ekalavya narrated in the *Mahābhārata*. Ekalavya was refused admission to his school of archery by Droṇa on the ground that he was a Nishāda. Ekalavya had however implicit faith in Droṇa; unable to get the guidance of Droṇa in flesh and blood, he prepared an image of his Guru and successfully finished his studies in archery under the inspiration that he received from the inanimate representative of his animate Guru.[5] It was not only Hindu thinkers that attached great importance to the teacher; Buddhist thinkers are found to hold

---

1 *Va. Dh. S.*, 28,38-9; *Gau. Dh. S.*, I, 1, 10; Manu, II, 170.
Cf. आचार्य उपनयमानो ब्रह्मचारिणं कृणुते गर्भमन्तः। *A. V.*, XI, 5, 3.

2 *Bau. Dh. S.*, I, 2, 48.

3 Āp. *Dh. S.*, I, 10, 11.

4 Cf. यथा घटप्रतिच्छन्ना रत्नराजा महाप्रभाः।
अकिंचित्करतां प्राप्तास्तद्वद्विद्याश्चतुर्दश ॥
Quoted by Aparāka on Yāj. I, 212.

5 Ādiparvan, 143, 43 ff.

similar views. Buddha has laid down that every Saddhivihārika or pupil must have an Upajjhāya or teacher to guide him for a long time; in the 7th century A. D. Buddhist novices used to be under the control and guidance of their Gurus for ten long years[1].

The high reverence which was primarily intended for the teacher of the Vedas, was extended in course of time to his humbler confrere, who initiated the young pupil in the mysteries of the 3 R's. or taught him the technique of a profession. The teachers on their part recognised the responsibility of their position. There was often competition among them for getting more students in their classes;[2] but their conduct was usually honourable. In this connection there is a very interesting story narrated in the *Gopatha Brāhmaṇa*.[3] There was a discussion between two teachers, Maudgalya and Maitreya, in which the latter was proved to be not well grounded in a certain branch of knowledge. He immediately closed his classes and dismissed his students, observing that it was now incumbent upon him to learn the subject in which Maudgalya had specialised before he could continue his school. The debate between Śankara and Maṇḍanamiśra was held on the condition that the vanquished should become the pupil of the victor.

---

[1] Legge, I-tsing, p. 104.

[2] See, *Tai. Ār.*, VII, 4; *Pār, Gr. S.*, II, 10; *Vā. Gr.S.*, 7

[3] I, 1, 31.

The great importance that was attached to the teacher in the Hindu Education System is not difficult to understand. Since the earliest times the Vedic learning is being transmitted orally in India from one generation to another. This continued to be the case even when the art of writing came to be well known. The Mahābhārata condemns to hell a person who commits the Vedas to writing. Great importance was attached to the proper accent and pronunciation in the Vedic recitation, and these could be properly learnt only from the lips of a properly qualified teacher. The continuous transmission of the store of the Vedic knowledge, which society regarded as priceless, was possible only through the instrumentality of the teacher, and his importance therefore could not be exaggerated. With the rise of the mystical systems of philosophy in the age of the Upanishads, the reverence for the Guru became still more intensified; for spiritual salvation depended almost entirely upon his proper guidence.[1] This deification of the philosophical Guru was not without its reaction in favour of the ordinary teacher. In the case of professions, even when books exist in plenty, a good deal more has to be learnt from the teacher. So a well-trained Guru, who would unreservedly place at the disposal of his pupil the essence of

---

[1] नैषा मतिस्तर्केणापनेया प्रोक्तान्येनैव सुज्ञानाय प्रेष्ठ । *K. Up.*, 11, 9.

तद्विज्ञानाय गुरुमेवाभिगच्छेत्समित्पाणिः श्रोत्रियं ब्रह्मनिष्ठम् ॥

*Mu. Up.*, 1, 2, 3.

all his experience could hardly be over-venerated by artisan apprentices working under him. Books in ancient India were dear, rare and written on materials that were very fragile and easily perishable; we can therefore well understand the prejudice against the learning aquired from books alone.[1]

## TEACHER'S TRAINING.

Though the teacher was held in high reverence, it does not appear that any institutions like Teachers' Training Colleges of the modern times existed in the past. In theological circles a person was held competent to teach the Gāyatrī Mantra only when he had recited it for 12,000 times.[2] This recitation would be increasing the spiritual worth of the teacher, but it could hardly have had any effect on his teaching capacity. One of the Mantras recited at the Samāvartana Homa prayed that the graduate, who was performing it, may have the good luck of attracting students from all quarters.[3] It is therefore clear that no further training was deemed necessary for the graduate in order to qualify him for the teaching profession. The reasons for this are not far to seek. Students received individual attention and lessons

---

1 पुस्तकप्रत्ययाधीतं नाधीतं गुरुसंनिधौ ।
भ्राजते न सभामध्ये जारगर्भ इव स्त्रियः ॥

Nārada quoted by *Pa. Ma.*, at I, 38.

2 Bṛihanmanu quoted in *VMS.*, p. 409

3 *Bau. Gr. S.*, II, 6.

in Vedic studies from their teachers, as will be shown in Chapter IV. During their educational course they could note how precisely teachers used to pronounce and intone the Vedic Mantras, when teaching them to their students. As far as the study of other branches like grammar, logic, rhetoric, philosophy, etc. was concerned, no special training was necessary for fostering and developing the powers of exposition and elucidation of students specialising in them. In the modern system of education students can get their degrees by listening to their teachers in the class-rooms and answering the question papers in the examination halls. Such was not the case in ancient India. Several times during his course the student was called upon to pass through the fiery ordeal of *Śāstrārtha*, when he was called upon to defend his own positon and attack that of the opponent in heated discussions. Powers of debate and discussions were thus remarkably developed by the time the student finished his education. Advanced students were also given opportunities of teaching the beginners in most of the educational institutions[1]. The Snātaka therefore had a fairly large teaching experience to his credit by the time he left his Gurukula or *alma mater*. The absence of training colleges therefore did

---

[1] See *Suta-soma-jātaka* No. 537. Of the advanced scholars at Nālandā and Valabhi, I-tsing says that they passed two or three years in these Universities, ***instructed by their teachers and instructing others.*** I-tsing, p. 177.

not materially tell upon the efficiency of the teachers at least as far as higher education was concerned. Of course this does not mean that all the teachers in ancient India were of a high calibre; the average efficiency, however, must have been fairly remarkable in teaching in the traditional method. Some, however, were profound scholars, while others were particularly apt in teaching. The great poet Kālidāsa has observed that these qualities need not necessarily coexist in all cases[1]. The ideal teacher was expected to combine deep scholarship with tact in teaching.

## Social Position of the Teacher.

The vast majority of teachers in Ancient India consisted of householders. Such was undoubtedly the case as far as the primary education was concerned. In higher education, the majority of Hindu teachers were married men, leading lives of plain living and high thinking, and subsisting on what their pupils and rulers could provide for them. Some of these teachers like Kaṇva and Divākaramitra (of the *Harsha-charit*) were Vānaprasthas or Sanyāsins, leading retired lives in forests away from the bustle of the city or the village life; but they formed a small minority. As far as the teachers in Upanishadic, Jain and

---

[1] Cf. श्लिष्टा क्रिया कस्यचिदात्मसंस्था संक्रांतिरन्यस्य विशेषरूपा ।
यस्योभयं साधु स शिक्षकाणां धुरि प्रतिष्ठापयितव्य एव ॥
Mālavikāgnimitram, Act I.

Buddhist circles were concerned, they were all Sanyāsins, who had renounced the world and its temptations; but we are not concerned here with such teachers.

Our sources do not enable us to get any adequate idea of the normal income of the teacher in the various periods of ancient Indian history. In ancient times in India as in the West, there was no Government Education Department prescribing a scale of salaries, which was more or less followed in private institutions. Nay, educational institutions themselves were evolved in India after about the 4th century A. D. For several centuries, or rather throughout the ancient Indian period, the teacher had no fixed income except in those rare cases where he belonged to an institution, where his salary was provided for by an endowment. The Dharma-śāstra literature throws no light on the pecuniary position of the Veda teacher. Universities at Nālandā and Valabhi were richly endowed; but they were more monastic than educational in their outlook and organisation. Teachers in these places were generally monks who had renounced the world and were in no need of salaries. At Vikramaśilā the adminstration had to spend for each monk-teacher just the amount necessary for the maintenance of four ordinary monks.[1]

The Jātakas, which supply us a good deal of interesting information, about Takshaśilā and its educational

---

[1] Bose, *Indian Teachers of Buddhist Universities*, p. 35

activities, are altogether silent about the income of the 'world-renowed' teachers of the place. If we are to take for granted that each of these 'world renowned' teachers had 500 students under him, and each of the latter offered him 1,000 coins, (which are obviously intended to stand for the contemporary silver Karshāpaṇas, each being slightly heavier than the modern silver four anna piece,) then these Takshaśilā teachers, we shall have to conclude, must have been fairly rich men. But these Jātaka statements cannot be taken at their face value. As will be shown in Chapter IV, normally speaking a Sanskrit teacher used to be in charge of not more than 20 students. The honorarium of 1000 coins was further paid only by rich parents like kings or merchant princes. Ordinary parents must have offered much less. Further, we do not know whether this sum did not include the boarding expenses of the scholar also, for many of these scholars, who used to pay in advance the fee of 1,000 coins, are described as living happily in their teachers' house like their eldest sons. The sum was intended as the fee for the whole of the course,[1] and we do not know its precise duration.

---

[1] There are some indications to show that the course probably extended over five years. If we suppose that each teacher used to train about 20 students who were on the average paying, for their tuition only, 500 four anna pieces, the average income of the Takshaśilā teacher would be equal to 500 tolas of silver. We have no definite information

*P. T. O.*

South Indian inscriptions belonging to the 11th and the 12th centuries throw some welcome light on the teacher's income. From one of these inscriptions[1] we learn that in the Sanskrit college at Ennayiram the Vedanta teacher used to get a daily allowance of $1\frac{1}{3}$ *kalam* of paddy towards the beginning of the 11th century. The allowance for the Vyākaraṇa and Mīmānsā teachers was one *kalam* of paddy a day. At this time the village accountant used to get an annual salary of 200 *kalams* of paddy; so the income of the Sanskrit teacher was about double the pay of the village accountant. An adult at this period required about twenty *kalams* of paddy for his annual food expenses[2]; so the Sanskrit teacher with his annual income of about 400 or 500 *kalams* could have led a life of moderate comforts, neither very luxurious nor very penurious.

---

(*Continued from the last page*)

about the cost of living during this period, and thus can form hardly any adequate idea of the financial condition of the Takshaśilā teacher, even if the links in the above argument were all correct.

[1] No. 333 of *S. I. E. R.*, 1917

[2] The annual expense for a daily sumptuous feast was $37\frac{1}{2}$ *kalams* of paddy (S. I. I., II., No. 28); that for a daily ordinary meal must therefore have been about 20 *kalams*. See also Altekar, *The Rāshṭrakūṭas and their Times*, *pp. 393-8*. The quantity of the *kalam* varied with localities, but usually it was about a maund.

This seems to have been the average salary of the Sanskrit teacher. The teacher at the Malkapuram Sanskrit college used to receive a salary, which was equal to twice the wages of the carpenter.[1] The carpenter at this time used to receive about 150 *kalams* of paddy for his annual wages,[2] so the Sanskrit teacher's salary was about 300 *kalams* per annum.[3]

To conclude, the teachers in the organised educational institutions of south India used to receive during the 11th and the 12th centuries an income which was about twice the amount necessary for keeping an

---

[1] *S. I. E. R.* for 1917, pp. 122-4

[2] *S. I. I.*, II, p. 320

[3] In the Sanskrit college at Tirumukkudul in Chingleput district, the Veda teacher used to receive only 60 *kalams* of paddy, (*S. I. E. R.*, 1915, No 182), but he was there a part time teacher as will be shown in Chap. VIII. The summary of one inscription given in *S. I. E. R.* for 1918 pp. 145ff. seems to show that the teachers in the south Indian college described in that record used to receive about 1440 *kalams* of paddy per year. This seems to be a very high salary, but until the inscription is published in extenso, we cannot draw any definite conclusion. In the Salotgi Sanskrit college, the principal was given an endowment of 50 *nivartanas* of land. We however do not know the exact dimensions of the *nivartana* in vogue in the locality, nor are we informed whether the land was wet or dry. So this inscription does not help us much in this matter. ( See, *E. I.*, IV. p. 60 ).

ordinary Brahmana family in moderate comforts. The same probably was the case in earlier periods, though we have no definite evidence on the point. The Sanskrit teacher was thus neither running mad after wealth nor shunning it. He was content to lead a life of moderate comforts. About the financial condition of the primary teacher we have next to no information about any period in ancient Indian history. In pre-British days he used to eke out more or less a precarious existence from the voluntary contributions that he used to receive from the guardians of his pupils, which were now and then supplemented by special gifts on festive and religious occasions. It does not appear probable that the primary teacher was at any time as well off as the village accountant.

## THE TEACHER AND THE CASTE SYSTEM.

The general view that the teaching profession was a preserve jealously guarded by the Brahmanas in ancient India requires several modifications. It is undoubtedly true that the vast majority of teachers in ancient India was that of Brahmanas; it is doubtful if the ambitious Kshatriya or the clever Viashya would have cared to exchange the horse or the counter for the teacher's *gādi*. The theory that none but the Brahmana could teach the Vedas gained ascendancy in the age of Smṛitis; in the earlier times, however, there are several examples of kings like Aśvapati, Janaka and Pravāhaṇa Jaivali attaining wide fame as teachers and imparting instructions to all, including the Brahmanas.[1] Nay, the *Kāṭhaka Saṁhitā* has a ritual calculated to promote the fame of a non-Brahmana, who had mastered the Vedas but was not prospering;[2] the fame must obviously be referring to his reputation as an efficient teacher.

We learn from some Jātaka stories that training in several practical professions like the military art, medicine, snake charming etc. was being imparted by Brahmanas at Takshaśilā.[3] Caste system had not yet become very rigid, and the professions were not yet strictly predetermined by birth. Stray Kshatriya teachers of the Vedic learning existed down to the Upanishadic times, and the keen intellect of the Brahmana was being utilised to further the bounds of human knowledge in several spheres of non-Vedic learning. To a certain extent Buddhism was a revolt against Brahmanical supremacy, but strangely enough many of the noted Buddhist teachers like Moggalāna, Sāriputra, Nāgasena, Vasubandhu, Nāgārjuna, etc. were Brahmana converts to Buddhism. It is not

---

[1] See *Br. Up.*, II, 1, 14; *Ch. Up.*, V. 4. 1.

[2] Cf. योऽब्राह्मणो विद्यामनूच्य नैव रोचेत स एतांश्चतुर्होतॄन् व्याचक्षीत ।
एतद्वै देवानां ब्रह्म निरुक्तं यच्चतुर्होतारस्तदेनं निरुच्यमानं प्रकाशं गमयति॥

काठकसंहिता IX 16

[3] Bhīmasena Jātaka, No. 3; Parantapa Jātaka, No 416, Mahāsutasoma Jātaka, No. 537; etc.

improbable that an appreciable section of the Buddhist teachers in the heyday of that religion was originally of Brahmana extraction.

In course of time, however, religious and literary education became confined to the Brahmanas, and higher professional education to the various non Brahmana castes and guilds concerned in the matter. This development had a disastrous consequence on the welfare of the country, as will be shown in the last chapter of this book.

Primary education was largely in the hands of the members of the village priestly families. There must have been a good sprinkling of Vaishya teachers also. This appears probable when we note how a large percentage of primary teachers in some provinces like Bengal and the United Provinces was drawn from the Kāyastha caste at the advent of the British rule owing to the writing profession having become a practical monopoly of that caste.

## Admission Qualifications

Birth as a bar to admission operated only in the case of the Vedic education. Smṛitis are positively against the admission of the Śūdras and Ati-śūdras to theological schools. Some earlier texts are in favour of the admission of the Rathakāra (carpenter) to the privilege of Upanayana and Vedic studies; but the conclusion sometimes drawn from this circumstance that some classes of the Śūdras were admitted to Vedic schools is not sound. For, the important profession of chariot-making and carpentry, which had revolutionised warfare and established the Aryan supremacy over the non-Aryans, must have been a monopoly of a section of the Kshatriya or the Vaishya communities.[1]

It is undoubtedly a pity that a section of the community should have been excluded from the Vedic education, but it is very doubtful if this prohibition would have been enforced if the art of writing were known in early Vedic times and utilised for the purpose of preserving the Vedic texts. The Aryan theologians believed that if there was the slightest mistake in the accent or the pronunciation of the Vedic Mantra, it would bring about ruin and disaster.[2] It was feared that the Vedic Sanskrit not being the mother tongue of the Śūdras, the sacred hymns would be transformed out of all recognition if they were transmitted hereditarily in non-Aryan families. This seems to have been

---

[1] *Vaj. Sam.* XXVI, 2 यथेमां वाचं कल्याणीमावदानि जनेभ्यः। ब्रह्मराजन्याभ्यां शूद्राय चार्याय च स्वाय चारणाय च ॥ is taken by some as referring to the admission of the Śudras to the Vedic educatiuon. This, however, is a very questionable interpretation; *Kalyāṇī vāk* refers to courteous speech and not to Vedic Mantras.

[2] Cf. मंत्रो हीनः स्वरतो वर्णतो वा मिथ्याप्रयुक्तो न तमर्थमाह।
स वाग्वज्रो यजमानं हिनस्ति यथेन्द्रशत्रुः स्वरतोऽपराधात् ॥

*Pāṇiniśikshā, v. 52*

the chief reason for the exclusion of the Śūdras from the Vedic education. This exclusion however did not amount to the total denial of religious education to the Śūdra community; for the members of that community were permitted to study Smṛitis, epics and Purāṇas.[1] Vidura, though a Śūdra, was very well grounded in several branches of non-Vedic learning.

There were no caste restrictions to the admission of students in Buddhist educational institutions. There is no direct evidence on the point, but what is stated above is a natural corollary from the circumstance that even admission to the Order was open to all with the exception of a few classes like kings' servants, slaves, debtors etc., whose initiation was calculated to affect the rights of third parties.

## Admission Test.

Very little information is available about the admission test at the time when students were enrolled in educational institutions. In the ancient Indian education system there were, generally speaking, no examinations and degrees, as will be shown in Chapter IV. Every student therefore had to undergo a severe test before he was admitted to particular classes of higher educational institutions. There were no migration certificates or certificates of efficiency to afford a student any shelter at the time of his admission.

[1] See *Sānti P.*, 50, 40; 328, 49

This would become clear from what we know about Nālandā; Yuan Chwang informs us that only two or three out of ten seeking admission to that University would succeed in gaining their object[1]. Both at Nālandā and Vikramaśilā a Dvārapāla (lit. a door-keeper) used to be appointed at each gate from among very distinguished scholars, whose duty it was to test the calibre and equipment of those anxious to secure admission.[2] Probably this principle was followed also in other educational centres, though we have no definite information on the point.

## Mutual Relations Between the Teacher and the Student.

The teacher's profession had a very high code of honour in ancient India. The duty to teach has been regarded as an imperative one since very early times, and has been enjoined as such on every Brahmana. He could refuse no properly qualified student, though there may be no prospects whatever of his receiving any honorarium from his student on account of his poverty. Nay, the teacher was expected to arrange for the boarding, lodging and clothing of his students in case they were very poor. That this duty was

1 Watters, II, p. 165; Beal, II, pp. 170-171

2 Bose *Indian Teachers of Buddhist Universities*, p. 47, p. 61 See also Chap. VIII, sections on Nālandā and Vikramaśilā.

recognised as binding would be clear from the fact that down to quite recent time the *Tol* teachers in Bengal used to make arrangements for the boarding of their pupils by collecting subscriptions for the purpose.[1]

The teacher was bound to commence the education of his pupil within a year of his coming to him for that purpose. If he did not do so, all the sins of the pupil were to be transferred to him.[2] Gods become angry, says the *Chhāndogya Upanishad*,[3] if a teacher capriciously withholds instructions from his properly qualified students. The *Smriti-Kaustubha* narrates

---

[1] *Nadia Gazetter*, p. 182

[2] Cf. संवत्सरोषिते शिष्ये गुरुर्ज्ञानमनिर्दिशन् ।
हरते दुष्कृतं तस्य शिष्यस्य वसतो गुरुः ॥

*Kū, p.*, in *VMS.*, p. 515.

[3] IV, 10, 2. It is no doubt true that some Tantra works recommend that nothing should be taught to a pupil till he is tested for about five years; ( e. g. *Tantrarāja-tantra*, II. 37-8 ) In Upanishads also we sometimes come across cases like those of Indra and Vairochana where instructions are given after a period of 32 years. ( *Ch. Up*., VIII, 7, 2-3 ) But these cases refer to the teaching of mystical philosophical doctrines, which could be imparted only if the student possessed the necessary bent of mind. A long period of waiting was therefore necessary to test the sincerity and *vairāgya* of the candidate. As far as ordinary education was concerned, its beginning could not be postponed on any account to a period longer than one year.

the story of a teacher condemned in the next birth to the life of a tree for his failure to impart Vedic knowledge[1]. Medical writers urge that a six month's period of waiting should be regarded as sufficient in the case of medical students to enable the teacher to find out their seriousness and intellectual calibre.[2] Profit or no profit, knowledge ought to be imparted to the deserving; gift of the greatest conceivable merit, according to Bṛihaspati,[3] is the gift of knowledge.

There were a few rational exceptions to the imperative duty to teach. These, it will be seen, are all in the interest of education. Persons who were morally or intellectually unfit to receive education were not to be admitted as students.[4] Smṛiti writers lay particular emphasis on moral disqualifications, because they have primarily the teaching of the sacred texts before their mind. The rule against the admission of intellectually incompetent students was not enforced very rigorously; Jātaka stories record several cases of dullards being admitted to educational institutions at Takshaśilā and Benares.[5] These dull students were advised discontinuance of education, when it was

---

[1] Cf. स चूतवृक्षो विप्रोऽभूद्विद्वान्वै वेदपारगः ।
विद्या न दत्ता विप्रेभ्यस्तेनैव तरुतां गतः ॥ p. 174.

[2] *Ashṭāṅga-hṛidaya*, *Sūtrasthāna*, chap. 2.

[3] Quoted in *SCS.*, p. 145.

[4] *Nirukta*, II, 4.

[5] *E. g.* Naṁgaliśa Jātaka, No. 124.

discovered that no amount of efforts on the part of the teacher was of any avail in developing their intellect.

There was no fixed scale of monthly or sessional fees prescribed for the students of the different grades or classes in ancient India. The duty to teach was imperative; no student could be turned out merely because he was too poor to pay any fees. Kālidāsa deprecates a teacher who regards his learning as a mere means of livelihood,[1] and Smṛities hold that a person who stipulates for fees is too impure to be invited for a Srāddha. *Saura Purāṇa* goes a step further and declares that if instructions are imparted for fixed fees, both the teacher and the student will go to hell.[2]

It should be however clearly noted that what is condemned by the Hindu thinkers is not the mere receiving of any honorarium or fee, but the stipulation at the time of admission that the student would be admitted to the school only if he agrees to pay certain fees, and not otherwise.[3] Judged by this standard all modern education is based upon a fundamentally wrong conception, for we do not admit students unless they agree to pay a certain scale of fees.

---

[1] यस्यागमः केवलजीविकायै तं ज्ञानपण्यं वणिजो वदंति ।
*Mālavikāgnimitram*, Act I, v. 17

[2] X, 42.

[3] Cf. भृतिः संप्रतिपत्तिपूर्वकमेवाध्यापनम् प्रतिषिद्धम् ।
इतरस्य तु वृत्तिहेतुत्वेनाविरोधात् । *SCS.*, p. 140.

It is interesting to note that there existed a similar prejudice in pre-Periclean Greece against the practice of charging fees from students. It was held that the relation between the teacher and the student should be based upon mutual esteem and regard and not on any financial considerations. It was the sophists who first introduced the custom of offering instruction to any person in any subject he chose, if he offered sufficient remuneration. This procedure was first despised by public opinion, but it was almost universally adopted by all the heads of educational institutions before the 3rd century B. C.[1] In India, however, education still continues to be free in the *Pāṭhaśālās* (Sanskrit schools) of the old type.

The Hindu theory was that the teacher's honorarium becomes payable only when the whole course was over. Yājñavalkya repeatedly refused the offer of Guru-dakshiṇā (fees) by his royal pupil Janaka on the plea that he had not finished teaching the king all that he knew.[2] This course dictated by high idealism was not, however, very convenient either to the teacher or to the student's guardian. For, the imperative duty to teach imposed on the teacher did not exempt the guardian from the payment of the teacher's fees; for our texts declare that there is no object in this universe, however precious it may be, which can be regarded as an

---

[1] Munroe, *A Text Book of History of Education*, p. 112.
[2] *Br. Up.*, IV, 1.

adequate fee for even that teacher, who teaches only one letter of the alphabet.[1] This is of course in the hyperbolic strain, but it was necessary to resort to it, because the actual amount of the teacher's honorarium was made dependent upon the guardian's ability. To pay the whole fee in a lump sum at the end of the course, even when proportionate to one's ability, could not have been very convenient to guardians; many must have preferred making part payments during the course, though there is no actual instance recorded of this procedure. Jātakas record several cases of rich persons like princes and merchants paying the teacher the whole honorarium at the beginning of their wards' education.[2] When Bhīshma invited Droṇa to teach Kaurava princes, he paid the teacher handsomely before he commenced his labours.[3] The same was done by the father of Nāgasena, when he sent his son for Vedic education.[4] It is therefore clear that rich guardians

---

[1] Cf. एकमप्यक्षरं यस्तु गुरुः शिष्ये निवेदयेत्।
पृथिव्यां नास्ति तद् द्रव्यं यद्दत्वाऽनृणी भवेत्॥
Laghu-Hārita in Par.-Mād., I, ii, p. 53

It is interesting to note that Luther's view was similar. 'I tell you a teacher who faithfully trains and teaches boys can never receive an adequate reward, and no money is sufficient to pay the debt you owe him.' Monroe, *A Text book*, p. 414

[2] Jātaka Nos. 55, 61, 445, 447, 522, etc.

[3] *MBH.*, I, 142, 1.

[4] *Mil. Pan.*, I, 17.

did not take advantage of the rule that the teacher should be paid only when the education of the student was over. None, who could afford to do so, was allowed by public opinion to escape from his liability to pay the teacher's fees. The gentleman in ancient India regarded it a very great disgrace that a report should get abroad about him that he had not paid the teacher's fees, although properly instructed by the latter. When Nāgasena, being a monk, expressed his natural unwillingness to accept the rich and luxurious gifts offered by his royal pupil, Menander, the latter begged him to change his mind in order to save him from the scandal getting abroad, that though he was convinced, he would give nothing in acknowledgment to his teacher.[1]

Poor students, who were unable to pay any honorarium, used to do house-hold work in the teacher's house, as we shall soon see. When the education was over, they used to make efforts for raising funds for the purpose of paying at least some fee to their teachers. In this connection we have the example of Kautsa in the *Raghuvanśa* and of several other students in the Jātakas.[2] To refuse the request of such students was regarded as highly disgraceful; whatever they required for the purpose, it was the duty of the king and the gentry to supply. In the *Mahā-*

---

[1] *Mil. Pan.*, I, pp. 134–5.

[2] Canto V; Jātaka No. 478

*bhārata* we find king Poshya directing his wife to present her costly earrings (Kuṇḍalas) to a Snātaka named Uttaṅka, because he was asked to secure them as his fee by his teacher at the desire of the latter's wife. King Raghu is said to have contemplated an expedition against Indra, because he was anxious that a report should not get abroad that a Snātaka had to seek another donor on account of his inability to pay him his Gurudakshiṇā amount, although it was due to his having just then performed Viśvajit sacrifice, which required him to offer all his belongings as Dakshiṇā.[1]

If any gifts were received by the student during his education course, they legally belonged to the teacher.[2] If the teacher was in distress, he was authorised to appropriate a third part of the alms collected by the student.[3]

To sum up, regular fees payable by instalments were not insisted upon in ancient India. It was the duty of the Brahmanas, who were the custodians of ancient culture and literature, to teach all qualified students free. Even if such students were poor, they could not be turned out; the teacher had to teach them in return for their personal services and in expectation

---

[1] Canto V.

[2] *Ā. Dh. S.*, I, 2, 7, 19; *Vā. Gr.* S., 7.

[3] Śaṅkha in *VMS.*, p. 487.

of some lump sum to be received later, when students had finished their education and were in a position to collect money for the purpose. As far as the rich were concerned, the educational thinkers have emphatically pointed out that no amount of money could be regarded as an adequate return for the education that was being imparted to their sons by the custodians of national culture. They ought to pay the maximum that they could spare for the purpose. This arrangement is on the whole fair, for it fostered a proper sense of responsibility on both the sides.

We have seen already how the teacher was regarded as the spiritual father of the pupil. The relations between the two were therefore naturally more or less filial in character. Both Hindu and Buddhist teachers are emphatic on the point. Yāska quotes a verse of high antiquity to the effect that the teacher, who extends the limits of knowledge, should be revered by the pupil as highly as the parents.[1] Āpastamba says that a teacher should regard his students as his own sons.[2] Buddha lays down that an Upajjhāya or teacher ought to take all possible care of his pupils, arranging for their robes, bowls, etc.[3] That such was

---

[1] Cf. य आतृणत्यवितथेन कर्णौ अदुःखं कृण्वन्नमृतं सम्प्रयच्छन् ।
तं मन्येत पितरं मातरं च तस्मै न द्रुह्येत्कतमच्चनाह ॥

*Nirukta*, II. 4.

[2] Cf. पुत्रमिवैनमनुकांक्षन्... । *Āp. Dh. S*, I, 2. 8.

[3] *Digghanikāya*, III, p. 189

actually the case in Buddhist institutions would become quite clear from the testimony of I-tsing, who found the Buddhist teachers of the 7th century A. D. actually nursing their students when ill.[1]

Owing to the filial conception of the teacher-pupil relationship, extra-academic duties of the teacher were far more numerous in ancient India than they are in modern times. We can get a fairly adequate idea of these duties from the *Milindapañha,* which may be regarded as depicting the state of affairs at about the beginning of the Christian era. The teacher must always keep guard over his pupil. 'He must let him know what to cultivate and what to avoid; about what he should be earnest and what he may neglect. He must instruct him as to sleep, and as to keeping himself in health, and as to what food he may take and what he may reject............He should advise him as to the people whose company he should keep, and as to the villages and Vihāras he may frequent.......'[2]

The teacher was to teach all that he knew to his students. He was to teach nothing partially, keep nothing secret, and hold nothing back[3] through any selfish consideration of maintaining his relative superiority. When Sukeśa Bhāradvāja apprehended that his royal pupil Hiraṇyanābha was under the

---

1. Takakusu, I-tsing, p. 120.
2. I, p. 142.
3. *Ibid*, p. 143.

impression that he was withholding deliberately from him the gospel about the *Shoḍaśa-kala-purusha,* he vigorously protested; how could he be guilty of such conduct when he knew full well that it would lead to his utter moral and material degradation?[1] Suśruta requires a medical teacher to take a vow in the presence of the Upanayana fire that he would withhold nothing from his pupil.[2] How generous and large hearted teachers usually were in this connection can be judged from the conduct and exclamation of Alāra Kalāma, when the Buddha had finished his studies under him. 'Happy friend are we, in that we look upon such a venerable one, such a fellow ascetic as you. The doctrine which I know, you too know, and the doctrine which you know, I too know. As I am so are you, as you are so am I. Pray, sir, let us be joint wardens of this company.' The Buddha feelingly exclaims, 'In such wise did Alāra Kalāma, being my master, set me his pupil on precisely the same footing as he himself.[3]

In theory the teacher could accept no fees before he had finished teaching all that he knew. King Janaka, surprised by the depth and originality of the successive philosophical theories of Yājñyavalkya,

---

1 Cf. नाहमिदं वेद । यद्यवेदिषं कथं ते नावक्ष्यमिति । समूलो वैष परिशुष्यति योऽनृतमभिवदति तस्मान्नार्हाम्यनृतं वक्तुम् । *Pr. Up.* VI, 1.

2 Sūtrasthāna, Chap. 2.

3 *Further Dialogues of the Buddha*, Ariya-parivesana-sutta, p. 116,

offered him repeatedly a heavy honorarium ; the Guru however refused to accept it on the ground that he had not finished teaching him all that he knew about the point in discussion.[1] All ordinary teachers may not have followed this high ideal, but a system is to be judged by the high ideals repeatedly emphasised rather than by the conduct of a few black legs.

As we shall soon see, the student was expected to do all kind of work in the teacher's house. In practice, however, teachers used to expect service only from poor students, who were unable to offer any fees. The preceptor was, however, required to see to it that the work did not interfere with the studies of his pupils.[2] The teacher was further responsible for the safty of the students ; if a student died while executing a commission of his teacher, the latter was required to undergo a very difficult penance.[3] In practice a few teachers like Dhaumya may have been unsympathetic, but there were others like Baida, who were so kind as never to take any service or work from their pupils.[4] The story of Dhaumya and of his three pupils seems,

---

[1] Cf. पिता मेऽमन्यत नाननुशिष्य हरेतेति । *Br. Up.*, IV. I.

[2] Cf. न चैनमध्ययनविघ्नेन आत्मार्थेषूपरुंध्यादनापत्सु । *Āp. Dh. S.*, I, 2, 8.

[3] गुरुप्रयुक्तश्चेन्म्रियेत ( शिष्यः ) त्रीन्कृच्छ्रांश्चरेत् । *Bau. Dh. S.*, II, 1, 27.

[4] *MBH.*, Ādiparvan, Chap. 1–3.

moreover, to be intended more to illustrate the virtue of obedience among the students and the supernatural powers of the old sage than to typify the normal temperament of a teacher. Some teachers must have been unsympathetic, but majority seems to have more or less conformed to the ideal.

Normally there was a perfect accord between the teacher and his pupils. There must have occasionally arisen situations where refractory students had to be corrected by the use of physical force. There is a difference of opinion among educational thinkers as to whether physical punishment should or should not be used in extreme cases. Manu grows eloquent over the virtues of gentle persuasion,[1] and Āpastamba recommends that in the case of refractory students the teacher should try to improve matters by ordering a fast, cold bath or banishment from his presence.[2] Gautama, on the other hand, while laying down as a general rule that the rod should be spared as far as possible, realises that physical punishment would be sometimes necessary. He however lays down that it should be mild and not brutal. Only a thin cane or rope was to be used for the purpose, and the pupil was to be beaten only on the back ; a transgression of this rule would make the teacher liable for legal prosecu-

---

[1] II, 159-161.

[2] 1, 2, 8. 30.

tion.[1] When the teacher in the Tilamuṭṭhiya Jātaka[2] orders a few blows to be given on the back of the prince of Benares, when he found that the latter would not give up his stealing habits, he exclaims that the use of the rod cannot be altogether tabooed by the teacher. He takes up the position of Gautama, which represents the *via media* and which seems to have been generally followed in ancient India.

Many students used to live under their teachers' roofs, and the affection which existed between the teacher and the taught must have often led to matrimonial connections. Later writers have prohibited a marriage with one's teacher's daughter, and Kacha refuses the request of Devayānī to accept her hand on the ostensible plea that one cannot marry one's teacher's daughter. This rule was a salutary one, and must have been intended to prevent complications likely to arise in practice, when many young students used to live and board with their teachers. But earlier practice seems to have been different. In Silavimansa Jātaka[3] we find a teacher of Benares marrying his daughter to one of his pupils, who had proved himself to be most virtuous;[4] from Mahāummagga-Jātaka[5] we learn that

---

[1] Cf. शिष्यशिष्टिरवधेन । अशक्तौ रज्जुवेणुविदलाभ्याम् । अन्येन घ्नन् राज्ञा शास्यः । I, 2, 48-50.

[2] No. 252.

[3] No. 305.

[4] No. 546.

the custom of selecting a son-in-law from amongst the pupils was so deep rooted in some teachers' families at Takshaśilā that the selected pupil had no option in the matter. In the above Jātaka story, the student married the teacher's daughter though he positively disliked her, for the simple reason that he did not wish to displease his teacher. It is quite probable that this custom may have prevailed in several other localities as well.

Let us now survey the duties of students towards their teachers. The student was to hold his teacher in deep reverence[1]. His outward behaviour must be in conformity with the rules of decorum and good manners; he ought to get up and salute his teacher in the proper way, he ought not to occupy a higher seat or wear a gaudier dress. Reviling and backbiting are severely condemned. It however did not follow that the student was to connive blindly at his teacher's misconduct. Āpastamba, who holds that the teacher ought to be revered like a god, also lays down that the student should draw his teacher's attention in private to his failings;[2] Gautama points out that the duty of obedience comes to an end when the teacher transgresses

---

[1] Manu, II, 200 ff. Cf. also Charaka, Vimāna-sthāna, VIII, 4, :-

तमग्निवच्च देववच्च राजवच्च पितृवच्च भर्तृवच्चाप्रमत्तः परिचरेत् ।

[2] Cf. प्रमादानाचार्यस्य बुद्धिपूर्वकं वानियमातिक्रमं रहसि बोधयेत् ॥

I, 2, 6, 13.

the limits of Dharma.[1] His commands were to be regarded as *ultra vires*, if they were likely to jeopordise the student's life or were against the law of the land.[2]

The student was expected to do personal service to the teacher 'like a son, suppliant or slave.'[3] He was to give him water and tooth-stick, carry his seat and supply him bath water. If necessary, he was to cleanse his utensils and wash his clothes.[4] He was further to do all sundry work in his teacher's house, like bringing fuel or guarding cattle. This custom is very ancient; it is mentioned in the *Gopatha Brāhmaṇa*[5] and the tradition asserts that even great personages like Srikṛishṇa had deemed it an honour to do all kind of menial work in their preceptor's house during their student days.

There were, however, limitations to this duty to work, The teacher was prohibited, as shown above, from assigning any work that was likely to interfere with the studies of the student. Secondly, the duty to do manual service was more nominal than real in the case of paying scholars. We have seen already that the duty to teach was imperative, and a teacher could not refuse a student merely because he was poor.

---

1 Cf. आचार्याधीनो भवति अन्यत्राधर्माचरणात्। III, 1, 15.

2 Charaka, Vimāna-sthāna, VIII, 7.

3 Cf. पुत्रवद्दासवदर्थिवच्चानुचरता त्वया··· । *Ibid.*

4 *Mahāvagga*, I, 25, 2.

5 I, 2, 1-8.

Poor students were admitted if they were willing to help the teacher in his household or field work; this duty to work was effectively operative only in their cases. At Takshaśilā the students, who used to pay their teachers' honorarium in advance, used to stay in their houses like eldest sons, doing no manual work and spending all their time in study. Free students, Dhammāntevāsikas, on the other hand used to do all kind of manual work for their teachers. They used to work by day, when paying scholars were receiving their lessons; teachers used to hold special classes for them at night with a view to see that their education did not suffer on account of their day time work in the field or in the house.[1] At Nālandā also secular students, who saught free boarding, lodging and education, had to do some manual work for the monasteries.[2]

In ancient India for several centuries the relations between the teacher and the student were direct i. e., not through any institution. Buddhism had its own Saṅghas or monasteries, which developed into educational institutions in course of a few centuries; but as far as Hinduism is concerned, we do not so far find any regular educational organisations or institutions till about the beginning of the 9th century A. D. For

[1] Cf. धंमंतेवासिका आचरियस्स कम्मं कत्वा रत्तिं सिप्पमुग्गण्हंति आचरियभागदायका गेहे जेट्ठपुत्ता विय हुत्वा सिप्पमेव उग्गण्हंति।

Tilamuṭṭhijātaka, No. 252.

[2] Takakusu, I-tsing, p. 106.

centuries Hindu teachers like Hindu Sanyāsins had no organised institutions. We come across seveal Jātaka stories about the students and teachers of Takshaśilā, but not a single episode even remotely suggests that the different 'world renowned' teachers living in that city belonged to any particular college or university of the modern type. Each of them was conducting an independent educational institution. European travellers of the 17th century have noted a similar state of affairs at Benares. Bernier says, 'Benares was a kind of university, but it has no colleges or regular classes but resembles rather the schools of the ancients, the masters being spread over in diferent parts of the town in private houses.[1]

Though the relations between the teacher and the pupil were thus entirely private and personal, there was usually a surprising constancy. The tendency to desert one teacher for another out of mere freakishness did not exist. Ātreyī no doubt leaves Vālmiki, but that was because she was too dull to pull on with Kuśa and Lava.[2] Such cases were, however, few.[3]

---

1 *Travels of Bernier*, p. 334

2 *Uttara-Rāma-charit*, Act II.

3 In Upanishads and Buddhist canonical literature, we come across some cases of disciples leaving one spiritual Guru for another, when they found his system to be unsatisfactory. But these cases refer to the spiritual quest, and have not much bearing on ordinary education.

sophical theories and communicated them to their disciples in sylvan solitudes. The same was the case with celebrated teachers like Vālmiki, Kaṇva and Sāndīpani, who used to stay in forests, though they had made arrangements in their Āśramas for instructions in secular subjects lika grammar, philology, astronomy and civics in addition to Veda, religion and philosophy.[1] One of the Jātakas also records the story of a Benares teacher who left that city for the Himalayan forest, because he wished to be altogether free from the disturbances of city life. The few and simple needs of this teacher and his students were supplied by surrounding villagers, who vied with each other in being of use to the educational colony.[2]

But the vast majority of students in ancient India, who were engaged in literary or professional education, did not live in forests; they used to stay with their teachers who were usually householders living in towns or villages. The numerous references to Takshaśilā teachers and students in the Jātakas show that they were living in the metropolis of Gandhāra and not away from it in any adjoining forest. Smritis prescribe a holiday when a death occurs in the village or when it is infested with thieves;[3] if the students and teachers were both living away in forests, there would have been

---

[1] *MBH.*, I, 91.

[2] Tittiri Jātaka, No. 438.

[3] E. g. Manu, IV, 108; 118.

no necessity for suspending studies for these disturbances in villages.

It would however appear that even those who had to carry on the educational work in towns and cities were quite aware of the beneficial results proceeding from study in quiet places ; and wherever possible, they tried to repair to adjoining gardens and orchards for the purpose of imparting instructions to their pupils. This practice existed in Benares during the 17th century A. D.,[1] and may be going back to the ancient Indian period. The case of Buddhist Monastic Universities like Nālandā and Vikramaśilā was peculiar; they were like modern University towns of Oxford, Cambridge and the Benares Hindu University, independent University settlements, where arrangements were made for the lodging and boarding of the students who flocked there in thousands. They combined the advantages both of the town and forest life.

The precise nature of lodging and boarding arrangements for students in Hindu centres of education is but imperfectly known. In the Sanskrit college at Salotgi in Bijapur district, there existed a number of boardings for the students who flocked there from distant provinces[2]. In the college at Ennāyiram in south India arrangements for free lodging and boarding were made for all the 340 students that were admitted there

---

[1] Bernier, p. 330.

[2] *E. I.*, IV, p. 60.

in the 11th century[1]. In the college attached to Veṅkaṭeśa Perumal temple in Tirukkudal there was both a hostel and a hospital attached to the institution in 1062 A. D.[2] In Vijayanagar, schools and colleges were attached to the more important temples and the moffusil students were probably lodged in the extensive temple out-houses. Most of the *Agrahāra* villages assigned to learned and distinguished Brahmanas were centres of higher education, but very little is known about the boarding and lodging arrangements in them for students. To judge from the examples quoted above, boarding houses existed in places where there were organised educational institutions. But we do not know anything about the boarding arrangements at places where organised institutions did not exist, and teaching was done by individual scholars on their own responsibility. Such was the state of affairs throughout India before the rise of Buddhist centres of education. The custom in these days, as disclosed by the Smritis, was for the student to stay with his teacher under the latter's roof. This was more or less indispensable in the case of Brahmana students specialising in sacrificial rituals; they could learn the practical details of the ritual only in their Guru's Yajñaśālā (sacrificial hall). Uddālaka Āruṇi, while studying the sacrificial lore, was staying in the spacious house of his preceptor

---

[1] *S. I. E. R.*, No. 333 of 1917.
[2] *Ibid*, No. 182 of 1915.

Patañchala,[1] and other students of that branch must have done the same. When Upakośala resolves to resort to fast, his teacher's wife tries to disuade him[2]; this shows that the student going on fast was probably a boarder with his teacher. Teachers in early times used to take responsibility for about 10 to 15 students only,[3] and they were well-to-do enough to arrange for the lodging of this number in their own houses or near their vicinity. Those students who were poor used to subsist on alms, the rest used to board with their teacher and note that fact while paying their *Gurudakshiṇā*. In Tilamuṭṭhi Jātaka, we find the teacher making the boarding and lodging arrangement of the Benares prince in his own house, when he learns that he is going to be a paying scholar[4]. Most of the Takshaśilā teachers were probably doing the same. Some rich students were probably staying in their own bunglows.' Such was the case with prince Juṇha, who, one night, emptied the begging bowl of a poor man, while returning home from teacher's house.[5] It is possible that there may have been some hostels at

---

1 *Br. Up.*, III, 7, 1.

2 *Ch. Up.* IV, 10, 3.

3 Jātakas often represent Takshaśilā teachers as having 500 students under them; this figure is, however, conventional and cannot be taken as literally true. See Chap. IV, under 'Method of teaching.'

4 No. 252.

5 No. 456.

Takshaśilā for moffusil students, but so far we have not discovered them either in literature or in excavations.

Hindu educationalists preferred, as shown above, that students should, as far as possible, live and board with their teachers. When, however, his course was over, he was permitted to stay with his preceptor for not more than four months.[1] Similarly the privilege of living on alms was withdrawn the moment he became a Snātaka. When the youth was properly trained, it was naturally expected that he should no longer be a burden to his teacher or to society. He must stand on his own legs.

### COLLEGE TERMS AND HOLIDAYS.

Information about the duration of the annual term is not satisfactory. Upākarma ritual, as we have shown already, was performed in the month of Srāvaṇa (August-September), when students assembled at the beginning of the annual session, and Utsarjana ceremony was celebrated in Pausha or Māgha (February-March) to mark the termination of the Vedic term. The time of these two rituals would suggest that the annual session lasted for about five or six months. Such was probably the case in pre-historic times when only the Vedic Saṁhitās formed the curriculum of study, and even Brāhmaṇa literature was yet to come into existence.

---

[1] Cf. अथाशुचिकराणि समावृत्तस्य भैक्षचर्या तस्य चैव गुरुकुले वास ऊर्ध्वं चतुर्भ्यो मासेभ्यः । *Bau. Dh. S.*, II, 1, 46.

In course of time religious and semi-religious literature began to develop at a very rapid rate; Brāhmaṇa literature assumed voluminous proportions and several treatises came to be written on the important branches of grammar, exegesis, philology, astronomy, mathematics and liturgy. Vedic schools had to extend their curricula so as to embrace these new branches, and a six months term was soon found to be utterly inadequate for the purpose.

There are ample indications in later literature showing that the Vedic studies did not stop with Utsarjana but continued practically throughout the year. Jaimini expressly states that even after Utsarjana ceremony,—which was intended to mark the termination of the Vedic studies,—teaching of the Vedas was to continue throughout the year.[1] Manu advises that after the Vedic studies had formally terminated with Utsarjana in February, bright half of the remaining months of the year should be devoted to the cultivation of the Vedas and the dark half to that of the Vedāṅgas.[2]

Sāma-veda circles recognised that it would be a self-contradiction to state that Utsarjana was to mark the termination of the Vedic studies, and prescribe in the same breath the study of Vedas and Vedāṅgas during the remaining months of the year. Sāma-veda school educationalists tried to get over this anomaly by

---

[1] *Jai. Gr. S.*, I, 15.

[2] IV, 98.

prescribing two Upākarmas, one in Bhādrapada ( September ) and the other in Māgha ( March ), the former to mark the beginning of the study of the Vedas and the latter that of the Vedāṅgas[1]. The original significance of Upākarma and Utsarjana seems to have been clearly forgotten even in the Smriti period. The inconsistency of celebrating the Utsarjana ceremony in February and continuing the Vedic studies still further was not realised, and so the Sāma-veda remedy of two Upākarmas did not become popular.

It is therefore clear that for several centuries before the Christian era the annual session of schools and colleges extended over more than six months. The exact months covered by the session and the duration of the annual vacation, if any, are not known. Transport difficulties were immense in ancient India and the students from Rājagṛiha and Benares used to return from Takshaśilā only when the whole course was over[2]. It is, therefore, very doubtful whether any long annual vacations existed in ancient India. Indications from the *Arthaśāstra* of Kauṭilya also show the same. Kauṭilya lays down that when a husband has gone out for education and does not return, his wife should wait for ten or twelve years before marrying again or resorting to Niyoga[3]. It is therefore clear that students studying at

[1] See the texts quoted by Chandrakānta at Go. Gr. S., III, 3, 14.

[2] Tilamuṭṭhi Jātaka, No. 252, *ante*, pp. 94-5.

[3] Cf. ब्राह्मणमधीयानं दशवर्षाण्यप्रजाता द्वादश प्रजाताः । III. 4.

distant centres of education could not normally get an annual vacation long enough to go and stay at home. Present day custodians of Sanskrit learning are also unaware of any tradition about a long annual vacation. Students could get occasional holidays for a few days when their presence was urgently required at home. Those, whose homes were near by, could take advantageof this concession and go home occasionally. But entire teaching does not seem to have been stopped for any part of the year. Work was not much disturbed by different students going home at different times, for, generally speaking, individal attention was given to each student as will be shown in the next chapter.

We come across a systematic list of holidays only in post-Vedic literature[1]. But many of these go back to early times. Regular holidays were four in the month at an interval of a week, the new and full moon days and the eighth days of each fortnight. External causes were, however, responsible for frequent stopping of the work. The school was closed when the peace of the settlement was disturbed by an invasion or by incursions of robbers or cattle-lifters, or when the king or a Brahmana of the locality had met with an accident or died. Arrival of distinguished guests led to the suspension of studies ; for a good deal of the time and energy of both the teacher and the students had to be devoted to make the guests comfortable.

---

[1] *Gau. Dh.* S., II, 7; *Bau. Dh. S.*, I, 11; Manu, IV. 100 ff.

Abnormal weather conditions giving rise to untimely clouds, thunder, heavy showers, frost, dust-storms etc. were also regarded as sufficient causes to suspend studies. Holidays for these causes seem to go back to hoary antiquity, when students and teachers lived in humble cottages and were engaged in agricultural pursuits. It must be further remembered that the teaching and learning of the Vedic Mantras in the manner in which it is done traditionally was physically impossible when a storm or lightning was thundering abroad. In later times when teachers were well-to-do men living in towns and villages and not directly concerned with active agricultural pursuits, it is doubtful if studies were suspended when there was a dust-storm or frost. The same observation will have to be made about the holidays when the howling of jackals, crying of wolfs, screeching of owls, braying of donkeys or barking of dogs was heard. Suspension of Vedic studies for these causes seems to have been dictated partly by superstitious beliefs and partly by the notion that the Vedic study was so sacred an affair that it could be prosecuted only under ideally pure circumstances. It was apprehended that gods would become angry if the sanctity of the Vedas was defiled by their being studied on such occasions[1].

[1] Cf. छिद्राण्याहुर्द्विजातीनामनध्यायान्मनीषिणः ।
छिद्रेभ्यः स्रवति ब्रह्म ब्राह्मणेन यदर्जितम् ॥
आयुः प्रजां पशून्मेधां कृंतामि सुकृतं च यत् ।
अनध्यायेष्वभ्यसतः ब्रह्म व्याहरतस्तथा ॥
quoted by Aparārka on Yāj. I, 142-151.

In course of time most of the holidays mentioned in the last paragraph were abolished. Curriculum was getting heavier and some reasons had to be found for departing from the old tradition. Baudhāyana, therefore, started the theory that prohibition of studies under abnormal weather condition referred only to loud recitations; silent reading was not intended to be interdicted.[1] The view of Āpastamba was the same[2]. Manu thinks that Vedāṅgas and non-Vedic works could be studied on the official holidays.[3] The view of the *Kūrma-Purāṇa* was the same; it recommends the reading and study of Vedāṅgas, history, Purāṇas, and law on holidays.[4] It would appear that in later times discretion was given to different institutions as to what holidays should be permitted by them to their students. Holidays allowed to the youngsters were to be more numerous than those to be allowed to advanced students.[5] This was certainly a very sound educational principle. In the case of serious students, apart from the four monthly holidays, studies seem to have been suspended only when they themselves or the place they were studying was impure.[6]

---

[1] I, 11, 40

[2] Cf. मनसा चानध्याये । I, 3, 11, 24

[3] II, 105.

[4] नानध्यायोऽस्ति चांगेषु नेतिहासपुराणयोः ।
न धर्मशास्त्रेष्वन्येषु पर्वण्येतानि वर्जयेत् ॥ I, 2, 14, 84.

[5] तत्र सर्वत्र प्राज्ञाप्राज्ञाध्येतृविषयेण गुरुलघुकालानां व्यवस्था ज्ञेया । *VMS.*, p. 536

[6] Manu, IV, 127.

## DURATION OF THE COURSE.

There is a general unanimity among the Smriti writers that Vedic education should extend over a period of 12 years. This period was regarded as sufficient for mastering one Veda. In modern times students master the Ṛig-veda, in both its Saṁhitā and *pada* texts, along with its six subsidiary branches in about eight years. In the earlier period holidays were re numerous and twelve years may have been equired. Svetaketu's studies extended over twelve years[1] and the story of Upakośala shows that the normal period of Brahmacharya extended over the same period.[2] We have seen how the *Arthaśāstra* requires a Brahmana wife to wait for 10 to 12 years before remarrying, when her husband had gone out for education; this would suggest that the course did actually extend over 12 years in the case of serious students. If the subject was mastered earlier, an earlier return was permitted. Those, who did not aim at a thorough mastery,

---

1 *Ch. Up.*, VI, 1, 2.

2 *Ibid*, IV, 10. In the Upanishads we find Indra and Virochana spending 101 years as Brahmachāris, and in the Mahābhārata we find Kacha staying for a thousand years with his Guru. But these are mythological cases and refer to the acquisition of carefully guarded doctrines. It must be further noted that the life of Indra, Virochana and Kacha was supposed to be so immense in duration, that the time they spent in Brahmacharya was only a very small fraction of their entire lives.

used to return in six or three years. Those, on the other hand, who wanted to master the complicated details of the Vedic rituals, had to spend a few years more.[1] Those, who wanted to master several Vedas, were advised to devote 12 years to the study of each of them; in practice, however, a shorter period may have been sufficient, for many of the Mantras of the different Saṁhitās are common. Specialisation came into the field early, functions of the priests were differentiated, and so in actual practice mastery of the four Vedas by one individual was not necessary. Students spending 36 or 48 years for mastering three or four Vedas must, therefore, have been very few in practice. Some social thinkers were positively opposed to studenthood extending over 36 or 48 years, for they held that one ought to marry in the prime of youth and not when one's hair had grown gray.[2] Śukra goes to the extent of recommending that the king should banish or imprison persons who were seeking to avoid family responsibility by extending their education aimlessly and indefinitely.[3]

---

[1] In Madras presidency, twenty years were required for mastering the Mantras and rituals of the Kṛishṇa Yajurveda, so as to enable the scholar to superintend every ritual and perform every ceremony of that Veda.

*Report of the Madras Prov. Committee, Edu. Com.*, 1882, p. 6.

[2] Cf. कृष्णकेशो ह्यग्नीनादधीतेतिश्रुतेः । *Bau. Dh. S.*, I, 2, 31.

[3] Cf. विना कुटुंबभरणात्तपोविद्यार्थिनः सदा ।
द्वीपे निवासितव्यास्ते बद्धा दुर्गोदरेऽथवा ॥ IV, 1,105.

Unfortunately there in no sufficient evidence to show what was the duration of the course in the case of non-Vedic students. Owing to the growing unpopularity of Vedic sacrifices and the rise of a number of new branches of knowledge like grammar, philology, logic, philosophy and astronomy, Vedic education lost its earlier hold. Only a small section of the Brahmana community continued to address its energies to the task of memorising the Vedic texts. The rest contented themselves with the knowledge of the few Vedic Mantras necessary for normal purposes, and specialised in one of the new branches mentioned above. Our sources supply no information about the time these students spent over their courses.

We find that students used to go to Takshaśilā when they were about 16, but strangely enough Jātakas throw hardly any light on the duration of their stay in that famous centre of education. We are told that they used to master the three Vedas and eighteen sciences before they returned home; it is, however, clear that no one, who was studying the three Vedas, was mastering the eighteen sciences and vice versa. The whole curriculam was also not finished at Takshaśilā. It is, therefore, not possible to determine the duration of the literary course at Takshaśilā from the information available with any amount of certainty.

In ancient India there were no successive classes, examinations and clear cut courses, as they exist in modern systems of education. Knowledge was regarded,—and rightly too,—as unlimited and no period that one could spend over its acquisition was regarded as really adequate for the purpose. The parable of Indra and Bhāradvāja narrated in the *Taittirīya Brāhmaṇa*[1] is very interesting in this connection. Bhāradvāja had spent three successive lives as a Brahmachārin in attempting to master all the Vedas. On learning that he would spend his fourth life also for the same purpose, Indra showed to him three mountain-like objects, and taking a handful from each, told Bhāradvāja that the Vedas or branches of knowledge were infinite and that, what he had learnt bore the same ratio to what remained to be mastered as his three handfuls bore to the three mountains before them. Sanskrit literature teems with proverbs pointing out the infiniteness of knowledge and the impossibility of mastering it completely. The duration of the course was, therefore, left to the will, capacity and convenience of the student. Jīvaka is known to have spent seven years for his medical course at Takshaśilā; Arts students were probably spending more or less the same number of years and return home at about the age of 22 or 24. In the seventh century A. D. also a person had to spend about 16 years in order to be called a cultured person. Grammar course alone extended over ten years.[2] Those who desired to be specialists in logic, or philosophy or Dharmaśāstra

---

[1] III, 10, 11, 3.

[2] Takakusu, Itsing, pp. 170-77.

were probably finishing their grammar course in a shorter period, but they had to spend about eight or ten years in getting a mastery of their special subjects. They could have returned home only at about the age of 25. Those few, on the other hand, who were anxious to get a mastery over several branches like grammar, logic or philosophy, had to continue their studies for some years even after 25. Megasthenes obviously refers to such passionate devotees of learning when he refers to students studying for 37 years[1]. The tradition continued to modern times, for Colebrooke also found some students at Nadia who were 37.[2] Normally, however, in order to be well up in his own branch, a student had to spent about 12 to 16 years from the commencement of his Sanskrit education, and could return home at the age of 24 or 25. A longer period of studentship for ordinary persons was disapproved by the Hindu social thinkers as we have seen already.

Students usually forget a good deal of what they learn in their student life. However extensive an educational course may be, it can never cover the whole field of knowledge in any particular branch. In order to promote the cause of learning some educationalists of ancient India like Śvetaketu proposed that even after his marriage, a person should spend two months at his

---

[1] Fragment No. 41.

[2] *Nadia Gazetteer*, p. 182.

*alma mater* in order to extend the sphere of his knowledge.[1] Svetaketu pointed out that his own scholarship became much deeper because he followed this course. The advice of Svetaketu was followed by those who were anxious to master new theories or discoveries.[2] Other thinkers like Āpastamba were unwilling to recommend Śvetaketu's theory for universal acceptance. They pointed out that there were practical difficulties in following Svetaketu's advice ; householders had their duties and could not possibly spare two months' time in the year for spending it at the Gurukula. Āpastamba, however, accepted the underlying principle of Śvetaketu's theory and recommended that if a graduate felt that he was week in any particular subject, he should repair to his teacher to perfect his knowledge.[3] How far this principle was accepted by society we do not know. Jātakas, however, show that students living in University centres like Benares or Takshaśilā were often accustomed to attend the lectures of their former teachers, even when they had married and settled down in life.[4]

---

[1] Cf. निवेशे वृत्ते संवत्सरे संवत्सरे द्वौ द्वौ मासौ समाहित आचार्यकुले वसेद्भूयः श्रुतमिच्छन्निति श्वेतकेतुः। तच्छास्त्रैर्विप्रतिषिद्धम्। निवेशे वृत्ते नैयामिकानि श्रूयंते। *Ap. Dh. S.*, I, 4, 13, 19-21.

[2] *Br. Up.*. VI, 2, 1-7 ; *Ch. Up.* V, 3.

[3] यया विद्यया न विरोचेत पुनराचार्यमुपेत्य नियमेन साधयेत्। II, 2, 5., 15.

[4] Kosiya Jātaka, No. 130.

The cordial relations that existed between the teacher and the student continued also in their after life. Āpastamba lays it down that even when the student had returned home after his education, he should frequently call on his teacher, bringing him some present, it may be even a tooth-stick.[1] Teachers also used to return these visits.[2] Koseya Jātaka shows that many students used to follow this advice in practice. The teacher's visit was not without its benefit to the student ; he used to utilise the occasion to ascertain how far the ex-student was keeping up his reading and studies. In the Anabhirati Jātaka,[3] the ex-student informs his teacher that he was quite up-to date in his studies for some time after he had left his school, but admits that he had forgotten some of his Vedic Mantras since the time he was married ; he however promises to mend the matters without delay. The mutual contact between the teacher and the student continued in the after life and was not without mutual benefit.

---

1 *Āp. Dh. S.*, I, 2, 8, 22.

2 No. 130.

3 No. 185.

# CHAPTER THIRD

## STUDENT'S LIFE.

Some aspects of the student life have been already considered incidentally while discussing the mutual relations between the teacher and the student; others will now be dealt with. This chapter will be mainly dealing with students prosecuting higher religious and literary education; life of primary and professional students will be reviewed in course of the chapters V and VI.

## DAILY LIFE.

Students were expected to rise early in the morning at about 4-30 A. M. After finishing the morning duties they were to take a bath. Then they were to offer the morning prayer (*sandhyā*) and attend to the fire-altar. *Agnihotra* was universal in India in Brahmana priestly families down to the 10th century A. D.; so students living with their Brahmana teachers must be regularly performing this fire service. Brahmana students must have paid special attention to fire sacrifices and their details. All of them were required to keep the sacred fire after their marriage, and some of them were expecting to follow the priestly profession, where proficiency in ritualism was a *sine qua non* of success. It is not known whether in later times, when

Brahmanical colleges came into vogue from about the 8th century A. D., there used to be maintained an institutional *Agnihotra.* In Vedic colleges like that at Ennāyiram[1] this must very probably have been the case, otherwise Vedic education would have remained sadly incomplete. In the second millennium of the Christian era, *Agnihotra* became less and less common; students of grammar, logic, poetics and philosophy were not probably spending any time daily in the fire-worship ritual in the days of Rana Pratap and Shivaji.

Strangely enough our authorities supply no information about the school hours. Probably these varied with different provinces, teachers, students and courses. We have seen already that free students at Takshaśilā used to receive lessons at night. It is clear that the classes for the paying scholars must have been held by day. Very probably they had a morning school of three or four hours which they used to attend after their morning prayers. This was the usual practice in Buddhist colleges.[2] Then followed the meal and noon rest, after which studies started again and continued till the evening. Down to the end of the Upanishadic age (c. 600 B. C.) the evening time was spent in visiting adjoining forests and fields for the purpose of collecting sacred fuel for the sacrificial fire. All students used to go together, spending their time in merry

---

1 See Chapter VIII for an account of this college.

2 Takakusu, I-tsing, p. 117.

conversation.[1] This compulsory evening trip to forests must have given good exercise to students and improved their health. It is not known how students used to spend their evenings when daily trips to fetch sacred fuel became no longer necessary owing to the progressive decline of Vedic sacrifices subsequent to about 600 B. C. Probably they were spending that time in physical exercises; our sources are, however, silent on that point. At sunset they used to offer their evening prayer and then attend to the work at fire altar. Then came the supper which was after a while followed by retirement to the night's rest. The interval between the two may have been utilised by advanced students for the home work. It should be however noted that there was hardly much home work to do in ancient Indian schools; books were very rare, paper and printing were unknown, and so most lessons were committed to memory in the school in teacher's presence. The only home-work possible was the revision and recapitulation of lessons memorised at school.

We have already seen that daily begging of food was prescribed for students by the Smritis. Whether this rule was actually followed by the vast majority of students in ancient India is the question that we have to investigate now. There are express injunctions that a Brahmachārin should subsist on food obtained

---

1 See Sanjīvaka Jātaka, No. 150.

in the daily begging trip;[1] nay, some texts lay down that he ought to beg both morning and evening.[2] No food is so holy for the student as the food he obtains by begging at the midday.[3]

This injunction to subsist on alms goes back to Atharva-veda;[4] are we then to conclude that all students in ancient India used to live on alms obtained at midday by begging from door to door?

There are several injunctions in sacred texts themselves to suggest that such was not the case. The *Gopatha Brāhmaṇa*[5] and the *Baudhāyana Dharma Sūtra*[6] prescribe different penances for failure to beg at least once in a week. It is therefore clear that daily begging of alms was not practised by all. Hindu Sanyāsins and their spiritual disciples used to follow this rule without exception, but here we are not concerned with them. Sumantu lays down that a Brahmachārin should take his food early in the morning before his 8th year, at about 9 o'clock before his 12th year and

---

[1] *Go. Gr. Ś.*, II, 10; *Dr. Gr. Ś.*, II, 5, 16; Manu, II, 65.

[2] *Jai. Gr. Ś.*, I, 18; *Āp. Dh. Ś.*, I, 1, 3, 24-5.

[3] Cf. शाकभक्षाः पयोभक्षा ये चान्ये यावशाकिनः ।
सर्वे ते भैक्षभिक्षस्य कलां नार्हति षोडशीम् ॥ Atri in *SCS.*, p. 111.

[4] XI, 5, 9.

[5] I, 2, 1-8.

[6] I, 2, 52.

at noon in later life.[1] It is clear that no cooked food could have been collected early in the morning by begging, and so the Brahmachārins under 12 could not be living on food obtained by begging. As far as grown up students are concerned, we have got definite evidence to show that many of them did not beg. Well-to-do students staying at Takshaśilā for their higher education used to live comfortably in their teachers' houses like their eldest sons. Smritis also contemplate this arrangement, for they say that a Brahmachārin should either take his food at his teacher's house or subsist on alms.[2] Manu defines a Guru as one who performs the various Sanskāras and provides boarding for his students.[3] We have further to note that there were some schools and colleges in Ancient India like those at Sālotgi, Ennāyiram and Nālandā, where the institutions had made arrangements for free boarding of students out of endowments received for the purpose.[4] It would have been an impracticable proposition for students at centres like Takshaśilā, Nālandā and Valabhi to subsist on begging. The student population at these

---

[1] Cf. अश्नीयादष्टवर्षस्तु ब्रह्मचारी प्रगे सदा।
तदूर्ध्वमाद्वादशाब्दादश्नीयात्संगवे सदा।
तदूर्ध्वं गृहिवद्भिक्षां भोजनं च समाचरेत्। quoted in *VMS.*, p. 486. The view of Karshṇājini is the same; see *VMS.*, p. 486.

[2] Cf. भैक्षाचार्यवृत्तिः स्यात्। *Mā. Gr. S.*, I, 1, 2.

[3] II, 142.

[4] See Chapter VIII for detailed information.

places was several thousand strong, and the inhabitants of these places, how-so-ever liberal they may have been, could hardly have been rich enough to offer sufficient alms to all of them. Yuan Chwang attributes the fame of Indian scholars for deep scholarship to the circumstance that students in India have not to worry about their food, clothing and medicine[1]. We know from Losaka Jātaka[2] that rich citizens of Benares had arranged for the free feeding of poor students reading at that place. The same arrangement existed at Benares during the 17th century, for Bernier informs us that rich citizens of that city used to supply *khichḍi* (rice cooked with pulses) free to poor students[3]. In such cases there was no necessity to beg food from door to door every noon. Alberuni undoubtedly observes that Brahmana students of the 11th century used to beg alms every day,[4] but his information on this point seems to be more a summary of the Smriti rules than a result of actual observation.[5] His testimony therefore

---

1 Beal, *Life*, p. 113.

2 No. 41.

3 Bernier, 335.

4 Vol. II, p. 131.

5 For instance, at p. 131 of Vol. II, he states that students used to marry at 25, but later on at p. 155 he informs us that Hindus marry at a very young age, and therefore their parents arrange the marriages of their sons. The first of the above statements is based upon the theoretical rules in Smritis, the second on contemporary practice.

does not invalidate the conclusion that begging was not universal in the student population in the 10th and 11th centuries A. D.

The rule of begging was laid down for the student in order to teach him humility and make him realise that it was due to the sympathy and help of the society that he was learning the heritage of his race. The rule that every one ought to beg during his student life removed the distinction between the poor and the rich and brought education within the means of the poorest. Teachers in ancient India could not refuse students because they were unable to pay any fees; if the teacher himself was poor or in distress, he was authorised to appropriate a part of the alms obtained by his students.[1] And finally the rule of begging was intended to make society realise its responsibility about the education of the rising generation. Civilisation will not progress if each generation does not take proper steps to transmit its heritage to the next. Hindu thinkers therefore made it an incumbent duty on all householders to offer cooked food to the begging student;[2] to refuse his request was to invite serious spiritual and material disaster.

---

[1] Cf. भोजयेद्याचितमन्नं त्रिधा कृत्वैकभागकम् ।
अग्नौ व्याहृतिभिः स्थाप्य भागमेकं गुरोरपि ॥
एकं भुञ्जीत............ Śaṅkha in *VMS*, p. 487.

[2] Cf. स्त्रीणां प्रत्याचक्षाणां समाहितो ब्रह्मचारी इष्टं दत्तं हुतं प्रजां पशुं ब्रह्मवर्चसमन्नाद्यं वृङ्क्ते । *Āp. Dh.* S. I. 3, 24-25.

In actual practice begging was resorted to only by those who were too poor to maintain themselves. Hindu educationalists realised full well that begging for daily food could not be a reality in the case of rich students; they therefore have laid down that the formality of begging should be gone through by all at least once in the course of the week.[1]

The caste restrictions were not very rigid about inter-dining down to the 5th or 6th century A. D.; so the sacred texts permit the Brahmachārin to collect his alms from all with the exception of men of bad character.[2] He was, however, to collect just the necessary amount of food; if he collected more or retailed it, he would be guilty of theft[3].

Before closing this section, it may be observed that while begging was an honourable duty for the Brahmachārin, it was a positive disgrace for the Snātaka. Society was morally bound to support every poor boy, who was honestly struggling to educate himself; the moment his education was over, he was expected to stand on his own legs. Hence we find a number of

---

[1] Cf. न चैनं ससम्यभिक्षितात्तीयात्। *Bau. Dh.* S., I, 2, 52.

[2] Ap. Dh. S., I, 1, 13, 24-25.

[3] Cf. आहारादधिकं वर्णी न कचिद्भैक्षमाचरेत्।
युज्यते स्तेयदोषेण कामतोऽधिकमाहरन्॥
Manu in *VMS.*, p. 486.

authorities prohibiting begging for the student who had finished his education[1].

## Rules of Student Life.

Rules governing students' life have been given in detail in several Smritis. Students were to treat with deep reverence their teachers and elderly relations. High morality was to characterise their life; lying, gambling and slandering were out of question. Foppishness was severely condemned. Students were either to shave their heads clean or grow matted hair. They were to take a bath once in the day, but pleasure baths were forbidden. Plain living was to characterise their life; shoes and umbrellas were not to be used, dress was to be simple, and collyrium, ointments and unguents were not to be touched. Food was to be simple; meats, sweetmeets, spices etc. were not to be used normally[2]. Of these rules those relating to moral conduct were strictly enforced; modifications were permitted in the case of the rest. Some of these modifications are expressly stated in some of our texts. Thus the prohibition of the use of shoes and umbrellas was intended to operate in the case of movements within the village or town; *Drāhyāyaṇa Gṛihya Sūtra*

[1] Cf. समावृत्तस्य भिक्षाऽशुचिकरा । *Bau. Dh.* S., II, 1, 63; see also *Śa. Br.*, XI, 3, 3, 7.

[2] For the rules of the student life, see Manu, II, 175 ff.; Yāj., I, 28 ff.; *Gau. Dh. S.*, I, 2; *Āś. Gr. S.*, I, 22; *Dr. Gr. S.*, II, 5; etc.

says so expressly, and we find that the princes and merchants' sons who used to journey to Takshaśilā from Rājagriha or Benares were usually provided with shoes and umbrellas[1]. The prohibitions against the use of these articles was an impracticable proposition in the burning summer of Benares or Takshaśilā. Similarly occasional exceptions were permitted in the case of oils and sweetmeets; an eleventh century inscription from south India records an endowment made *inter alia* for the purpose of meeting expenses in connection with the weekly oil baths of the students studying at Tirumukkudal college[2]. Very probably exceptions were generously permitted also in the case of the use of cots in swampy or snake infected localities.

The rules of the student life were on the whole reasonable for the age. Asceticism is no doubt at a premium in India, but educationalists have refrained from laying down that students should, like Sanyāsins, kill their passions or starve themselves. It was recognised that the student life was a period when body is being built up; fasting therefore has not been held as an ideal to the student, he is urged to eat as much food as his system demanded[3]. Similarly rules about food were liberally relaxed when medical considerations so

[1] Tilamuṭṭhi Jātaka, No. 252.

[2] *S. I. E. R.*, No. 182 of 1915.

[3] Cf. अष्टौ ग्रासा मुनेर्भक्ष्याः षोडशारण्यवासिनः ।
द्वात्रिंशतं गृहस्थस्यामितं ब्रह्मचारिणः ॥

*P. T. O.*

required[1]. In the light of these facts the observation of a recent writer that student's life in ancient India "requiring a stay at a stranger's, demanding a beggar's or menial's life, and denied all pleasures of life was very severe'[2] will appear to be considerably wide of the mark. Society did not regard the student life as a fit occasion for enjoying pleasures of life; all that was required for plain living and high thinking was generally permitted to the student. Great emphasis is laid on the moral side and that is natural and essential. Relaxations were permitted in the case of some of the rules when demanded by local conditions. Further concessions were given in the case of primary students as will be shown in Chapter VI.

## GURUKULA AND ĀŚRAMA.

Where were students living during their education is the next question to be considered. Smritis lay down that immediately after his Upanayana the student

---

(*Continued from the last page*)

आहिताग्निरनड्वांश्च ब्रह्मचारी च ते त्रयः ।
अश्नंत एव सिध्यंति नैषां सिद्धिरनश्नताम् ॥
गृहस्थो ब्रह्मचारी च योऽनश्नंस्तु तपश्चरेत् ।
प्राणाग्निहोत्रलोपेन अवकीर्णी भवेत्तु सः ॥

*Bau. Dh. S.*, II, 7, 31-33. Devaṇabhaṭṭa attributes the first of these verses to Vasishṭha and the second to Āpastamba; *SCS.*, p. 114.

1 *Bau. Dh. S.*, II, 1, 29.

2 Bokil. *The History of Education in India*, part I, p. 151.

should go to his preceptor and live under his roof. *Antevāsin*, the normal term used to denote the student, primarily means one who stays close to his teacher, i. e. under his roof. The term *Samāvartana*, which roughly corresponds to the modern convocation, literally denotes the return of the student to his own house (from that of his preceptor's.) *Chhāndogya Upanishad* describes the student as 'Āchārya-kula-vāsin' 'one who dwells in the house of his preceptor.'[1] The rules which require the student to rise earlier and sleep later than his teacher, to show him the alms that he gathers at the midday, and to attend to the night service of his Agnihotra,—all these tend to prove that the student was living under his teacher's roof. The same conclusion has to be deduced from the story of Nābhānedishṭa; his father divided the family property among his brothers during his absence at his preceptor's house without reserving any share for him; when Nābhānedishṭa on his return claimed his share, his father explained to him how he had not been really passed over by him, though he was absent.[2] Smritis have further laid down that the Law of Limitation shall be relaxed in favour of a Brahmachārin studying at the Gurukula.[3]

---

1 II, 23, 2.

2 *Ait. Br.*, XXII, 9.

3 Cf. ब्रह्मचारी चरेत्कश्चिद्व्रतं षट्त्रिंशदाब्दिकम्।
समावृत्तो व्रती कुर्यात्स्वधनान्वेषणं ततः॥
पंचाशदाब्दिको भोगस्तद्धनस्यापहारकः। Kātyāyana in *Pa. Mā.*, Vol. III, i. p. 148.

The reasons why a stay at the preceptor's house away from home was preferred by ancient Indian educationalists can be gathered from the Tilamuṭṭhiya Jātaka. Although in their own capitals there lived teachers of world renown, kings of Rājagṛiha and Benares, we are told, used to send their sons for education over a great distance to Takshaśilā away from the borders of their kingdoms, for they thought that in this way their pride and haughtiness would be broken, they will learn to bear heat and cold and learn also the ways of the world.[1] It is clear from this passage that the Gurukula system, requiring the student to pass his studenthood under the teacher's roof or under his direct personal supervision, was preferred because it better facilitated studies, toned down personal idiosyncracies, and helped the student to become more resourceful and self-reliant and better aquainted with the world and its ways. When the college was near, students could go home on short leave on special occasions; the wonderful Tittiri birds of the Tittiri Jātaka, who are said to have been able to give lessons in Vedic recitations, were killed because the Āśrama was for the time being without any students, as all the inmates had gone home for a certain festival. When, however, Rājagṛiha or Benares students were sent to places like Takshaśilā, more than a thousand miles from

[1] Cf. पोराणिकराजानो अत्तने पुत्ते 'एवं एते निहतमानद्प्पा सीत-ण्हक्खमा लोकचरितञ्ञू भविस्संति' अत्तनो नगरे दीसापामोक्खे आचरिये विज्जमानेपि सिप्पुग्गहणत्थाय दूरे तिरोरट्ठं पेसंति । Jātaka No. 252.

their homes, a return home before the end of the course was impracticable in ancient times when there were no quick means of transport as in modern days. Parents used to congratulate themselves that they had seen their sons returning home in their own life-time when they used to come back from distant places like Takshaśilā at the conclusion of their education.[1]

The Gurukula system was regarded as very beneficial and was followed wherever circumstances permitted. But it is not to be supposed that it was universal, or that it embraced the entire education course. Primary students stayed with their parents as will be shown in Chapter VI. Smritis no doubt prescribe that immediately after his Upanayana at about the age of 8 or 10, the boy should migrate to his teacher's house for the higher education. We however find students proceeding to Takshaśilā for studying 'the three Vedas and eighteen sciences' usually when they had attained the age of discretion ; many of them are expressly stated in Jātakas to be 16.[2] Poor boys probably left their homes very early ; they had to beg their daily food, work in their teacher's house and carry on the studies in the spare time Well-to-do parents however used to send their sons to the teacher's house and town for higher education, when they had become old enough to take care of themselves. When competent teachers existed in the

1 दिट्ठा मे जीवमानेन पुत्तो दिट्ठो । *Ibid.*

2 *Jātakas* Nos. 51, 252 etc.

town itself, it must have been only princes and merchants, who were suffering from a superfluity of money, who may have sent their wards to distant Gurukulas. Normally when the teacher and the parents belonged to the same locality, it is very doubtful whether the local students lived and boarded with their teachers in preference to their guardians. It must, however, be noted that at present there is no evidence to prove either alternative.

It is often asserted that education used to be imparted in ancient India in sylvan solitudes, away from the throng of the village and city life. This statement, like many others that one often hears about ancient India, is neither wholly true nor wholly untrue. Dr. Rabindra Nath Tagore's observation that the forest and not the town is the fountain head of Indian civilisation[1] is undoubtedly true of its religious and philosophical achievements. Vedic study was regarded as a specially holy affair, and there are indications to show that in early times it was carried on in quiet places away from the haunts of men. Both the *Gopatha* and *Sāmavidhāna Brāhmaṇas* lay down that a Brahmachārin was to enter village only for begging his daily alms;[2] the rest of the time he was expected to spend in quiet localities on the outskirts of the village settlement. Upanishadic and early Buddhist thinkers undoubtedly thought out their deep philo-

---

[1] *Vishvabhāratī Quarterly*, April 1924, p. 64.

[2] I, 2, 1-8; I, 1, 4, 1.

## MARRIAGE AND STUDENT LIFE.

The theory required that a student should not marry before he had finished his education. Such was the case with the majority of students in early times, when marriage of girls also used to take place at an advanced age. It is, however, doubtful whether in the age of the Smritis when the pre-puberty marriages of girls had become common, students could remain unmarried till the end of their educational courses. The *Arthaśāstra* refers to Brahmana ladies anxiously awaiting the return of their husbands for ten or twelve years when they had gone out for education.[1] Students falling in love and marrying before the end of their courses are not unknown to the Jātakas.[2] Sometimes Jātaka teachers are seen consoling their students who had discovered that their wives were far from being ideal spouses.[3] A natural consequence of lowering the marriageable age of girls to 10 or 12 was to lower the age of the bridegrooms also to 16 or 18. Probably quite an appreciable percentage of students was marrying before their education was over from about the beginning of the Christian era.

## LIFE-LONG STUDENTS (NAISHṬHIKA BRAHMACHĀRINS).

Some persons in ancient India preferred to remain unmarried in order to devote their whole time and

[1] III, 4. [2] Jātaka No. 64.

[3] Anabhirati Jātaka, No. 185.

energy to the cause of religion and education. They were known as Naishṭhika Brahmachārins.[1] The ideal of Naishṭhika Brahmacharya must have been unknown in the Vedic age; life-long and continuous maintenance of the sacred fires and the proper performance of the various daily and periodical sacrifices were then regarded as the most incumbent duty[2] and the sacred fires could be installed only at the time of marriage. The Vedic view of life was also different. The world and its good things were regarded as real and worth striving for; a life of austere and life-long austerities was at a discount.

The ideal of Naishṭhika Brahmacharya seems to have come into vogue in Upanishadic times when the spiritual urge was inducing several well-to-do persons to abandon their comfortable homes in search of the Eternal. The primary motive for Niashṭhika Brahmacharya was spiritual salvation, but it was to be achieved not by austerities or meditations but by the dedication of a life of chastity to the cause of the sacred lore. From Yuan Chwang we learn that like Sanyāsins Naishṭhika Brahmachārins used 'to promenade through life away from human affairs' unmoved by honour or reproach. They were held in the highest veneration by society, but they did not care to mix with it. Their

---

1 *Nishṭhā* means death; *Naishṭhika Brahmachārin* is one who keeps celebacy till his death.

2 Cf. वीरहा वैष भवति योऽग्निमुत्सादयति । quoted by Śankara at *Ch. Up.*, II. 23. 1.

sole concern was 'a thorough acquisition of knowledge'. 'Forgetting fatigue' says the Chinese pilgrim 'they expatiate in arts and sciences; seeking for wisdom... they count not 1000 *li* (roughly equal to 200 miles) as a long journey. Though their family may be in affluent circumstances, such men make up their minds to be like vagrants and get their food by begging as they go about. With them there is honour in knowing the truth and there is no disgrace in being destitute[1]'.

The Naishṭhika Brahmachārin was theoretically required to be under his teacher till the latter's death, but in practice he may have soon separated from him in search of new knowledge as the account of Yuan Chwang shows. In many cases he may have founded new centres of education for imparting the extensive knowledge that he had acquired. Famous teachers like Kaṇva, Jābāli and Divākarasena (of the *Harshacharit*) who were chancellors (*Kulapatis*) of their sylvan universities, were all Naishṭhika Brahmachārins. The ideal of the Naishṭhika Brahmachārin is peculiar to India and has contributed largely to the striking achive-ments of Ancient India in the sphere of learning and philosophy. It is a great pity that we have no reliable knowledge of the extent to which this ideal appealed to the different ages of ancient Indian history. The history of education would have become considerably

[1] Watters, I, pp. 160-161.

richer if we had true and detailed biographies of some of these life-long devotees of knowledge.

Naishṭhika Brahmacharya was dictated partly by spiritual and partly by educational considerations. In later times, however, its true significance was forgotten, and persons who were forced to remain unmarried owing to physical defects or incapacity were regarded as following the course of Naishṭhika Brahmacharya. No greater parody of the great ideal can be conceived. That a number of medieval writers like Devaṇabhaṭṭa,[1] Mādhava[2] and Mitramiśra[3] should have gravely advised dumb, deaf and impotent persons to practise Naishṭhika Brahmacharya shows that the age they lived in had become incapable of realising the true nature of some of the noble ideals that were the main springs of Ancient Indian culture and civilisation.

---

[1] *SCS.*, p. 171.

[2] *Par. Mād.*, I, ii, p. 51

[3] *VMS.* p. 551; Cf:-

पंग्वादीनामनंशत्वादसामर्थ्याच्च शाश्वतः ।
नियतं नैष्ठिकत्वं स्यात्कर्मस्वनधिकारतः ॥
(Attributed to Saṅgrahakāra)

कुब्जवामनजात्यन्धक्लीबपंग्वार्तरोगिणाम् ।
व्रतचर्या भवेत्तेषां यावज्जीवमनंशतः ॥
(Attributed to Vishṇu)

# CHAPTER IV.

## CURRICULA, METHOD OF TEACHING, AND EXAMINATIONS.

*(Literary Side)*

Smritis are most disappointing as far as information about the curricula, method of teaching and examinations is concerned. They are content to observe that Brahmanas, Kshatriyas and Vaishyas should study the Vedas exclusively in the monsoon term, and the Vedas along with the Vedāṅgas during the rest of the year. How far this advice was followed by the Kshatriyas and Vaishyas will be discussed in the next chapter, but a little reflection will show that even the Brahmana community could not have been following this stereotyped curriculum throughout the several centuries of Ancient Indian History. The rise of new branches of knowledge must have affected the curriculum; let us try to find out its scope age by age.

### EARLY VEDIC PERIOD.

(Upto about 2000 B. C.)

There was a deep prejudice in the matter of requisitioning the services of the art of writing for the purpose of preserving or transmitting the Vedic literature. Down to modern times Vedic hymns have been transmitted from one generation to another by oral tradition.

The same was the case in the early Vedic period, when probably the art of writing also was not known.[1] What literature, other than the Vedic hymns, the Aryans brought with them in India is not known. The Rig-veda itself presupposes or refers to no other types of literature. The Atharva-veda, however, attests the existence of *Itihāsa, Purāṇa* and *Nārāśansī Gāthās.*[2] It is almost certain that the antiquity of this semi-historical and semi-legendary literature would go back to the early Rigvedic period, though the Rig-veda itself does not refer to it. As Tilak has shown in '*The Arctic Home in the Vedas*' the Vedic Aryans were in possession of some traditional information about their earlier life beyond the borders of India. Their tradition may also have preserved some information about the exploits and achievements of distinguished hereos of hoary antiquity. This must have supplied the subject matter to the *Itihāsa, Purāṇa* and *Nārāśansī Gāthās* first mentioned in the Atharva-veda, but probably existing since much earlier days.

In the literary schools of the early Vedic period, Vedic hymns along with *Itihāsa, Purāṇa* and *Nārāśaṅsī Gāthās* must have been the main topics of study. In that early age, these however were studied in a way quite different from that in which they came to be studied from the later Saṁhitā period downwards.

---

[1] See *ante*, pp. 3-4.

[2] XV, 6, 10.

The later belief that a Vedic Mantra, if recited with the least deviation in accent or contents, would bring down a disaster, did not exist in this period. In the 11th century A. D. it was regarded as a sacrilege, says Alberuni[1], to compose a poem in imitation of a Vedic *ric*. The creative period of the Vedic literature subscribed to no such theory. Vedic hymns were studied more or less as specimens of literature, to be freely imitated or improved by any one who felt equal to the task. Later Vedic poets are often seen comparing,—sometimes not without an air of complacency or boastfulness—their own compositions with those of the ancient *Ṛishis*[2]. The hymnal activity spread over several centuries. New hymns were being cotinuously composed, some of which were finding admission into Saṁhitā collections. Hence it is that in the Rig-veda we find references to poets of early, middle and later ages[3]. The careful analysis of the Rigvedic repititions made by Bloonfield has shown that nearly one-fifth of the Rig-veda i repitition. The book itself is found to be a mixed fina precipitate of a later time, and to some extent also the clectic choice of a comparatively later age. 'The hymns of the Rig-veda as a body, are

---

[1] Sachau, I, p. B5.

[2] Cf. आदित्या रुद्र वसवो जुषन्त इमं ब्रह्म क्रियमाणं नवीयः ॥
VII, 35, 14.

नव्यं नु स्तोममग्नये दिवः श्येनाय जीजनम् । वस्वः कुविद्वनाति नः ॥
V, 15, 4.

[3] Cf. यः स्तोमेभिर्वावृधे पूर्व्येभिर्यो मध्यमेभिरुत नूतनेभिः ॥ III, 32, 13.

largely epigonal, or born after a long period of hymn production, which must have been once upon a time much freer from conventional thought and mechanical utterance'.[1]

Vedic hymns and the poems and ballads, constituting *Itihāsa, Purāṇa* and *Nārāśansī Gāthās* were studied in this period as specimens of literature, to be understood, admired, imitated and excelled. Professional priests must have committed the hymns to memory, but not so meticulously as not to permit even a slight departure in accent. The mass of the people consisting of agriculturists, artisans and soldiers must have committed to memory only some selections in the same way in which some choice poems and songs of medieval saints are memorised by the Hindu masses in the present times. Selections of different groups may have been different, and some changes in synonyms and construction must have been consciously or unconsciously introduced in order to make the contents clearer.

It would appear that the different members of the priestly families were studying just those portions of the Vedic hymns and formulæ that were necessary for their professional duties in after life. Thus a would-be Hotṛi would learn only those hymns that he would be called upon to recite, an would-be Udgātṛi those songs that he would have to sing to the

[1] Bloomfield, *Rig-Veda Repitions*, p. 21 See also p. 646.

tune in the sacrifice, and an would-be Adhvaryu those formulæ and Mantras that were necessary to be muttered while conducting the multifarious details of different sacrifices. This specialisation led to the differentiation and classification of the mass of hymns and formlæ into the Rig-veda, Sāma-veda and Yajur-veda.

A portion of the time in the school was devoted to the purpose of explaining the full versions of the historical and legendary incidents referred to in some of the hymns. Principles of prosody must have been expounded, and some time must have been devoted to develop the powers of versification of the young scholars. Those who intended to take up the priestly profession must have been required to master the details of the rituals associated with the hymns they had memorised. Elements of geometry, necessary to construct the altars of the various sacrifices, must have been expounded. The knowledge of elementary astronomy, which enabled the Vedic age to find out the difference between the lunar and the solar year, was probably imparted to all. Grammar and etymology did not trouble the students of this age, because these sciences were yet unknown.

### Late Vedic and Brahmanic Period.

### (*C.* 2000 B. C. to *C.* 1000 B. C.)

During this period considerable changes were introduced in the curriculum of schools and colleges.

A portion of what is known as Sruti or revealed literature was canonised. The notion that the canonical literature ought to be preserved exactly in its pristine form seems to have become popular during this age. The Vedic dialect, once the spoken language, was progressively become more and more different from the current form of speech, which was tending to develop dialectical differences owing to the wider distribution of the Aryans over the plains of the Punjab and the western Gangetic plain. The non-Aryans in the Gangetic valley seem to have been stronger and more civilised than those in the Punjab, and the conquerors started the practice of taking wives freely from the conquered population. The purity of Sanskrit speech, which had become already differentiated from the Vedic dialect, was thus considerably threatened in some of the Aryan households on account of the presence of non-Aryan wives speaking non-Sanskritic speech. It was felt that though the ordinary language may be modified by the contact with the non-Aryan forms of speech, the sacred hymns should be saved this desecration. They ought to be preserved in their pristine purity, otherwise there was the serious danger of gods not listening to the prayers of the suppliant.

A good deal of the energy of the students and teachers of this age was devoted to the task of preserving the old Vedic hymns,—which were now regarded as revealed or inspired,—in their precise traditional form. It is, however, doubtful whether the students of this age had to face the arduous task of committing to memory the *Pada-pāṭha, Jaṭā-pāṭha and Ghana-pāṭha,* for these devices to preserve the purity of the Vedic texts seem to have been evolved in the next period. The Brāhmaṇa literature was in the process of formation and must have been studied more or less in the same way in which commentaries are studied now. It does not seem to have been studied or preserved as carefully as the Mantra literature; otherwise we cannot account for the fairly large number of unidentified Brāhmaṇa passages occuring in the *Nirukta.*

The Vedic exegesis must have formed a part of the school curriculum, for the spoken language had begun to differ from the Vedic dialect. Several lists of difficult Vedic words, which were later known as Nighaṇṭus, were prepared for meeting the needs of the student population. The average Vedic student of this period was not only expected to memorise the Vedic Mantras but also to explain their meaning; authors like Yāska pour ridicule on persons who were unable to interpret properly the Vedic stanzas they could recite.[1]

---

[1] Cf. *Nirukta* I, 18-19 :—

स्थाणुरयं भारहारः किलाऽभूदधीत्य वेदं न विजानाति योऽर्थम् ।
योऽर्थज्ञ इत्सकलं भद्रमश्नुते नाकमेति ज्ञानविधूतपाप्मा ॥

यद्गृहीतमविज्ञातं निगदेनैव शब्द्यते ।
अनग्नाविव शुष्कैधो न तज्ज्वलति कर्हिचित् ॥

A passage from the *Śatapatha Brāhmaṇa* shows that Itihāsa, Purāṇa and Nārāśansī Gāthās continued to be studied in this period.[1] The study of this literature must have been to some extent useful in understanding the references in the Vedas and the Brāhmaṇas. Vedic scholarship has sustained an irreparable loss by the disappearance of the major portion of this literature, which was recited for the delectation of the persons assembled at sacrificial sessions during the intervals of rituals.

The sacrifice became a very complex and complicated affair by this time, and a good deal of the time and energy of the Vedic student, who intended to become a professional priest, must have been devoted to master its details and intricacies. A strenuous and thorough study of not less than 12 to 15 years must have been required to get the necessary facility to participate in or to preside over the various Vedic sacrifices mentioned in the Brāhmaṇa literature.

We come across stray speculations upon grammar and etymology in the Brāhmaṇas. The development of these sciences was started in this period when two dissimilar forms of speech, the spoken and the Vedic dialect, came into contact with each other. It is, however, doubtful whether regular manuals were composed on these subjects and studied in schools. Astronomy, geometry, liturgy and metrology (*Chhandas-*

---

[1] XI, 3, 8, 8; see also *Tai. Ār.*, II, 9.

*śāstra*) must have figured in the school curriculum. Text books of these subjects, studied in this age, no longer exist; they have been superseded by the better successors of later times.

## UPANISHADIC, BUDDHIST AND SŪTRA PERIOD.
(From *c*. 1000 B. C. to *c*. 1 A. D.)

Thanks to a few passages occuring in the Upanishads, Buddhist canon, Jātakas and the Milinda-Pañha, we get a fairly good idea of the curriculum of the educational institutions of this period. The data supplied by the Dharmasūtras seem to be altogether inadequate and one-sided.

The most striking feature of this period seems to have been a combination of the liberal and professional education in the higher schools and colleges, which were usually managed by the Brahmanas. Probably the same was the case in the early Vedic period, as one may infer from the statement of a Rigvedic sage that he himself was a poet, while his father was a physician and maternal grandfather a mason[1]. From a passage in the *Chhāndogya Upanishad*[2] we learn that when Nārada came to learn higher philosophy from Sanatkumāra, he had already studied, besides Vedas and the allied branches, arithmetic (*rāśi*), archery,

---

[1] कारुरहं ततो भिषगुपलप्रक्षिणी नना ।
नानाधियो वसूयवोऽनुगा इव तस्थिम ॥

*Rig-veda*, IX, 114, 3.

[2] VII, 1, 2.

astronomy and astrology, (*Nakshatravidyā*) snake charming and antidotes against poisons (*Sarpavidyā*), and the arts of divination and finding out treasure-troves (*Daiva* and *Nidhi*). The average youth of this age obviously did not combine a knowledge of all these arts, but the reply of Nārada may be taken as showing that Brahmana youths at this time used to master some useful arts. Jātaka evidence shows the same. From several stories in the Jātakas it appears that the Brahmana and Kshatriya youths at this period used to study together at Takshaśilā; both of them are usually described as being proficient in the three Vedas and eighteen arts (*Sippas*). Of course from the very nature of things, he who was proficient in the three Vedas, could not be well versed in the eighteen arts, and vice versa; but the Jātaka statements on this point may be taken as showing that Vedic knowledge in this age was combined with a fair grounding in some useful profession, and that those who were experts in practical arts were not altogether strangers to general cultural education. From the *Milinda Pañha* also we learn that Brahmanas used to combine a knowledge of a portion of the Vedic literature with some grounding in one or more of the following useful branches of knowledge,—astronomy, astrology, arithmetic, and prognostications to be drawn from the flights of birds, falls of meteors, and interpretation of omens, dreams and signs.[1]

[1] Vol. I. p. 247.

The exact scope of the useful education, which was imparted along with the liberal education in this period, is difficult to determine owing to the silence of the Jātakas about the precise nature of the eighteen Sippas. From the various Jātaka stories we find that archery or the military art,[1] medicine,[2] magic,[3] snake charming[4] and the art of finding hidden treasures[5] were among the practical arts taught at Takshaśilā. These arts must have figured among the eighteen Sippas, and some knowledge of the rest may perhaps be obtained from a passage in the *Majjhima Nikāya*[6] where we are told that the eight principal Sippas were conveyancing or law, mathematics, accountancy, agriculture, commerce, cattle-breeding, *issattha* (?) and administrative training. Music, dancing, painting and engineering were probably also included in the eighteen Sippas, though they do not figure in any of the lists known so far.[7]

---

1 Bhīmasena Jātaka, No. 80 ; No. 537 also.

2 *Mahāvagga*, VII, 1, 6.

3 Anabhirati Jātaka, No. 185.

4 Compeyya Jātaka, No. IV, 256.

5 Parantapa Jātaka, No. 416.

6 I, p. 85. *Aṅguttara Nikāya* gives only the last five of the Sippas mentioned in the *Majjhima Nikāya*, (IV, pp. 281, 382 ). The meaning of the first three terms in the original is rather doubtful.

7 Most of the subjects, here enumerated as being included in the 18 Sippas, were very probably included under them.

*P. T. O.*

From the Jātaka evidence it would further appear that the three Vedas and eighteen Sippas were both taught by the Brahmanas. The same conclusion would follow from the Upanishad and Milinda Pañha passages

---

(*Continued from the last page*).

*Milinda-Pañha* (Vol. I, p. 6) mentions the following as the 19 Sippas mastered by king Menander :-'holy tradition and secular law; the Sāṅkhya, Nyāya, and Vaiśeshika systems of philosophy ; arithmetic, music, medicine, the four Vedas. the Purāṇas, and the Itihāsas, astronomy, magic, causation, spells, the art of war, poetry and conveyancing, in a word, all the nineteen (Sippas). This enumeration seems to have been partly influenced by the conception of the eighteen Sāstras, the study of which was enjoined for the Brahmana, viz., the four Vedas, six Vedāṅgas, four Upāṅgas, (Purāṇa, Nyāya, Mīmānsā and Dharmaśāstra) and four Upavedas (medicine, art of war, music and Arthaśāstra). Vide *Vishṇu Purāṇa*, III, 6, 28) Both these lists do not give any correct idea about the eighteen Sippas that were taught at Takshaśilā. The Jātakas separate the Vedas from the Sippas which neither the *Milinda-Pañha* nor *Vishṇu Purāṇa* does. Further, it has to be observed that Sāṅkhya, Yoga, Mīmānsā, Nyāya, Vaiśeshika, Itihāsa, Purāṇa, and Dharmaśāstra could hardly be included in the list of the Sippas. The basic idea underlying the term Sippa is an art or profession or work of special skill. Cf. (1) एतद्धि दिव्यं शिल्पं न मानुषम् । *Kathāsaritsāyara*, XXV, 175 'This a work not of human, but of divine skill' (2) त्रिवृद्धै शिल्पं नृत्यं गीतम् वादित्रम् ।

(*Śa. Br.* XXIX,5 as quoted in the *St. Petersberg Dictionary* under *Śilpa*.)

referred to above. Unfortunately towards the end of this period many of the practical professions became tabooed to the priestly class, and non-Brahmanas ceased to interest themselves in literary education and philosophical discussions. The result was an undesirable separation of the useful from liberal education, which had very unfortunate consequences on the progress of knowledge and national prosperity.

The period under review was the most creative one in the history of Hindu literature, philosophy and science. It recorded remarkable achievements in the realm of philosophy, literature, poetics, grammar, philology, astronomy, Dharmaśāstra, medicine, surgery, sculpture, architecture and ship-building. The curricula of the schools and colleges of this period must therefore have differed considerably from those prevailing in the earlier ages. Vedic religion, characterised by multifarious sacrifices, usually involving slaughter of animals, was getting unpopular in this period, as a consequence of the Upanishadic, Buddhist and Jain movements. In some sections of the Brahmana community the Vedas continued to be assiduously studied along with the Brāhmaṇa literature, which came to be canonised in this period. The nature and extent of the scholarship of a Brahmana Vedic scholar can be ascertained from several passages in the Buddhist literature. He could recite three Vedas by heart, could intone them correctly, could understand their meaning, fix the right place of each particular verse and grasp the mysteries they contained'. A knowledge about the Vedic prosody, grammar, lexicography and legends concerning Vedic characters was also possessed by him. *Pada-pāṭha, Ghana-pāṭha and Jaṭā-pāṭha* were evolved by this time and had to be mastered.[1] Meaning of the Vedic hymns was also taught; the Gṛihya-sutras declare a person ineligible for the Samāvartana ceremony or the conferment of the degree, if he was able to recite the Mantras but unable to interpret them.[2] Owing to the wide distribution of the Aryan culture over practically the whole of India, the number of the Vedic Sākhās and Charaṇas had immensely increased in this period. Normally a person used to study the works of his own Sākhā. Persons, who used to master the works of Sākhās other than their own, existed but their number was not considerable.

During the period under review the Vedic literature ceased to be the main topic of study in Brahmanical circles. Of course all the Brahmanas and a certain percentage of the Kshatriyas and Vaishyas used to memorise the Vedic Mantras necessary for routine religious purposes, but those who specialised in Vedic scholarship formed probably only about 15 per cent of

---

[1] Early in this period, the *Pada-pāṭha* was not regarded as infallible as the memory of its author Śākalya was still fresh. Yāska in one place points out a mistake in the *Pada-pāṭha* division; See *Nirukta*, VI, 28.

[2] See *ante*, p. 39.

the learned Brahmana population. Attention of the learned circles must have been captivated in this period by the new sciences that were developing,—grammar, philology, law, logic and philosophical systems, both orthodox and heterodox. Works on these branches that have been preserved to the present day formed but a small percentage of the books written in this period. This conclusion is forced upon us when we take into consideration the large number of predecessors that have been referred to or quoted by the *Nirukta, Upanishads*, Buddhist and Jain canons, the *Brahmasūtras* and the *Arthaśāstra* of Kauṭilya. It seems almost certain that after learning a few Vedic hymns and getting the necessary grounding in grammar, a vast majority of students who used to take the literary course must have commenced to specialise in one of the branches mentioned above.

It is a great pity that no definite information should be available about the various books prescribed for the different courses in grammar, logic, philosophy or Dharmaśāstra. Probably the books of the particular Ṣākhā or province, along with the works of the masters in the line, were studied in the different schools. In the advanced classes of philosphy, however, works of the opposing schools were also studied and examined. Philosophical and theological controversies among the followers of the different schools and sects of Hinduism, Buddhism and Jainism were continuous and animated, and this circumstance must have obviously necessitated a careful study of the works of the opposing schools.

From the ***Milinda-Pañha*** we learn[1] that Buddhist controversialists like Nāgasena used to master Brahmanical theological works. Hindu and Jain controversialists must have done the same in order to get a first hand knowledge of the systems they wanted to attack. It is, therefore, almost certain that the study of the Hindu and Buddhist works was carried on in the Buddhist and Hindu educational institutions respectively in what may be conveniently described as the post-graduate classes in theology and philosophy. Otherwise we cannot explain the large influence which the Hindu, Jain and Buddhist thought and institutions have exercised over one another.

## The Age of the Smritis, Purāṇas and Commentaries.

(*c.* 1 A. D. to *c.* 1200 A. D.)

Vedic curriculum remained more or less unchanged in this period. A number of writers emphasise the great importance of knowing the meaning of the Vedas. We are told that a person who does not understand the import of the Mantras is practically

---

1 1, 34. Buddhist commentators explain the term 'Vedic lore' occuring in such passages as referring to the Buddhist Vedas, i. e. the Tripīṭaka. This explanation is obviously wrong ; in the present passage the Vedic lore is mentioned in addition to the 'Three Baskets.'

of the same status as the Śūdra ;[1] he is merely a beast of burden. His effort can be compared to the pounding of chaff which can never produce any grain.[2] These observations and exhortations seem to be necessitated by the growing ignorance of the average Vedic scholar in this respect. We know from Alberuni also that very few persons could understand the meaning of the Vedic hymns in the 11th century A. D. The latter part of the period we are reviewing here was preeminently an age of the commentators, and yet only one Vedic commentary has been handed down to us, and that too refers to very few predecessors. Few attempts were, therefore, being made in this period to interpret the Vedic hymns which were becoming progressively more unintelligible. Very rarely we come across persons bearing surnames like '*Vedārthada*'[3] 'expounder of the meaning of the Vedas' in inscriptions; vast majority of Vedic scholars were able merely to recite the Saṁhitās. Liturgical studies also must have fallen in the background owing to the progressively growing unpopularity of the Vedic sacrifices. Their

---

1 Cf. योऽधीत्य विधिवद्वेदं वेदार्थं न विचारयेत् ।
स संमूढः शूद्रकल्पः पात्रतां न प्रपद्यते ॥
*Padma Purāṇa*, *Ādi-khaṇḍa*, 53, 86.

2 यथा पशुर्भारवाही न तस्य लभते फलम् ।
द्विजस्तथार्थानभिज्ञो न वेदफलमश्नुते ॥
Vyāsa in Aparārka on Yāj., I, 51.

3 *E. g. I. A.*, XIV, p. 69.

place was taken in the latter half of this period by the formulæ and procedure that was being evolved in connection with the new Pauranic Vratas.

Several donees in the copperplate grants of our period are described as *Chaturvedins, Trivedins* and *Dvivedins.* Persons mastering several Vedas were, however, getting progressively rarer even among the professional priests. Several authorities lay down that a person should not study another Veda or Śākhā without mastering his own.[1] Help of the ritual of another Sākhā was to be taken only when one's own ritual was silent on the point. Maxims like these must have discouraged a study of the Vedic literature on broad and comprehensive lines. The Vedic study itself was getting more and more unpopular. It is difficult to say whether the view of the *Sukra-nīti,*[2] that the Vedic study is detrimental to intellectual development and promotes inefficiency and incapacity for the affairs of the world, was generally shared in our age; we, however, find a writer of our period expressly permitting Brahmanas to devote their energy to the study of the Vedāṅgas, Smritis and Purāṇas to the entire exclusion

---

[1] Cf. एकवेदेऽपि शाखानां मध्ये योऽन्यतमां श्रयेत् ।
स्वशाखां तु परित्यज्य शाखारंडः स उच्यते ॥
Vasishṭha in *VMS.*, p. 505.

[2] Cf. नानुवाकहता बुद्धिर्व्यवहारक्षमा भवेत् ।
अनुवाकहता या तु न सा सर्वत्रगामिनो ॥
III, 281.

of the Vedas.[1] Such a statement would have been inconceivable in the preceding ages. It is quite clear that a Brahmana of our period, who intended to take up to Government service, trade or agriculture, or become an astronomer, astrologer, Paurāṇika or grammarian could hardly have taken the trouble of remembering more than the few Vedic Mantras that were necessary for daily religious purposes. The same was the case with those who intended to specialise in Vedānta, Mīmānsā, Nyāya, Yoga or Sāṅkhya. Among the college professors, however, there used to be many who were all-round scholars. A 7th century copperplate of the Eastern Chalukya dynasty[2] describes the donee's grand-father, who was a teacher at the local college, as well versed in two Vedas, with their *Pada*, *Krama* and *Anukramaṇikā*, *Kalpa*, *Upanishads*, *Purāṇas*, *Itihāsas* and many *Dharmaśāstras*. The donee himself was well grounded in Yajña rituals, *Upanishads*, *Mantras*, *Itihāsa*, *Purāṇa* and *Dharmaśāstra*. College teachers were thus following the advice of Sukra that it is essential for a scholar to be well grounded in several branches of knowledge.[3]

From Alberuni we learn that some Kshatriyas continued to study the Vedas down to the 11th

---

1 Cf. न वेदमनधीत्यान्यां विद्यामधीयेतान्यत्र वेदांगस्मृतिभ्यः ।
Saṅkha in *VMS.*, p. 511.

2 *S. I. E. R.*, 1927, p. 115.

3 Cf. बुद्धिमानभ्यसेन्नित्यं बहुशास्त्राण्यतंद्रितः ।

century A. D., but that the Vaishyas were excluded from the Vedic studies in direct opposition to the Smriti injunction on the point.[1] Vaishyas were by this time more or less completely assimilated with the Sūdras on account of the identity of professions, similarity in living and extensive inter-marriages, hence their loss of the privilege of the Vedic studies.

We can describe fairly accurately the curricula in the non-Vedic literary schools and colleges with the help of the information supplied by the 7th century Chinese travellers.[2] Boys began the alphabet at about the age of 6 and used to take about six months to master it. I-tsing is silent as to what was studied in the next year; probably it was devoted to the study of elementary arithmetic. The Sūtras of Pāṇini were mastered in the 9th year and the next three years were spent in studying *Ashṭadhātu*, *Uṇādi-Sūtras* etc. I-tsing is silent as to what the boys did for the next two years; very probably they were utilised in getting a good grounding in Kāvya (poetics), Sāhitya (literature) and Kosha (dictionary).

Specialisation and bifurcation of courses took place at this stage.[3] Only those students were admitted to

---

[1] Sachau, I, p. 125.

[2] This paragraph is based upon Chap. XXXIV of I-tsing's *Record of the Buddhist World.*

[3] I-tsing's account no doubt suggests that five more years were spent by all the students in mastering the *Kāśikā* and

*P. T. O.*

institutions of higher education, who on account of their mastery over ordinary grammar, literature and vocabulary, were in a position to understand without much difficulty advanced books on technical subjects. From Yuan Chwang we learn that besides grammar there were four other branches which were selected for specialisation. 'The second is that of skilled professions (concerned with) the principles of mechanical arts, the dual processes and astrology. The third is the science of medicine, the use of the stone, the needle and moxa. The fourth is the science of reasoning by which the orthodox and heterodox are ascertained and the true and false are saught out. The fifth is the science of the Internal, which investigates and teaches the five degrees of religious attainments and the subtle doctrine of Karma[1].'

Among these five subjects, grammar seems to have been most popular. Specialists in grammar according to I-tsing, used to study thoroughly *Kāśikā-Vṛitti* and *Pātañjala-Mahā-bhāshya* in about five or six years. The actual books selected for the higher course all over

---

(*Continued from the last page.*)
the *Pātañjala Mahā-bhāshya*, but he is here obviously referring to specialists in grammar. According to Devaṇabhaṭṭa also, proficiency in ordinary grammar, literature and vocabulary was sufficient for admission to higher educational courses.

[1] Watters, I, p. 155.

India may not necessarily have been those mentioned by I-tsing; the entire grammar course, however, must have covered a period of about 10 years as stated by the Chinese traveller. From Alberuni we learn that grammar held its position as the most popular subject in the 11th century also. In fact even today in Sanskrit Pāṭha-śālās no subject is so extensively studied as Vyākaraṇa. The reason is obvious, the teachers in ordinary Sanskrit Pāṭha-śālās were naturally expected to be well up in that subject. The demand for the grammarians is comparable to the demand for trained English teachers in modern India.

From the quotation given above from Yuan Chwang it appears that astronomy-cum-astrology and medicine were the most popular liberal professions of the age. Discussion about their courses will be undertaken in the next chapter; it may be noted at this stage that those who intended to take them up had to possess a fair grounding in ordinary grammar, literature and vocabulary. Logic and philosophy were the two branches of liberal education that were specialised in most of the higher educational institutions. The two were intimately connected with each other. In this as in the earlier period, Hindu students of metaphysics used to study the works of their opponents also. Some of them used to be specialists in Buddhism, enjoying a fame equal to that of celebrated Buddhist scholars. Yuan Chwang stayed for a month and half in southern Kośala in order to study the treatise called *In-ming* from a Brahmana scholar.[1] There must have been many such scholars in the Hindu colleges specialising in philosophy. This is quite clear from Bāṇa's description of the Āśrama of Divākarasena, who was originally a Brāhmaṇa but was later converted to Buddhism. We learn that students of Dharmaśāstra, Upanishads, and of Kāpila, Vaiśeshika and Laukayatika systems of philosophy stayed in his Āśrama and studied under him, along with the followers of Makkhali Gosāla and Svetāmbara and Digambara Jainism.[2]

The advanced courses in logic and philosophy, which commenced at about the age of 15, must have extended over a period of about eight years. I-tsing undoubtedly observes that the students, who used to proceed to Valabhi and Nālandā for the study of logic and metaphysics, used to stay there only two or three years. This does not, however, mean that the entire college course in these subjects extended over that short period. I-tsing is referring only to advanced students who had finished earlier part of their education elsewhere; he describes these students as 'being instructed by their teachers and instructing others.'[3] Specialists in logic and philosophy could not have finished their education before about the age of 24.

The study of Smritis and Purāṇas is not mentioned by the Chinese travellers probably by over-

---

[1] Beal, *Life of Hiuen Tsang*, p. 136.

[2] *Harsha-charit*, Uchchhvāsa VIII.

[3] Takakusu, Itsing, p. 177.

sight. These had a hold over the popular mind of our period, which was almost as great as the hold of the Vedas on the mind of the earlier generations.[1] It is, therefore, certain that Smritis and Purāṇas must have been taught in the vast mojority of even the second rate schools and colleges. Classical Sanskrit literature, drama, and poetics became extremely popular from about the 5th century A. D.; the extra-ordinary development of these branches would warrant the conclusion that subjects like Nyāya, Mīmānsā and Vedānta must have temporarily fallen in the background in the schools and colleges from about the 7th or the 8th century. The special course in Sāhitya comprised a study of grammar, metrics, poetics, popular literature, epics, Purāṇas, traditional stories and the works of the celebrities of the bye-gone times.[2] Ability to compose a poem was regarded almost as indispensable in this period as the ability to read and write in modern times. The large number of Smritis, Purāṇas, dramas, Kāvyas, and works on poetics that were composed in this period makes it quite clear that these subjects must have been cultivated with great care and assiduity in the schools and colleges of our period.

The curriculum of the Budhist institutions differed to some extent from that prescribed in Hindu Colleges.

---

1 Altekar: *The Rāshṭrakūṭas and their Times*, pp. 297-304.

2 *Kāvyamīmāṇsa*, pp. 49-50.

Mahāyāna Buddhism was in ascendancy in India at this time and most of its important works were in Sanskrit. Lay Buddhists like their Hindu brethren used to spend about seven or eight years in the study of grammar, literature and Kosha. At about 16 they started reading Buddhist works on logic and metaphysics like *Hetu-vidyā* and *Abhidharma-śāstra* and spent about seven or eight years in mastering them. Some select passages from the Vinaya were probably taught at an earlier stage *pari passu* with the elementary study of grammar.

Studies prescribed for the Buddhist monk were naturally somewhat different. For ten years after his ordination he was under the direct control and guidance of a teacher (Upajjhāya). He had to master both Pali and Sanskrit, because Buddhist scriptures and works that he had to study were written in both these languages. He had to study very thoroughly the *Vinaya, Sūtras, Pātimokkha* and the *Śāstras*. This usually took about ten years and then he became qualified to become a teacher himself. His education, however, did not stop here, for he was expected to be a life-long student like the Hindu Naishṭhika Brahmachārin. Of course, not all the monks had either the inclination or the intellectual calibre to go on mastering books after books; but it has to be admitted that many of the 7th century monasteries including those in out of the way places like Jalundar, Dhenukākaṭa and southern Kośala possessed celebrated monk scholars, who could detain Yuan Chwang several months for learning the special subjects cultivated in them.[1] Among the 10,000 monks that resided at Nālandā, in *c.* 635 A.D., 1,000 could explain 20 collections of Sūtras, 500, 30 collections and about 10, 50 collections.[2] The number of distinguished scholars among the Buddhist monks at this time seems, therefore, to have been fairly large.

Hetu-vidyā śāstra, Nyāyānusāra śāstra, Praṇyamūla śastra, Shaṭpadābhidharma śāstra, Kosha and Vibhāshā were among the principal subjects studied in Buddhist monastery-colleges of this period. Medicine was also studied probably to meet the needs of the huge monastic population. Hindu systems of philosophy like Vedānta and Sāṅkhya were carefully analysed in order to meet the Hindu opponent on his own ground. Even Yuan Chwang, who had undertaken the arduous and dangerous journey to India primarily for studying Buddhist scriptures, spent two fifth the period of his stay in India in studying the sacred books of the Hindus.[3]

New books were being produced in this period in quick succession on most of the subjects that were being taught in schools and colleges. If we had fuller information, we might probably have learnt that some authors in ancient times were not far behind their

---

1 Beal, *Life of Hiuen Tsang*, pp. 136, 137, 177.

2 *Ibid*, p. 112.

3 *Ibid*, p. 125.

modern successors in taking all possible steps to get their books introduced as text books in educational institutions. It is, however, very doubtful whether any pecuniary gain was likely to accrue to an author by his book being used as a text book, for there was no press and copyright in our period. Probably it was only the honour that was being coveted. One concrete and interesting case is known in this connection. Ugrabhūti, the teacher of king Anangapāla of the Punjab, (*c.* 1000-*c.* 1010 A. D.) had composed a book on grammar called *Sishya-hitā-vritti.* He sent it to Kashmir, but the scholars there refused to adopt it. The author then complained to his quondam royal disciple, who sent a sum of 2,00,000 *dirhams* (= Rs. 60,000) to Kashmir for being distributed among those who would study the book of his master. The book was then adopted in no time all over the country and there was a rush upon it.[1] Ugrabhūti's case need not be supposed to be the typical one; but some such funny episodes may be lying buried in the lost records of ancient Indian history.

The revival of Hinduism had led in our period to a revival of Sanskrit, which was so intense and effective that even the Buddhists and Jains discarded the precepts and examples of the founders of their systems and began to compose their sacred works in Sanskrit. Early in this period, down to about 300 A.D.,

[1] Sachau, Alberuni, I, pp. 135-6.

even public documents were composed in Prakrits, but we hardly get any copper plate grant or lithic inscription in a Prakrit language after the beginning of the 4th century A. D. The Sātavāhanas were the champions of Prakrit,[1] but their example was not emulated by any later kings. Nay, with the revival of Sanskrit some kings like Sāhasāṅka of Ujjayinī are said to have issued orders that Sanskrit alone should be spoken even in their harems.[2] As a consequence of all these factors the development of Prakrit and Apabhranśa dialects was arrested in our period. Even what may be described as primary schools were mainly engaged in the teaching of Sanskrit grammar and syntax. It appears almost certain that no attention was paid in our schools and colleges to the cultivation of the spoken languages of the people.[3] This had unfortunate consequences on the spread of knowledge among the masses, which will be discussed in the last chapter.

---

1 There was a standing order in their court that Prakrit alone should be spoken in their households. See Rājaśekhara's *Kāvya-mīmānsā*, p. 50.

2 *Ibid.* p. 50.

3 Cf. Alberuni's observation, 'Further the language is divided into a *neglected vernacular* one in use among the common people and a classical one, only in use among the upper and educated classes, which is much cultivated' Sachau, I, p. 18.

### METHOD OF TEACHING.

Wide divergence of opinion exists at present as to the best method of teaching suitable to students of different grades. Some think that no teaching is at all necessary at higher stages; it is quite sufficient for the teacher to supply a good bibliography. Some are in favour of careful tuition and home exercises. Others grow eloquent over the merits of the lecturing system, which in the hands of a competent professor, enlarges the student's vision and transports him to the higher regions.

In order to understand the method of teaching prevailing in ancient India, it is essential that we should visualise the state of affairs then prevailing. The art of printing was unknown and books were very costly, fragile and rare. The theory that the use of a carefully selected library is the best method of education was, therefore, naturally out of the mental vision of the age. The services of the art of writing were for several centuries not utilised for lightening the burden of the memory. The sacred character of the Vedic literature was partly responsible for this; it was probably feared that the most sacred possession of the race might pass into profane hands, if the Vedas were committed to writing. Great importance was attached to proper accent and intonation, and the necessary guidance in this respect could be had from the lips of an animate teacher and not from the pages of an inanimate book. Then there was the danger of the semi-illiterate scribe; even int he 11th century A.D. the most important conclusions of an author's work were often omitted from the copy by the negligence of the scribe. His book was often transformed out of recognition and used to be altogether unintelligible in the first or second copy.[1]

Owing to the above considerations learning was transmitted from generation to generation orally; this state of affairs continues down to the present times in Sanskrit Pāṭhaśālas of the older type. *Prātiśākhyas* give us a good glimpse into the traditional method of teaching the Vedas since very early times. Scholars used to recite the stanzas of the Vedic hymns taught to them by their teacher exactly in the same way and intonation.[2] The slightest mistake in intonation, accent or pronunciation was regarded as most fatal; each boy had, therefore, to be taught separately. Every day about two or three verses were committed to memory. The teacher used to pronounce only two words at a time and this number was reduced to one if the word happened to be compound one. The first pupil then recited the words exactly in the way the teacher had done, and if he had any difficulty it was explained to him. When the whole *praśna* was taught

---

1 Sachau, Alberuni, I, p. 18.

2 Cf. यदेषामन्योऽन्यस्य वाचं शाक्तस्येव वदति शिक्षमाणः।

*R. V.*, VII, 103, 5.

in this way, the next student was taken up.[1] Necessarily every student used to receive individual attention under this system.

It would appear that the Vedas were first committed to writing some time in the 8th or the 9th century A. D. Vasukra, an inhabitant of Kashmir, had the courage to undertake the task of writing out the text and explanations of the Vedic Mantras. The Mahābhārata condemns a man to hell for the sin of writing down the Vedic texts[2]; but Vasukra, we are told by Alberuni, was afraid that the Veda itself would be lost if it was not committed to writing.[3] Hence he undertook the task from which every one else had recoiled till then. Vasukra's step did not revolutionise the traditional method of teaching; it was too deep-rooted. Books, besides, were very rare, costly and fragile.

This method of teaching was also followed in Buddhist institutions. For several centuries the teachings of the Buddha continued to exist only in the memory of his disciples and followers. In the 2nd century B. C., Nāgasena learnt the Tripīṭaka

---

[1] *Ṛik-prātiśākhya*, Paṭala XV.

[2] Cf. वेदविक्रयिणश्चैव वेदानां चैव दूषकाः ।
वेदानां लेखकाश्चैव ते वै निरयगामिनः ॥

*Āśvamedhika Parva*, 106, 92.

[3] Sachau, Alberuni, I, p. 112.

by heart not from any books but from the lips of his teacher Dhammarakkhita.[1] Buddhist students used to have recourse to the same method in the 7th century A. D., though the Tripīṭaka was committed to writing at least as early as the time of Kanishka. The method of teaching then in vogue has been described by I-tsing; the teacher used to take up the Tripīṭaka passage of the day and gave a lesson that suited the circumstance without leaving any fact or theory unexplained.[2]

The fact that the Vedas and the Tripīṭakas were learnt by the heart has given rise to the impression that learning by rote was the only method followed in Ancient India. The impression, however, is wrong; explanation, exposition and elucidation were resorted to even in the Vedic schools when the etymology of difficult words, the interpretation of obscure passages and the changes that took place in the Saṁhitā text when it was converted into the Pada text and vice versa, had to be discussed with the pupils. A considerable portion of the Brāhmaṇa literature is of the nature of explanation and exposition of the Vedic texts; it really represents portions of the lectures that were delivered to the Vedic students in the class-rooms of that period. It is, therefore, clear that even in early times Vedic teachers were not content merely with teaching

---

1 *Mil. Pan.*, I, p. 21.

2 p. 120.

the text of the hymns. In the Tittiri Jātaka, the Veda teachers are represented as expounding the knotty points in the hymns as easily as a stream leaps down from a mountain peak.[1]

Sūtra works like those of Pāṇini, Jaimini and Bādarāyaṇa could never have been learnt merely by rote. They are too obscure and difficult to be learnt by that method. Teaching in such cases must have been accompanied by extensive explanations and expositions, which seem to have been partly incorporated in some of the extant commentaries on these works. Teaching of the various books on the Vedānta, Mīmānsā, Nyāya, Vaiśeshika and Buddhist metaphysics was hardly possible without exhaustive discussions pertaining to the views expounded and views controverted. In these discussions there was unravelling of the subject matter, distinctions and contradistinctions were drawn, and an effort was made to show the reasonableness of one's position and the errors of the opponent.[2] The students of the various schools of orthodox and heterodox systems of religion and philosophy, who were studying under Divākarasena, used to listen to the exposition of their respective systems, deliberate on their natures, discuss their features, raise doubts on obscure themes, determine for themselves the main

---

1 Tittiri Jātaka, No. 438.

2 *Mil. Pan.*, I, 46.

outlines and enter into discussion with their opponents.[1] This same procedure must have been followed in all the institutions engaged in teaching religion, philosophy, logic, law and poetics. Indian teachers in the 7th century A. D. were past masters in the art of explanation and exposition, and students from distant countries like Korea and China used to brave the dangers of the perilous journey to India, not so much because they wanted to learn by rote the scriptures of their religion, but because they were anxious to hear the explanations and expositions of obscure metaphysical passages which could be heard nowhere else. About his Indian teachers I-tsing says, 'I have been always very glad that I had an opportunity of acquiring knowledge from them personally, *which I should otherwise have never possessed.*'[2] What Yuan Chwang valued in his Indian Gurus was not so much their capacity to recite the texts as their remarkable ability in explaining obscure passages and offering illuminative suggestions on doubtful points.[3]

In several Jātakas we read that the 'world-famous' teachers of Takshaśilā used to have 500 scholars studying under them. This number of students seems to be more conventional than real, and was probably suggested by the repeated statements

---

[1] *Harsha-charit*, Uchchhvāsa VIII.

[2] P. 185.

[3] Beal, *Life*, pp. 76, 154, 160.

occuring in the Tripīṭakas that the Buddha used to be always accompanied by 500 disciples. For, all available evidence shows that generally speaking the Indian teacher used to take charge of about 15 or 20 students only. Nālandā used to provide for a teaching staff of a thousand teachers for its student population of about 9,000.[1] In the 11th century A. D., in the Vedic college at Ennāyiram, each teacher had about 20 students only under his charge.[2] At Benares, in the 17th century A. D. some times only four, and usually about 12 or 15 students, used to work under one teacher.[3] In the 19th century A. D., the number of students that used to study under a teacher in the *Tols* at Nadia used to vary from 10 to 20.[4] It therefore seems almost certain that the Jātaka statements that each of the famous teachers of Takshaśilā used to coach 500 students are not to be accepted as literally true, and that normally every teacher used to take the responsibility for about 15 to 20 students only. Individual attention to the needs of each student was therefore possible. Instructions were more of the nature of personal guidance than of lectures. Students used to receive personal instructions and guidance. This was one of the strongest points in the ancient Indian system of education. Lectures to

---

1 Beal, *Life*, p. 112.

2 *S. I. E. R.*, 1918, p. 145.

3 Bernier, p. 334.

4 *Nadia Gazetteer*, p. 182.

large classes of 100 or 200 students, which are unintelligible to some, superfluous to others and partially useful to the rest, were unknown in ancient India. Students could not afford to go to the class room, or to be more accurate, to the teacher without thorough preparation. There was a daily examination of every student and no new lesson was given until the old one was thoroughly mastered.[1] There were no annual examinations and mass promotions at fixed intervals. Clever students were not compelled to mark time for their dull companions as under the modern system of education. The educational system ministered to the needs and individual capacity of each student. If a student was intelligent and industrious, he could finish his education much earlier than is possible in modern times. The idle and careless student had not as pleasant a prospect of a merry college life as he has in the present age. Yuan Chwang says, 'When disciples, intelligent and accute, are addicted to idle shirking, teachers doggedly persevere in repeating instructions until their training is finished.'[2] The Chinese traveller was very favourably impressed by the capacity of Indian teachers to rouse their students to activity and urge them to progress.

In order to make personal supervision effective, the cooperation and help of advanced students were

---

[1] *Mil. Pan.*, I, p. 18.

[2] Watters, I, p. 160.

enlisted in the cause of education. They used to guide the studies of the juniors under the general supervision of their teachers. About the Valabhi college students, I-tsing observes that they used to pass two or three years 'instructed by their teachers and instructing others'.[1] This system also obtained at Takshaśilā; for instance, in the Mahāsuta-soma Jātaka we find that the Kuru prince Sutasoma aquired proficiency earlier, and was entrusted with the teaching of his brother prince, the heir apparent of Benares[2]. In some Jātaka stories we find senior students at Takshaśilā being put in charge of their schools during the temporary absence of their teachers.[3] This method of entrusting teaching work to brilliant students had a great educational value. It placed a high incentive before the student world. It afforded opportunities to intelligent students to learn the art of teaching, and thus indirectly performed the same service as the Teachers' Training Colleges discharge today. It increased the efficiency and decreased the cost of the school by affording intelligent and free assistance to the teacher.

When the teaching is individual and the knowledge of the student is tested every day by questions and answers, the dialogue method of teaching would often become inevitable. We find this method followed in some of the Upanishads and Buddhist Sūtras. In the

---

[1] p. 177.

[2] No. 537.

[3] E. g., Sukha-vihārai Jātaka, no. 10.

hands of a skilful teacher like the Buddha the method was most effective.

The value of observation and comparison was also recognised by some of the shrewd teachers. A teacher in Benares had an exceptionally dull but devoted student in his class who was a problem to him. After giving a careful consideration to his case he came to the conclusion that the best way to develop his intellect would be by questioning the young man on his daily return from the forest about something that he might have seen or done that day and then to ask him what it was like. 'For' thought the teacher, 'this would lead him on to make comparisons and give reasons and the continuous practice of comparing and reasoning on his part would enable me to impart education to him'.[1] In this particular case the experiment did not succeed, because the student was a dunce of an exceptionally high order. The story would, however, show that some teachers in ancient India tried to make education interesting and effective by enlisting the services of the faculties of observation and comparison. The *Hitopadeśa* would show that stories and parables were also utilised to make education lively and interesting.

To sum up, ancient Indian educationalists no doubt attached great importance to the teacher, but did not believe that education was a merely passive

[1] Mangalīśa Jātaka No. 124.

process, and that the teacher could achieve unaided all the ends desired. The cooperation of the student was esssential and a good deal depended upon his intellectual cali re.[1] Reflection on the part of the student was insisted upon, especially in the case of those who wanted to specialise in theology, philosophy and logic. Students were also encouraged to hold mutual discussions and their powers of comparison and observation were also developed. We find some of the Jātaka students undertaking tours at the end of their education, and Śukra describes graphically the various advantages to be derived from travelling and coming into contact with the scholars of different lands.[2] All this, however, could not give the finishing touch to education. Time was an important factor and maturity of intellect and scholarship would not come into existence the moment the course was over; time alone could achieve that consummation if properly utilised.[3]

## EXAMINATIONS.

We have seen already that there were no annual or periodical examinations in ancient India. New lessons

---

[1] Cf. वितरति गुरुः प्राज्ञे विद्यां यथैव तथा जडे ।
न च खलु तयोर्ज्ञाने शक्तिं करोत्यपहन्ति वा ॥
भवति च पुनर्भूयान्भेदः फलं प्रति तद्यथा ।
प्रभवति मणिर्बिम्बोद्ग्राहे न पुनर्मृदाञ्चयः ॥
*Uttara-Rāma-charit*, Act II.

[2] III, 131-7.

[3] Cf. आचार्यात्पादमादत्ते पादं शिष्यः स्वमेधया ।
पादं स ब्रह्मचारिभ्यः पादं कालक्रमेण तु ॥ *Subhāshitam.*

were given to students only when the teacher was satisfied after a searching oral examination that the old one was thoroughly mastered. The end of the education course was not marked by any lengthy and exhaustive examnation but by the pupil reciting and explaining the last lesson.[1] The modern practice to submit the student to what is known as *Śalākā-parīkshā*, where he is asked to explain the problems discussed on a page opened at random, is not mentioned in ancient books but may be perhaps old. Even if it goes to ancient times, it can hardly be compared to the modern system of examination.

At the end of his education the scholar was presented to the local learned assembly where occasionally some questions were asked.[2] From the Gṛihya-sūtras we learn that this presentation took place when the Samāvartana ceremony was over.[3] It is therefore clear that the eligibility of a student for Samāvartana or receiving the degree did not depend upon the opinion of the assembly but upon the opinion of his teacher.

Rājaśekhara describes the examinations held in the royal court[4] and Charaka refers to heated discussions held in learned assemblies to test the relative

---

1 *Mil. pan.*, I, p. 18.

2 *Br. U.*, VI, 2, 1 and 2.

3 *Dr. Gr. S.*, III 1, 26; *Āp. Gr. S.*, I, 11, 5.

4 *Kāvya-mīmāṅsā*, p. 55.

merits of the contending physicians.[1] These examinations were, however, fundamentally different from modern degree examinations. Each participant in these literary affrays was anxious to prove, not that he possessed certain minimum qualifications, but that he was the best poet or physician in the land, entitled to precedence, honour and annuities from the royal court. What Charaka or Rājaśekhara have in contemplation is not a routine examination but an intellectual combat among the distinguished physicians and scholars of the age.

Since there were no degree examinations, there were naturally no degrees or diplomas. From Tārānāth we learn that the Pāla kings of Bengal, who were patrons and chancellors of the Vikramaśila University, used to grant diplomas to students in a convocation held at the end of their education.[2] In medieval Bengal also learned bodies used to confer degrees like *Tarkachakravartī* and *Tarkālaṅkāra* on very distinguished scholars like Gadādhara and Jagadīśa. This practice of giving degrees and titles seems to be a new innovation of medieval times. Yuan Chwang informs us that unscrupulous scholars in the seventh century used to 'steal the name of Nālandā' in order to gain more respect[3]. This would not have been possible if the Nālandā University were in the habit of granting

[1] Vimānasthāna, 8.

[2] Bose, ***Indian Teachers of Buddhist Universities***, p.61.

[3] Watters, II, p. 165.

regular diplomas to those who had finished their courses there.

Students in ancient India had not to pass through the fiery ordeal of examinations; their lot, however, was by no means more enviable than that of the modern students. Armed with his irrevocable degree, the modern graduate can afford to forget all that he had learnt, and no one can question his competence. The scholar in ancient India could not take shelter behind the buttress of a degree. He had to keep his scholarship fresh and up-to-date, for he was liable to be challenged at any moment for a literary affray (*Śāstrārtha*) and the society used to judge his merit by the way in which he aquitted himself in such discussions. All that he had learnt he had to keep ready at the tip of his tongue; he could neither point to his diploma nor ask for time to refer to his note-books.

# CHAPTER V

## USEFUL EDUCATION.

In the last chapter we surveyed the higher courses in the literary line ; an attempt will now be made to discuss useful education and the problems connected with it. Military, medical and commercial education, training in various fine arts like sculpture, painting, music and dancing, and instructions in useful industries like spinning and weaving, masonry, carpentary, smithy, lapidary and mining and metallurgy come within the purview of the present chapter. Our sources of information are, however, few and poor; Smritis, which supply some information about theological and literary education, are with very few exceptions, silent about training in useful arts and professions, and earlier literature throws hardly any light on the subject. Observations of foreign merchants and pilgrims usually refer to liberal education, if the topic of education is at all touched by them. Had an Arabian or Chinese enquirer come to India to ascertain the methods of medical education or the processes of the great textile industry, or had a Smriti been written by a non-Brahmana interested in the methods and institutions of the various branches of professional education, or had an inscription been discovered making an endowment for a technical institution, our knowledge of the subject would have been much more complete than it is today.

## SECTION I.

### CASTE SYSTEM AND USEFUL EDUCATION.

The traditional division of professions among the various castes would suggest that the students who used to receive useful and industrial education must have predominently belonged to non-Brahmana classes. This *a priori* conclusion, however, does not bear close examination. In the Vedic period the caste system had not become rigid and we find a respectable sage, whose poems have been canonised, informing his readers that he himself was a poet, his father a doctor and his maternal grand-father a stone-cutter.[1] People used to follow useful and lucrative professions in accordance with their individual tastes. In course of time, however, the caste system became theoretically rigid, and sacred texts began to enjoin that the Brahmana should follow a life of voluntary poverty in the interest of religious and cultural education, and should abstain from lucrative careers in useful professions. A section of the Brahmana community followed this ideal, but the rest were unable to do so either because the sacrifice demanded was too high, or because they thought that their sacred duty to teach referred not only to Vedic lore but also included useful and industrial arts.[2] Brahmanas endowed with less than ordinary intelligence were naturally unfit to become the teachers of language

---

[1] R. V. IX, 112, 3.

[2] राजन्यवैश्यकर्म्मा विद्याहीनः । *Gau. Dh. S.*, I, 6, 16.

and literature. Gautama permits them to follow industrial arts[1] and several Jātakas show that this liberty was fully availed of. We find several Brahmanas learning and following the professions of the trader, the soldier, the serpent-charmer and the cultivator. Nay, in one Jātaka story we come across a Brahmana priest of holy Benares sending his son to Takshaśila for gaining proficiency in archery[2]. The Jātaka evidence is also supported by the Smritis; they lay down that Brahmanas, who are traders, physicians, navigators, trainers of horses and elephants and dealers in dogs and camels should not be invited for a Srāddha.[3] Obviously the number of Brahmanas following such professions must have been not insignificant, otherwise express rules for their exclusion would not have been laid down. The military profession and the government service also were by no means the exclusive preserves for the Kshatriyas. The army used to be recruited from all classes, and in the seventh century A. D. when Yuan Chwang visited India, kings of Ujjain, Maheśvara, and Assam were Brahmanas, those of Pariyātra and Kanauj Vaisyas, and those

1 In Jātakas we find several Brahmanas teaching archery, magic, snake-charming etc. *Dhanurveda Saṁhitā* (1, 4) lays down that either a Brahmana or a Kshatriya should be a teacher of the military arts. Droṇa, the teacher of the Kshatriya Kaurava princes, was himself a Brahmana.

2 Śarabhaṅga Jātaka, No. 522.

3 E. G., Manu, III, 152 ff.

of Matipura and Sindh Śudras. Śuṅga, Kaṇva and Kadamba rulers were Brahmanas by caste. When therefore we are thinking of useful and professional education, we need not suppose that students for these branches came exclusively from non-Brahmana groups. Down to about 500 A. D. intercaste marriages were not tabooed either by the Smritis or by society and the caste system did not have a dominant voice in determining the careers of the ambitious youths in the rising generation. A useful profession like the medical one was followed by the members of all the castes in the 2nd century A. D.[1]

A large majority of students who took up useful arts were naturally non-Brahmanas, among whom a fair percentage belonged to Kshatriya and Vaishya castes. Members of these castes were eligible for Upanayana and Vedic studies, but there is a wide divergence of opinion as to the extent to which they availed themselves of that privilege. Let us therefore try to ascertain the nature and extent of the Vedic and literary education of Kshatriya and Vaishya boys, who used to take up useful professions like commerce, industry or mining and metallurgy.

We have seen already how Upanayana was not a compulsory Sanskāra down to about the Upanishadic times (c. 800 B. C.) In this early age Vedic studies could obviously not have been universal among the

1 Charaka, Sūtra-sthāna, 30, 26.

Kshatriyas and Vaishyas. Brahmanical tradition itself has, however, recognised that some of the composers of the Vedic hymns like Vainya and Viśvāmitra were Kshatriyas, and in the Upanishads some Kshatriya kings are seen to be taking a leading part in philosophical development. Some of the important esoteric doctrines are admitted even by the Brahmanical tradition to have been for a long time in the exclusive possession of Kshatriya circles headed by kings like Ajātaśatru,[1] Pravāhaṇa Jaivali,[2] Aśvapati Kaikaya[3] etc. The *Kāṭhaka Saṁhitā* contains a ritual for the benefit of a non-Brahmana, who had studied the sacred lore but had not become famous.[4] Whether the term '*abrāhmaṇa*' in this passage would justify the conclusion that Vaishyas also like Kshatriyas were in some cases studying and teaching the Vedic texts it is difficult to state, for actual cases of Vaishya teachers or philosophical celebrities are not known. The number of Vaishyas taking deep and active interest in Vedic religion and philosophy seems to have been always much smaller than that of the Kshatriyas. The available evidence seems to show that in early times the intellectual sections among the Kshatriyas, and to a less extent, among the Vaishyas were often taking a deep interest in Vedic and Upanishadic

---

1 *Br. Up.*, III,1, 14.

2 *Ibid*, IV, 1, 1; *Ch. Up.*, IV, 4, 1.

3 *Sat. Br.*, X, 6, 1, 1.

4 Cf. योऽब्राह्मणो विद्यामनूच्य नैव रोचेत । IX, 16.

studies and problems, perhaps as a recreation for their leisure hours.

We have already seen how at about 800 B. C. it was deemed necessary to conscript the services of the whole Aryan society for the preservation of the Vedic lore, and how Upanayana came to be prescribed as a compulsory Sanskāra for Brahmanas, Kshatriyas and Vaishyas. The Smriti rules, if taken at their face value, would lead us to the conclusion that the Kshatriya and Vaishya youths also, like the Brahmana ones, were expected to study the Vedas for twelve long years after their Upanayana. The problem to be investigated into is whether the Kshatriya and Vaishya youths did really perform the Vedic Upanayana, and if so, whether they spent so long a time in Vedic studies.

We must first note that Upanayana was at this time regarded as a bodily (*śārīra*) Sanskāra and its non-performance was deemed to degrade an Aryan to the status of a Sūdra. It is clear that other Sanskāras like *Nāmakaraṇa* or *Chūḍākarma* were performed by the Kshatriyas and Vaishyas and there is therefore no reason to doubt the general prevalence of Upanayana also among these classes till about the 2nd century B. C. Otherwise it is difficult to understand how Smritis should be laying down very minute rules about such trivial points like the difference in the height of staffs, the textures of the sacred threads and girdles, and the formulæ at the time of begging that were to be used by the Brahmachārins of the different castes. Unfortunately specific historic instances of the performance of Upanayana like that of the Hoysala king, Narasiṁha III, which took place on the 25th of February 1255 when he was in his fifteenth year, are not on record; but that is due to the circumstance that historic documents, such as have been preserved, are not concerned with such matters. It seems, however, very probable that Upanayana was universal among those Kshatriyas who were anxious to be recognised as such, down to about the 11th century A. D., for Alberuni notes that in his time the members of the warrior caste used to study the Vedas though they could not teach it.[1] The case of the Vaishyas seems to have been different. They became assimilated to the position of the Sūdras very early on account of indiscriminate marriages[2]; already at the time of the Mahābhārata, (*c.* 200 B. C.) they were classed with the Sūdras among the fallen sections of the society.[3] In the 11th century A. D. we know from Alberuni that the Vaishyas like the Sūdras were prohibited from the reading and study of the Vedas.[4] Alberuni's testimony

---

1 Sachau, Vol. 1, p. 125.

2 Cf. अनिर्यंत्रितकलत्रा वैश्यशूद्रा भवन्ति... ।

*Bau. Dh. S.*, I, 11, 4.

3 *Gītā*, IX 32. When Drupada learns that an obscure person has won his daughter, he hopes that he is not at least a Vaishya or Śūdra. *MBH.*, I, 186, 16.

4 Sachau, I, 125.

is very important; he knew that theoretically the Vaishyas were perfectly entitled to study the Vedas, and yet he notes that in practice they were regarded as much ineligible as the Sūdras. Upanayana and Vedic studies must have disappeared from the Vaishya community as a whole before the beginning of the Christian era. A few respectable Vaishya families may have succeeded in preventing their assimilation with the Śūdras for a few centuries more. In their case Upanayana may have continued to be a reality followed by a nominal study of a few Vedic Mantras. They must, however, have formed an infinitesimal section of the Vaishya community.

When towards the close of the Upanishadic period the Kshatriyas could no longer become Vedic teachers, it is obvious that they would hardly have cared to spend as many as twelve years for their Vedic studies. The precise amount of the Vedic education of the Kshatriyas is difficult to determine. Some Jātaka stories no doubt represent Kshatriya princes as learning one entire Veda or even all the three Vedas, but these statements cannot be taken at their face value. For, we are gravely informed that these princes used to study all the three Vedas and all the eighteen practical arts and professions[1]. In a short period of six or eight years, no prince, howsoever clever he might have been,

---

[1] Cf. सोळसवस्सपदेसिको हुत्वा तक्कसिलायां सिप्पं उग्गण्हित्वा तिण्णं वेदानं पारं गत्वा अट्ठारसानं विज्जट्ठानं निप्फत्तिं पापुनाति। Dummedha Jātaka, No. 50.

could have mastered all these subjects. Similarly the *Mahābhārata* represents the Kaurava princes as being experts in Veda, Vedānta and the various branches of the military profession[1]. But a perusal of the relevant passages shows that the author of the epic was more anxious to represent his heroes as being well versed in all the known important branches of knowledge than in recording the authentic tradition in the matter, if any such had existed in the 3rd century B. C. The *Rāmāyaṇa* represents Rāma and his brothers as students of the Veda, but refrains from claiming for them any expert knowledge in that branch[2]. Serious military education could hardly have commenced before the age of 14 or 15, and it is quite probable that the youths in respectable Kshatriya families may have utilised a part of their early life in getting some grounding in the Vedic literature. The Jātakas usually represent the Brahmana and Kshatriya youths as being instructed together by the same teachers in the Vedas and Sippas[3]. It is therefore probable that the average Kshatriya youth may have had some grounding in the Vedic learning. Kauṭilya and Manu also prescribe that Veda and philosophy should form part of a prince's education. The controversy that was going on at this period as to whether the sciences of politics

---

[1] Ādiparva, Chaps. 118 and 133.

[2] Bālakāṇḍa, Chap. 18.

[3] Cf. खत्तियमानवा ब्राह्मणमानवा च तस्सेव संतिके सिप्पं उग्गण्हितुं गच्छंति। Asadisa Jātaka, No. 181; Thusa Jātaka No. 338.

and economics should not form the exclusive topics of study of a Kshatriya prince would show that by about the beginning of the Christian era the average prince and Kshatriya used to possess only a very limited knowledge of the Vedas and philosophy, probably not extending much beyond the capacity to recite a few Vedic Mantras and Upanishadic passages. The more religious-minded among them continued to ground themselves more deeply in the Vedic literature down to the time of Alberuni, but their number must have been very small[1].

## SECTION II

### VEDA-BRĀHMAṆA PERIOD.

( upto *c.* 800 B. C. )

Let us now proceed to discuss the history of Useful Education age by age. Very little is known about the state of affairs in the Veda-Brāhmaṇa age. In this period the followers of the manual arts were not regarded as plebian, but were held in high esteem. We have seen already how in the families of Vedic sages some were following the profession of the physician and some that of the stone-cutter[2]. The carpenter ( *Rathakāra* ) was so important a member of the society that the chief of his guild was included among the

---

[1] Hence the observation of Ḍalhaṇa, a medieval writer, at *Suśruta, Śārīra*, X, 52, **यथावर्णमिति ब्राह्मणास्त्रयीं राजन्यो दण्डनीतिं वैश्यो वार्तामिति ।**

[2] *R. V.*, IX, 112, 3.

twelve courtiers ( *ratnins* ) to whose house the king had to repair in order to offer him an oblation at the time of his coronation[1]. But perhaps the most vivid idea of the reverence that was shown to useful arts and industries would be gained from the mythological story about the *Ṛibhus*, which states that they were originally men but were later on raised to divinity as a reward for their high artistic skill. The doctor's profession was highly honoured unlike in later times ; the Aśvins also were like the *Ṛibhus* originally human princes and physicians who were later elevated to the pantheon for their medical skill.

Quite a large percentage of the Aryan society must be following the various useful professions, for Vedic studies had not yet become either universal or exacting. Archery, horsemanship, charioting, smithy, carpentry, medicine and mining were the principal useful arts of the age.[2] The continuance of the supremacy of the Aryans over the non-Aryans depended on the Aryan superiority in the above arts and professions, and the Aryans, therefore, must have taken all possible steps to ensure that as large a percentage of the rising generation as possible was well trained in the above arts. Unfortunately, however, the extant literature gives no idea

---

[1] *Mai. S.*, II, 6, 5 ; IV, 3, 8 ; *Śat. Br.*, II, 3, 1, 1.

[2] See Macdonel and Keith, *Vedic Index*. About mining, see *Vāj. S.*, 18, 13 :—हिरण्यं च मे अयश्च मे श्यामं च मे लोहं च मे सीसं च मे त्रपु च मे…।

of the arrangements made in this connection. Some of these professions may have been hereditary in several families; in such cases fathers must have been instructing their sons in the processes of their arts and industries. Ambitious princes like Sudās must have organised huge factories for the manufacture of bows, arrow-heads, chariots and saddles: their victory in war depended on the quality of the above material they could obtain at the time of war. Several youths may have joined these factories as apprentices and received training in smithy and carpentry. Not impossibly some of these professions may have been already organised into guilds and made arrangements about the training of the rising generation. All this is however a pure though probable conjecture; actual evidence is sadly lacking.

## SECTION III

### (*c.* 800 B. C. TO *c.* 250 B. C.)

Upanishads, Gṛihya-sūtras and Dharma-sūtras throw very little light upon the useful education of this period. The *Arthaśāstra,* Greek writers and Pali literature give some important information, but it is hardly sufficient to satisfy modern curiosity.

This period probably did not record any remarkable advance in sculpture and architecture, but decisive progress seems to have been made in the realms of weaving, ship-building, medicine, mining and metallurgy. Strabo, who complains that Indians do not pursue accurate knowledge in any line, admits that they were remarkably efficient in medicine.[1] The Greeks were particularly struck by the efficacy of the Indian medicine against snake-biting. The followers of *Garuḍa-vidyā* and *Sarpa-vidyā* mentioned in the *Gopatha Brāhmaṇa*[2] and *Chhāndogya Upanishad*[3], and the students who learnt at Takshaśilā the art of serpent-charming, must obviously be specialising in studying and devising antidotes against serpent poison. It is difficult to visualise the precise progress made in the medical science at this period, because no books of the age have been handed down. The Saṁhitā of Agniveśa, on which the present *Charaka Saṁhitā* is based, belongs to this time, but its precise contents are not known. The medical course, however, was a long one; Jīvaka was very reluctantly permitted by his teacher to go home at the end of seven years; the teacher however asked the home-sick student to note that he had got only a working knowledge of the profession and was far from being a master of the art.[4] The Takshaśilā medical course included practical training in surgery and pharmacy. Several surgical operations seem to have been taught to the students. On his way back to Pāṭaliputra Jīvaka attempted with success two

---

[1] Strabo, XV, C. 706; Nearchus Frag. 15.

[2] 1, 10.

[3] VIII 1-2.

[4] *Mahā-vagga*, VIII, 1.

surgical cases, one of a deep cranial abscess, and the other of intestinal displacement.[1]

Strabo avers that the Indians at this period were inexperienced in the arts of mining and smelting,[2] and used to work their gold and silver mines in a primitive fashion. It is, however, doubtful whether the Greek invaders of India, who had stayed here only for a few months, had any accurate and first hand knowledge of the mining and smelting processes of the Indians. The *Arthaśāstra* of Kauṭilya[3] disclosces a fairly accurate knowledge of the nature of the ores of gold, silver, copper and some other metals and of the processes by which they were to be purified. Mines were a state monopoly and some arrangements must have been made by the government for ensuring proper instructions in mining and metallurgy. No information is, however, available about the nature of these arrangements.

The apprentice system of education described by some of the later Smritis seems to have been the usual method of training in industrial arts in this period also. The inscription on the statue of a Yakshiṇī, who is being worshipped as Manasā Devī at Jhing near

---

1 *Mahāvagga*, VIII, 1.

2 Strabo, XV, c. 700.

3 Book II, chaps. 12 and 13. There is a difference of opinion about the date of this book, but the present writer thinks that its main contents belong to the Mauryan age.

Mathura, records that it was carved by Nāka, an apprentice of the sculptor Kuṇika.[1] This statue belongs to the Mauryan age and shows that the apprentice system of training was followed in the sculptor's profession. The same probably was the method by which the rising generation was trained in other branches of useful arts and industries like weaving and ship-bulding. This last mentioned industry was in a flourishing condition at this time, as there was immense riverine, coastal and foreign trade carried on at this time. Elementary knowledge of śpinning and weaving seems to have been imbibed by the whole population, both male and female. Some of the Gṛihya-Sūtras lay down that the garment to be offered to the boy at his Upanayana should have been spun and woven in the house just before the occasion. The *Arthaśāstra* refers to the arrangements made by the state for purchasing the yarn spun by widows and other destitute women.[2]

Industrial training that was given at this time seems to have raised the general intelligence to a fairly high level. Nearchus speaks highly of the cleverness of the Indian craftsmen of the 4th century B. C.[3] Indians took no time in manufacturing scrapers, oil-flasks and sponges that they first saw being used

[1] *A. S. R.*, 1922-3, p. 165 ; Cf :—सा पुतेहि कारितो पखि लाआवा कुनिकातेवासिना [नाके]न कता ।

[2] II, 40.

[3] Nearchus, Fragment 7.

by the Macedonians. Fine thread and wool was used to manufacture sponges, and they were then dyed so that they looked similar to the Macedonian articles. The effciency of the Punjab ship-builders may be inferred from the fact that they could supply to Alexander a huge fleet, probably about a thousand strong, in less than three months' time. Arts and crafts were not held in low estimation by society; in Kuśa Jātaka (No. 531) we come across a prince who was a great expert in the art of sculpture. Injury to an artist was a capital offence under the Mauryan administration.

It was in this period that empire building was started in India and she came into contact with foreign invaders. This must have given a great impetus to military training and the allied industries. Large armies required an enormous supply of bows, arrows, wheels, chariots, lances, armours, etc.; and this must have given an impetus to mining, smithy and carpentry. The states in Magadha, Kalinga and Āndhra, which are known to have been maintaining huge armies, must have organised big factories for the manufacture of these articles, where senior workmen may have been required by the state to train apprentices from among the youths of the rising generation.

A perusal of the Greek accounts of Alexander's invasion leaves the impression that the Macedonian hero was in many cases opposed not so much by state forces as by whole populations in arms.[1] It would appear that among many of the republican tribes of the Punjab like the Kaṭhas and the Mallois, the military training was imparted to almost the whole of the male adult population. Hence some of the republics were known as *Āyudhajīvi-sanghas* and used to supply fairly well-trained recruits to the state.[2] The *Arthaśāstra* also refers to villages exempted from taxation in return for their agreeing to supply an agreed quota of soldiers to the state army.[3] Such soldiers were known as *Maula* or hereditary soldiers. Military training seems to have been universal in such villages and in *Āyudhajīvi-sanghas*. It seems to have been organised by popular bodies in other villages also, for Kauṭilya expects every new village to be able to defend itself.[4] The average recruits to the state army in this period must have been of a fairly high calibre, well-trained in the use of the main arms of the day.

In addition to the popular village arrangements for the military training, there were some famous centres of military education. Takshaśilā was one of them; Brahmanas and Kshatriyas from all over India used to flock to this frontier city for acquiring

---

[1] M'crindle; *Ancient India, its invasion by Alexander the Great*, p. 140.

[2] *Arthaśāstra*, IX, 1.

[3] *Ibid*, II, 34.

[4] Ibid, II, 1.

mastery in archery and other branches of militrary profession. In one military college we learn that as many as 103 princes from different parts of India were being trained in the different branches of the military art.[1] Unfortunately we get no information as to whether these military institutions were subsidised by the state. The duration and precise nature of the course is also not known.

When soldiers were recruited to the army, the army authorities used to subject them to regular training. We are, however, not concerned here with the internal military organisation and discipline and so need not prosecute the enquiry further.

## SECTION IV.

### (From *c.* 250 B. C. to *c.* 800 A. D.)

During this period of about 1000 years, fine, useful and industrial arts of India reached their zenith. Almost all that is valuable in Indian achievements in the realm of medicine, sculpture, architecture, ship-building, mining, smelting etc. was achieved in this age. The arrangements to impart education in these branches must have been efficient in order to render this progress possible.

Medical education seems to have been imparted on very scientific lines. Sanskrit was the medium of instruction and the student was naturally expected to

[1] Sūta-soma Jātaka, No. 222.

get a good grounding in that language before he was admitted to the new course. Learning by rote was condemned ; Suśruta compares a person having only a verbal knowledge of the medical texts to a donkey, conscious of the heaviness but not of the quality of the weight it carries. Specialisation was encouraged, students were expected to master the different branches of the science from different experts.[1] Practical training in pharmacy and surgery and constant discussion of abstruse points among students and professors were some of the important features of the training.[2]

The *Milinda Pañha* contains an interesting passage giving a fairly good idea of the training of a doctor. The medical teacher used to accept students for training in consideration either of a fee or of manual and professional help. He used to train the student thoroughly 'in holding the lancet, in cutting, marking or piercing with it, in extracting darts, in cleansing wounds, in causing them to dry up, in the application of ointments, in the administration of emetics, purges and oily enemas'.[3] This passage refers to the surgical training, but we may infer from it that the medicinal training must have been equally comprehensive. Suśruta emphasises the importance of dissection for perfecting the student's knowledge and points out that mere book

---

1 Suśruta, Sūtrasthāna, IV, 4, 4-8.

2 Charaka, Vimānasthāna, 8, 4.

3 II, pp. 254-255.

learning cannot give a clear idea of the actual internal constituents of the human body.[1] Corpses used to be decomposed in water and students were then required to dissect them and visualise the nature of skin, muscles, arteries, bones and internal organs.[2] Anatomical knowledge that was thus imparted was fairly high when compared with the contemporary standards elsewhere. Unfortunately soon after Suśruta's time dissection of human bodies went out of vogue to the great detriment of the progress of the medical science.

Suśruta gives a good idea of the way in which practical training was given in surgery. Students used to learn the surgical methods by operating upon pumpkins, water melons, cucumbers etc. under the teacher's direction. Puncturing was demonstrated on the veins of dead animals, the manner of holding the probe on dry Alābu fruits, scarrification on stretched pieces of leather covered with hair, sewing on thin pieces of cloth or skin, application of bandages on stuffed human figures and the use of caustics on soft pieces of flesh.[3] This passage obviously refers to absolute beginners; later on they must have been afforded opportunities to try their hands on real cases, if the hospital conditions in the locality permitted it The training outlined above was fairly thorough for the

---

1 Sārīra-sthāna, 5, 49.

2 *Ibid.*

3 Sūtrasthāna, Chap, 9.

age, and before the decline of surgery, operations seem to have been performed in ancient India for cataract, hydrocele, abscesses, extraction of dead embryos etc. Failure to discover proper anæsthetics seems to have stood in the way of further progress in surgery. Wine seems to have been administered in a fairly large dose to render the patient less sensitive to pain.[1] *Bhojaprabandha* refers to a *Mohinīchūrṇa* used on such occasions, but it is not known to medical writers.

The exact duration of the medical course is not known. In the previous period it covered a period of about seven or eight years; probably the same continued to be the case in this age also. Charaka observes that no one can obtain real all-round efficiency in the Āyur-veda; he does not enlighten us about the normal duration of the course.

Early in this period, education was imparted by individual teachers to such students as were accepted by them. This was the method at Takshaśilā. Public educational institutions seem to have been evolved in India by the 4th century A. D. Nālandā had a medical course, but we do not know anything about its nature and duration. We have not yet come across a detailed description of any medical educational institution. Not impossibly in the big hospitals that existed at metropolitan centres like Pāṭaliputra there was provision made also for the training of efficient

[1] Suśruta, Sūtrsthāna, 17.

doctors. These hospitals seem to have been very well organised, for Indian doctors were imported by the Abbaside Khalifas to supervise their own hospitals in the 8th century A. D. It is to be regretted that Fa Hsien should have contented himself by making only a passing reference to the hospitals then in existence. If he had given a detailed description, we would probably have known a good deal about the methods of the medical education in the 5th century.

Charaka and Suśruta observe that it is the king's fault if incompetent doctors practise the medical profession.[1] Śukra prohibits a person from practising the medical profession without the king's license.[2] Neither of these writers discloses the condition on which royal licenses were issued under efficient administrations. Very probably they were issued to students, who were certified to have finished their course either by state hospital superintendents or by famous private practitioners.

The convocation address to the medical graduates exhorted them to follow a very high course of professional conduct. They must relieve distress in all quarters. They must strive for the welfare of the humanity. They must not desert a patient, even when their own life is in danger. They must continue study

---

1 Charaka, Sūtra-sthāna, 29, 8; Suśruta, *Sūtra-sthāna*, III, 52; X, 3.

2 I .304.

and research to the end of their life. This advice seems to have been followed in a large number of cases. India continued to be famous for its medical skill down to the 8th century A. D. In the latter half of that century, Khalifa Harun sent several scholars to India to study Hindu medicine and pharmacology, and induced about twenty Indian doctors to come to Baghdad to become chief medical officers of the state hospitals and to translate Sanskrit medical works into the Arabic. Most celebrated among them was Manakā, who was originally invited to cure an ailment of Sultan Harun, which had defied the skill of Arab physicians. He was successful in his treatment and was later induced to become the director of state hospitals and to translate Suśruta into the Arabic. Sāleh bin Bahalā and Ibn Dahan are the names of two other colleagues of Manakā as they have been preserved in the Arabic. The Sanskrit forms of these names are not easy to guess, but probably Manakā may have been Māṇikya and Dahan Dhanvantari.[1]

Hindu kingdoms at this period used to maintain big cavalries and elephant forces and this must have given a good impetus to veterinary science and education. The science was already well developed in the days of Asoka, who did not forget dumb animals

---

1 S. S. Nadvi, *Arab aur Bhārat ke Sambandha,* Hindi translation, pp. 103-123, (Hindusthānī Academy, U. P.;) Sachau, Introduction to Alberuni, p. XXXI.

when he provided medical relief throughout the length and breadth of his wide empire.[1] From the Mahābhārata we learn that both Nakula and Sahadeva possessed great skill in the veterinary line[2]. Kauṭilya enjoins that the army authorities should engage the services of competent elephant and horse doctors,[3] who were to advise on the regulation of food and the treatment of the diseases of the animals concerned. Śālihotra is the traditional founder of Aśvāyurveda, which deals with the diseases and disorders of the horse. *Aśvavaidyaka* of Jayadatta and *Aśvachikitsā* of Nakula are other works dealing with the same topic. *Hastyāyurveda* is attributed to the sage Pālakapya, who is said to have expounded it to king Romapāda of Champā.[4] Definite dates of these authors are not known, but they seem to have belonged to the period we are discussing. This literary activity will also show that the veterinary science was regularly developed in our period. Obviously there must have been in existence some efficient arrangement for the training of veterinary doctors in order to meet the large demand of military departments of the various governments of our age. We however do not find the description of any veterinary school or college in any period of ancient Indian history. Probably veterinary doctors,

---

[1] Rock Edict, II.

[2] Virāṭa-parvan, Chaps. 91 & 121.

[3] Book II, chaps. 30, 32.

[4] Winternitz, *Geschichte*, III, pp. 532-533.

were trained by the apprenticeship method similar to the one by which ordinary doctors were educated.

There are no indications whatever in earlier periods of physicians being held in low estimation by society. During this age, however, Smritis begin to look upon the medical profession with a contemptuous eye. We can understand the exclusion of a doctor from the Śrāddha ceremony, for highly learned Brahmanas alone were regarded as qualified for that ritual. But Smritis go further and pronounce the doctor to be a *Paṅkti-dūshaka*, i. e. a person, whose presence defiles a feast. The doctors were also declared to be members of a mixed caste, sprung from the union of a Brahmana father and a Vaishya mother.[1] Purāṇas also narrate a story to the effect that medicine became the profession of the illegitimate son of sage Gālava from his Vaishya maid-servant Ambā. Whether these curious theories were accepted by society we do not know. Sometimes we come accross grants made in favour of village doctors in inscriptions of this period.[2] Puritanical doctrines of meticulous purity were getting ascendancy at the end of this period, and they were probably responsible for the half-suppressed contempt felt for a profession, where filthy diseases had to be personally attended to. In course of time the sneering attitude of the Smritis may have disuaded at least a section

[1] *Bau. Dh. S.*, I, 8, 9.

[2] *I. A.*, VIII, p. 277.

of the Brahmana community from following the profession.

During the period we are reviewing in this section, *c.* 250 B. C. to *c.* 800 A. D., sculpture, architecture, coining and painting made remarkable progress in India. Most of the ancient valuable monuments belonging to these branches, that have been preserved to modern times, belonged to this period. Purushapura or Peshawar, Mathura, Vidiśā, Sanchi and Bharhut (in central India), Sarnath, Nālandā, Paṭaliputra, Karli, Ellora, Ajantha and Amaraoti (in the Andhra country) were famous centres of the plastic arts during this age. Possibly there may have been other centres also in existence whose work may have been altogether destroyed by the ravages of man or time. In all these centres the plastic arts were handed down from generation to generation not without considerable improvement. Before the time of Asoka, Indian architecture seems to have been mainly in wood. Asoka popularised stone arthitecture, which gave a new impetus to stone sculpture. We find carpenters and ivory workers of Sanchi taking to stone sculpture in order to meet the demands of the age[1]. No reference is however to be seen to the method by which students were trained in these plastic arts. In the last period at Mathura the apprenticeship method was in vogue in

[1] Cf. वेदिसकेहि दंतकारेहि रूपकंमं कतम्। *E. I.*, II, p. 378, No. 200.

the sculptor's profession; the same continued to be the case in this age also.

Leading sculptors and painters of the age could not have been illiterate artisans, if we are to infer from the quality of their work. A good knowledge of the Purāṇas and Hindu, Buddhist and Jain iconography was essential to their profession. Many of them must have acquired a working knowledge of Sanskrit before beginning to wield the chisel or use the brush.

Intensive and extensive training in architecture must have been obviously received by those unknown architects who were responsible for the beautiful Stūpas of Gāndhāra, the splendid caves and rock-cut temples of western India and the magnificent shrines of south India. This training included a grounding in Purāṇas, mathematics, painting and civil engineering.[1] How long the course extended and how and where it was taught we do not know. The student had to spend a good deal of time in getting practical training in civil engineering under the guidance of his teacher.[2]

Hereditary families specialising in painting, music and dancing excepted, education in these arts was usually confined to the members of royal and noble families. We no where find any recognition of the cultural value of

---

[1] *Vāstu-vidyā*, I, 12 ff. (Trivendram Sanskrit Series).
[2] *Ibid.*

music or drawing as a part of general education for the commoner. In this respect ancient Athens was in advance of ancient India, for it had given a due emphasis to the teaching of music and other fine arts in the general scheme of education.[1] Princes and rich persons used to maintain a music hall (Saṅgīta-śālā), where members of the household of both the sexes were given training in singing, music and dancing by specially appointed teachers. The latter do not seem to have belonged to any particular caste. They were required also to help the staging of dramas in the household of their employers.

Training in professions like those of the sculptor, the weaver, the carpenter, the miner, the goldsmith,[2] etc. was usually given by the apprenticeship method to which a reference has been made more than once. Our knowledge of the actual working of this system is based upon half a dozen verses from the Nārada Smriti.[3] There are two or three verses from Kātyāyana

---

[1] Monroe, *A Text-book of the History of Education*, p. 89.

[2] विज्ञानमुच्यते शिल्पं हेमकुप्यादिसंस्थितिः ।
नृत्यादिकं च तच्छिक्षन्कुर्यात्कर्म गुरोर्गृहे ॥

बृहस्पति in विवादरत्नाकर, p. 141.

Devaṇabhaṭṭa, while commenting on this, observes कंकणकटकादिनिर्माणविषयं नृत्यं गीतादिकरणविषयं चकारात्स्तंभकुंभादिरचनाविषयं च विज्ञानं शिल्पमुच्यते ।

[3] Cf स्वशिल्पमिच्छन्नाहर्तुं बान्धवानामनुज्ञया ।
आचार्यस्य वसेदन्ते कृत्वा कालं सुनिश्चितम् ॥ १७ ॥

*P. T. O.*

and Brihaspati preserved only in quotations, but they do not add materially to our information.

In liberal education the student could bid adieu to his teacher as soon as his course was over; under the apprenticeship method, however, the apprentice had to enter into an agreement with the consent of his guardian, binding himself to work under his teacher for an agreed number of years. This agreement was necessitated by the circumstance that the teacher was expected not only not to charge any tuition fees, but to offer free lodging and boarding to the apprentice. The duration of the apprenticeship period is not stated by our authorities, probably because the period must have varied with different professions. But it must have been fairly longer than the actual time required to master the art, for the teacher expected to be

---

(*Continued from the last page*).

आचार्यः शिक्षयेदेनं स्वगृहे दत्तभोजनम् ।
न चान्यत्कारयेत्कर्म पुत्रवच्चैनमाचरेत् ॥ १८ ॥

शिक्षयन्तमदुष्टं य आचार्यं संपरित्यजेत् ।
बलाद्वासयितव्यस्स्याद्वधबन्धौ च सोर्हति ॥ १९ ॥

शिक्षितोपि कृतं कालमन्तेवासी समाप्नुयात् ।
तत्र कर्म च यत्कुर्यादाचार्यस्यैव तत्फलम् ॥ २० ॥

गृहीतशिल्पः समये कृत्वाचार्यप्रदक्षिणाम् ।
शक्तितश्चानुमान्यैनमन्तेवासी निवर्तते ॥ २१ ॥

वेतनं वा यदि कृतं ज्ञात्वा शिष्यस्य कौशलम् ।
अन्तेवासी समादद्याच्च चान्यस्य गृहे वसेत् ॥ २२ ॥

नारदस्मृति, शुश्रूषाभ्युपगमप्रकरणम् ।

compensated for the trouble in teaching and the expenses in feeding the apprentice from the wages the fully-trained apprentice would be earning during the remaining period of his indenture.

Our authorities lay down that the apprentice should live under his teacher's roof for all the twenty four hours. This rule may not have been rigidly followed when the guardians of the student were living in the same village or town. But if the agreement to serve was for a much longer period than the time required to master the particular profession, then the apprentice must have been advised by his guardian to stay all the day long with his teacher and enjoy his stipulated hospitality with a view to imbibe the workshop atmosphere to the maximum degree.

Free students in the literary line were required to do a good deal of the honsehold work for their teacher. The artisan teacher, however, was required not to exact any service from his apprentice unconnected with the profession. This rule was in the interest of the teacher also; for if the time and the ability of the student were not frittered away by non-professional work, eventual gains that the teacher would get from the proceeds of the student's wages would be greater. If a teacher neglected his apprentice's education and exacted from him sundry work unconnected with the profession, the teacher became liable to be punished by the state, and the student was absolved from the agreement and permitted to leave the teacher.[1] If however the teacher was kind and considerate and anxious to teach all the technique of the profession, the student could not back out from the aggreement ; if he deserted his teacher he was brought back and compelled to stay and learn and work during the full period of agreement.

The art or profession was usually mastered by the apprentice much earlier than the expiry of the period of the agreement. The student had, however, to work during the remaining period in his teacher's workshop, and surrender to him his wages or the sale proceeds of his manufacture. This was in part compensation to his teacher for teaching the art. The student was also expected to offer a suitable honorarium to the teacher at the end of his course. He could then leave him and seek service elsewhere or start a business of his own. If, however, his teacher offered him suitable wages, he was expected to serve him in preference to a stranger.

Theoretical and practical training were both attended to in the workshop. Students of sculpture and painting had, for instance, to study carefully the Sanskrit manuals on iconography, which were so essential for their profession. They were further trained in making their own tools. A painter, for example, was taught to make his own brushes from out of roots or fibres, hair of squirrels or awns of various grasses.

---

[1] यस्तु न ग्राहयेच्छिल्पं कर्माण्यन्यानि कारयेत् । प्राप्नुयात्साहसं पूर्वं तस्माच्छिष्यो निवर्तते । Kātyāyana in Aparārka on Yāj. II, 84.

He did not rely on colours prepared by somebody else, but knew himself how to make them. A repousser was taught to make tools suitable for the work in hand. The craftsman was taught to rely on himself rather than on his tools.

The various stages in practical training of the painter may be mentioned with a view to give a general idea of the workshop training. The apprentice was first given a practice in drawing lines and curves. When the hand, eye and memory were trained in the use of fundamental curves in this fashion, traditional ornaments and decorative motives were then taught. Then followed a training in the drawing of the mythical animals and designs with men and beasts in them. The master would then take his apprentice to assist him in his work at the temple. At first the student would help the teacher only in grinding colours, then in priming the surfaces, then in applying ground colours and finally in filling in outlines sketched by his master. Experience was thus given in practical work. In course of time when the teacher was satisfied about the sincerity, devotion and ability of the apprentice, he would impart the trade secrets. Throughout the course the technique of the profession was taught in relation to real things and real problems.[1]

Nor was moral training neglected. The apprentice was reminded that he was expected to be a pious and

[1] Coomaraswami, *The Indian Craftsman*, pp. 83—90.

honest person faithfully abiding by the rules prescribed for the artists in the Śilpaśāstras.

Duration of the course varied with different professions and was determined by their varying requirements. There was no such notion as a twelve years course as was the case with the Vedic studies.[1] The training under the above system was of a fairly high order, because it was thoroughly practical and given in the workshop itself. It helped to raise the general level of skill and workmanship in several arts and crafts. Weaving industry could command the markets of practically the whole of the then civilised world. The skill in smelting and welding was also of a very high order; experts have been still wondering how the composition of the famous Iron Pillar near the Kutub Minar was made in such a skilful manner by the metallurgists of King Chandragupta II (of the Gupta dynasty), so as to prevent rusting inspite of the continuous exposure to the sun and rain for centuries together.[2] Sculptures, paintings and architecture of the age are also generally of a high order.

---

[1] प्रतिवेदं द्वादशाब्दः कालो विद्यार्थिनाम् स्मृतः।
शिल्पविद्यार्थिनां चैव ग्रहणान्तः प्रकीर्तितः॥

Nārada in *SMC.*, at *SBE.*, 30, p. 244.

[2] The mysterious Nāgārjuna is said to have contributed considerably to the development of the smelting processes of iron.. Cf. नागार्जुनेन मुनिना कारितमिह लोहशास्त्रमतिगहनम्। Ray, *Hindu Chemistry* Vol. I, p. 62.

How far this professional education was narrow it is difficult to judge. Prima facie the student learnt laboriously only what the tradition of his profession had to teach. There is, however, some historical evidence to show that many of the artists and artisans of the age used to possess a good amount of liberal and cultural education. In the weavers' guild at Daśapura (Mandsore in Malva), we find that some of its members used to take active interest in archery, some in folk-lore and some in astrology in the 5th century A. D.[1] There is no evidence to prove or disprove that what was true of the weavers at Daśapura was equally true of the average artisan of this period. The conclusion, however, may be hazarded that professional education at this time was not altogether narrow. Artists and artisans of the higher grades used to receive a fairly good amount of general education.

There is a certain resemblance between the Indian apprentice system outlined above and the guild education in medieval Europe. In Europe too the apprentice had to spend the earlier part of his indenture period in learning his craft, getting no wages. When he had learnt his art, he would become a journeyman, but he could undertake no work except through and for the benefit of his master. At the end of the agreed period, the student could start business of his own.[2]

---

[1] Fleet, *Gupta Inscriptions*, No. 18.

[2] Graves, *A History of education* Vol. II, p. 97.

In Medieval France, the guilds permitted an artisan to take only one apprentice at a time.[1] Whether there were such customary restrictions on the artist teachers in ancient India we do not know. Since, however, every apprentice had to be given a practical training, the admission of apprentices must have to a great extent depended upon the extensiveness of the factory or the business of the teacher. We have seen that in the literary line, a teacher used to take up only about 15 students; the number of apprentices working under an artisan teacher must have been still smaller.

Professions were usually hereditary in ancient India, and the principle of heredity became still more rigid towards the end of the period we are reviewing owing to the growing rigidity of the caste system. So in the majority of cases the boy was instructed by his father, uncle or guardian, who was himself an experienced artisan. From his very childhood the boy lived and breathed the atmosphere of the workshop, unconsciously picking up a number of manufacturing processes. When the father himself was the teacher, there was no question of any knowledge about any vital processes in manufacture being withheld from the apprentice. It was only when the circumstances of the family rendered home training impracticable, or when a boy wanted to learn a profession other than his hereditary one, that he was sent as an apprentice to an artisan teacher.

---

1 Graves, *A History of Education*, Vol. II, p. 97.

We can get some idea of the scope and nature of commercial education from the training prescribed for the Vaishya caste by Manu,[1] and the qualifications required by Kauṭilya in the superintendent of commerce.[2] First of all a knowledge of the varieties in quality of the articles to be dealt with was imparted. Then came commercial geography, for the trader was expected to know the places where the different articles were produced and the nature of the route by which they had to be imported. Customs barriers in the period we are discussing were numerous, and profits often depended on selecting a route where the customs duties were relatively light. The needs of the people of the various localities were to be carefully studied with a view to find out possible markets. A knowledge of different places and occasions of fares and pilgrimages was also imparted as it was necessary in this connection. The knowledge of the relative prices of different articles in different provinces and countries was also regarded as essential. Students were also taught the exchange value of articles and also of different currencies in different provinces and countries. Those who intended to deal with inter-provincial or inter-national trade were also given a working knowledge of the necessary languages. Principles of banking also formed part of the course.

---

[1] IX, 331-332.

[2] II, 16.

It is difficult to determine the percentage of persons who received so wide an education in the trading community. In the hereditary trading families of high status, all this education may have been a reality; much of it must have been unconsciously picked up by the youths in the family shops. In the case of petty merchants the extent of the education was probably determined by the needs of the situation.

Home education and the apprentice system seem to have been the usual methods adopted to train the new generation in the business line. These methods continued down to the 17th century, as we know from the observations of Tavernier.[1]

Most of the trades and industries of this time were organised into guilds which were often more permanent institutions than kingdoms and empires. These guilds had their own executives and guild funds. They are to be seen undertaking and financing a number of works of public utility; the famous Vīrabalañju guild used to maintain an Arts college at Dambal in the 12th century A. D.[2] It is however strange that we have not yet come across any inscription or document showing that part of the guild funds were also utilised for maintaining any industrial or commercial college. We have seen how down to the 5th century A. D. literary education was given by individual teachers

---

[1] Tavernier, *Travels in India*, p. 387.

[2] *I. A.*, VIII, p. 195.

and not in any organised institutions. Commercial and industrial education do not seem to have developed organised institutions even after the 5th century. Growing rigidity of the caste system at this time making most of the trades and industries hereditary seems to have rendered organised public institutions for industrial or commercial education unnecessary. The apprentice system was probably found to be sufficient to meet the needs of those who could not get education at home owing to family difficulties.

## Military Education

The method of military training continued to be more or less the same in this period also. The average youth of this period seems to have been fairly well trained in the use of the bow, the sword, and other ordinary weapons of offence and defence. The present writer has shown elsewhere how the village headman used to organise military defence and training in the village under his charge.[1] Deccan inscriptions of this period teem with references to fights among neighbouring villages in connection with cattle raids. These fights would have been impossible without regular village militias trained under the auspices of the village headman or Panchāyat. India was covered with numerous petty feudal chiefs, even when there existed big empires, and these were constantly engaged in official and

[1] Altekar, *A History of the Village Communities in Western India*, pp. 54 ff.

unofficial warfare. The fighting forces of the Gupta, Vardhana, Rāshṭrakūṭa, Pāla and Gurjara-Pratīhāra empires were usually more than half a million strong. A large part of this army was hereditary in profession. Several private captains used to make it a profession to train soldiers for the royal armies. They used to receive a 'capitation charge' on each trained soldier supplied to the royal army. This appears quite clearly from a simile in the *Milinda-Pañha* where we read of clever archers training soldiers in archery and afterwards presenting them to the king and receiving from him by way of reward money, land, horses, chariots and elephants.[1] The same passage shows that for teaching accurate aiming in archery targets of men of straw or masses of clay were used on the training ground. A 9th century Deccan inscription records the donation by a military captain, who is described as 'a marvel in training horses.'[2] It is not however known whether this skilful trainer of cavalry was conducting private classes like the officers mentioned in the *Milinda-Pañha*, or whether he was a regular professor in a military college maintained by the Rāshṭrakūṭa adminstration. The general impression left by literary and epigraphical evidence of this period is that a good deal of preliminary military training was given almost universally in all the villages under the aegis of the village Panchāyats. Organised institutions of military

---

1 II, pp. 153-4.

3 E. I., XIII, p. 187.

training did not probably exist in moffusil villages; retired members of the *maula* or hereditary forces were probably opening informal military classes in their own villages, which were attended by most of the able-bodied villagers. Further training was given in some places by adventurous captains, and final touches were given after the enlistment of the soldier in the state army in daily drills similar to those that are laid down in the epics, and are known to have been the order of the day under the Sungas and the Kaṇvas.

## SECTION V.

### (*c.* 800 TO *c.* 1200)

The state of affairs described in the last section continued to be more or less the same in this period also. No educational institutions as such were evolved even in this period for training students in different branches of useful and industrial education. The apprentice system continued, but the general culture of the average artisan became much inferior to what it was in the last period. As we shall see in the next chapter, primary education became restricted in this period to the higher strata of society ; the vast majority of workmen and artisans became illiterate by this time and knew only the traditional processes of their professions. It is extremely doubtful whether, for instance, members of any weavers' guild of this period were capable of taking any amateur interest in astrology and folk-lore as did those of the Mandsore guild in the 5th century A. D.

There was a general tendency in this period to make the courses easier and therefore more superficial. Medical courses in the earlier periods extended over seven or eight years; an observation of Vijñāneśvara would suggest that the course was now finished in about four years only.[1] Surgery seems to have been eliminated from the course. Sculpture of this period is much inferior to that of the preceding age, indicating a slackening of effort in this direction. The military education too seems to have degenerated in discipline and efficiency, as may be inferred from the easy manner in which Hindu armies were crushed by the forces of Islam.

The activity of the age was almost exclusively directed towards understanding and explaining the works of the earlier periods. There was hardly any new effort except in the realm of chemistry. The study of chemistry must have begun much earlier; the progress in metallurgy as illustrated by the successful smelting of the Delhi Iron pillar of the Gupta age would not have been possible without a good knowledge of chemistry. All extant books on chemistry, however, have been written subsequent to the 10th century A. D. The study of chemistry, however, was not cultivated

[1] On Yāj. II, 184; Cf. अंतेवासी गुरोर्गृहे कृतकालं वर्षचतुष्टयमायुर्वेदशिल्पशिक्षार्थं त्वद्गृहे वसामीति।

for its own sake; in India, as in the west, it was a bye-product of the search for the elixir of life. Medical science was vitally concerned in it and it is quite likely that the curriculum of the Āyurveda included at this period lessons in various chemical processes necessary for the purpose of the new mercurial and other preparations.

# CHAPTER VI.

## Primary Education.

It is very difficult to get any systematic information about primary education, its scope, method and organisation. Our sources of information fail us almost entirely with reference both to historic and pre-historic times. Secondary and higher education loom largely before the minds of the Smriti writers; primary education is forgotten altogether.

## Vedic and Brahmanic Times.

(Upto about 800 B. C.)

Early in this period the art of writing was probably unknown. Even when it became known, its use for the preservation of literature was tabooed for a long time; books continued to live only in the memory of scholars for many a century. Grammar was yet to be developed and commerce was in a primitive state not requiring any elaborate account keeping. Primary education in the sense of the knowledge of the 3 R's was therefore both impossible and unnecessary in the early Vedic period. Education commenced with the learning of the recitation of the Vedic and mythological songs. Upanayana Sanskāra at this time occupied the place of and was performed at the time when the

Vidyārambha Sanskāra was performed in later times.[1] Boys of 5 or 6 could not properly pronounce Vedic Mantras; so even the learning of the Gāyatrī stanza was postponed to a period about a year later than the time of the Upanayana.

During the latter part of this period, the art of writing became well-known and grammar, phonology and other subsidiary branches of the Vedic study were developed. It is probable that a knowledge of the alphabet was imparted at this time to all boys learning Vedic literature.[2] We cannot be, however, certain about this, for the aid of the art of writing was strictly prohibited for the preservation of the Vedic literature. It is quite possible that the conservative section of society may have looked askance at the new art like the feudal lords of Medieval Europe. We must further note that there was no Sanskāra like *Aksharasvīkaraṇa* prescribed by this age at the time of learning the alphabet. For initiation into Vedic studies a knowledge of phonology rather than that of the art of reading and writing was required in this period. If by primary education we mean the education of a child before the age of eight or nine, it must have at this time mostly consisted of a thorough grounding

---

[1] *Ante*, p. 17.

[2] In Greece, reading and writing was introduced in schools as late as about 600 B. C., and arithmetic and drawing were not introduced till a much later date. Monroe, *A Text-Book*, p. 94-6.

in the principles of phonology, metr cs and elementary grammar. *Taittirīya Prātiśākhya* lays down that a boy, who desires to study Vedic literature, should know the difference between short and long vowels and the rules about the varieties of accent, and lengthening, conjunction and disappearance of vowels. He must know the changes that take place in the original words when they are joined together in the *Saṁhitā-pāṭha,* and for this purpose elementary grammar, imparting a knowledge of the different parts of speech, was taught. It was this type of primary education that was imparted to boys before they were admitted to Vedic studies.[1] Kshatriya and Vaishya boys, who did not intend to specialise in Vedic learning, probably received no such primary education. As specimens of prayers, they must have learnt by heart some Vedic hymns and then turned to their practical professions. It is problem-

---

[1] Cf. गुरुत्वं लघुता साम्यं ह्रस्वदीर्घप्लुतानि च ।
लोपागमविकाराश्च प्रकृतिर्विकृतिः क्रमः ॥ ४ ॥
स्वरितोदात्तनीचत्वं श्वासो नादोऽगमेव च ।
एतत्सर्वं तु विज्ञेयं छंदोभाषामधीयता ॥ ५ ॥
पदक्रमविशेषज्ञो वर्णक्रमविचक्षणः ।
स्वरमात्राविभागज्ञो गच्छेदाचार्यसंसदम् ॥ ६ ॥

Chap. 24.

The view of Sāyaṇa, that the last verse refers to the approach of the Vedic scholar to heaven is untenable. The student's departure to the preceptor's house, and not to heaven, is referred to in the verse.

matical whether the boys of these classes were taught the art of writing, when it first became known or was invented in the latter half of this period. Commerce was not extensive and so the aid of the art of writing was not indispensable also to the trader. The proud Kshatriya, like the Earl of Douglas in the *Marmion*, may have looked with contempt on the new art and taken pride that 'he could never pen a line.'[1]

## SECTION II.

### (*c.* 800 B. C. TO *c.* 200 B. C.)

The art of writing became well known in this period, and there is no evidence of any prejudice against it except for the purpose of the transmission of the Vedic literature. Sciences of phonology, grammar, etymology etc. were well developed and Upanayana became, as we have already seen in Chapter I, a compulsory Sanskāra for all the Aryans. Vedic literature had become canonised and great importance was attached to its accurate preservation and transmission. The scope of the primary education was considerably enlarged by this time, and it must have been realised that a good grounding in it was essential for a boy in order to progress satisfactorily in Vedic studies. A knowledge of the 3 R's and of the elementary principles of grammar, phonology and metrics was imparted to the student before the commencement of the Vedic education. This primary

[1] *Marmion*, VI, 15.

education was commenced at about the age of five at the time of the tonsure ceremony[1] and finished at about the age of eight.

As we have seen already, the Upanayana ceremony became a compulsory Sanskāra during this period for all the Aryans, and it was a reality at least as far as 75% of the *Dvija* Aryan population was concerned. It was only towards the end of this period that the Vaishyas began to lose their Aryan status and became mixed up with the Sūdras.[2] Literacy, which Upanayana presupposed at this time, must therefore have been very high, perhaps as high as 75 per cent. King Aśvapati of the Chhāndogya Upanishad claims that there was no illiterate man in his kingdom.[3] Foreign and internal trade was also fast developing, giving a further incentive to the commercial classes to become literate.

There is a difference of opinion among scholars as to whether the publication of the Asokan message of Dharma in the different scripts and vernaculars of the various provinces does not prove a wide literacy among the masses of the age. It must be admitted that this circumstance alone cannot be regarded as affording

---

1 वृत्तचौलकर्मा लिपिं संख्यानं चोपयुञ्जीत । *Artha-śāstra*, 1, 2.

2 *Baudhāyana Dharma Sūtra* (I, 11, 4) is probably the first to mention the degradation of the status of the Vaishyas to that of the Śudras.

3 V, 11, 5.

a convincing proof to the conclusion of V. A. Smith[1] and others that literacy was widely diffused among the masses in the 3rd century B. C. But this fact, when considered along with the universal prevalence of Upanayana among all the sections of the twice-born community at this period, would show that at least 75 per cent of the latter were able to read and write. Without an elementary grounding in the principles of phonology and grammar, which at this time was not possible without a knowledge of the art of writing, an attempt at Vedic study was impossible in this age, when it was sincerely believed that the slightest mistake in pronunciation or accent of the Vedic hymns would entail most disastrous consequences.

The arrangements for imparting the primary education are not sufficiently known. One of the Jātakas refers to a son of a Benares merchant going out to learn his alphabet, when his wooden slate was carried for him by a servant of his household.[2] Obviously this refers to a boy going out to a primary school. But who conducted the primary schools of the age, and how they were financed we do not know. Probably the teacher, who was to carry on the Vedic education later, was expected to look after the primary education also. When literacy was so widely diffused, many members of the Aryan community must have

---

[1] Smith, *Asoka*, 3rd Edition, p. 138.

[2] Kaṭāhaka Jātaka, No. 125.

taken to primary education as a profession. Public institutions for the purpose did not exist. Buddhism was a local and an unimportant sect till the end of this period, when Asoka raised it to the position of an all-India religion. It had few monastaries worth the name, and the attention of their occupants was exclusively directed towards their own salvation. The Mahāyāna doctrine preaching an active effort for the salvation of humanity gave an impetus to the movement for the education of the laity, but this doctrine was yet to be evolved. It is extremely doubtful whether any of the monasteries endowed or created by Asoka, were imparting primary education.

## SECTION III.

### (*c.* 200 B. C. TO *c.* 800 A. D.)

Primary education was assigned in this period a definite place in the scheme of education by the exaltation of the beginning of the learning of the alphabet into a Sanskāra, known as Akshara-svīkaraṇa or Vidyārambha. Smritis are silent about the details of the primary course, because they were concerned mainly with theological and Sanskrit education. Vedic and Sanskrit education was impossible at this period without a good grounding in reading, writing, elementary grammar and phonology. Training in these subjects commenced at about the age of 5 or 6, which is the time usually prescribed for the Vidyārambha Sanskāra. The *Lalita-vistāra,*[1] the *Raghu-vanśa*[2] and the *Uttara-Rāma-charit*[3] represent Gautama, Raghu and Kuśa and Lava respectively as starting the study of the alphabet at about the age of five. I-tsing also confirms the testimony of the literary evidence on this point.[4]

The account of I-tsing enables us to get some idea of the scope of the primary education in the 7th century A. D.[5] The boys began the study of the primary and compound alphabet at about the age of six and spent about six months in mastering them. I-tsing is silent as to what was done in the next year, but it was probably spent in learning elementary arithmetic. Prakrits were well developed in this period, but it is not known whether their systematic study was included in the primary curriculum. Probably this was done in the earlier part of the present period when Prakrits were in the ascendancy, and when some kings like those of the Sātavāhana dynasty had passed orders to the effect that Prakrit alone should be used in their courts and households.[6] The revival of Sanskrit must have given a setback to the study and development of

---

[1] Canto X.

[2] Canto III.

[3] Act II.

[4] Chapter XXXIV.

[5] *Ibid.*

[6] Rājaśekhara, *Kāvyamīmānsā,* p. 50.

Prakrits. Sanskrit usurped their place in public documents and some kings like Sāhasāṅka of Ujjain are said to have enforced the use of Sanskrit even in their harems.[1] Naturally therefore after about 400 A. D. Prakrit studies in the primary stage must have been more or less perfunctory and boys must have passed to the study of Sanskrit grammar and *Koshas* as soon as possible. The secondary stage of education may be said to have commenced when boys commenced a systematic study of the higher grammar. This usually happened at the age of nine.[2]

Some of the books of this period refer to primary schools as *lipiśālās* (alphabet classes) and to the teachers thereof as *dārakāchāryas* (infant teachers).[3] The statement of the Jātakas and the *Lalita-vistāra* about the use of the wooden boards for writing purposes by the primary students is confirmed by the evidence from the Gandhāra art, where the Buddha at his primary school is seen sculptured as holding a rectangular board

---

[1] *Ibid.*

[2] Yuan Chwang states that the study of the Five Great Sciences commenced at the age of seven. (Watters, I. p. 154). This may have been possible only in highly educated families.

[3] Cf. *Lalita-vistāra*, Chap. X.
लिपिशालामुपनीयते स्म कुमारः । तत्र विश्वामित्रो नाम दारकाचार्यः ।

in his hand, on which he is seen writing the alphabet.[1] Chunam or some colour easily removable was used for writing. It is, however, equally probable that in the primary schools of the poorer classes wooden boards may have been covered with fine dust or sand and the alphabet written on them by fingers or wooden pens. This method prevailed in the Deccan till quite recent times. The teacher used to write one of the alphabets on the board and the boys used to shout out its name, as they went on writing it on their wooden slates. This method is graphically described in the *Lalita-vistāra.*[2] The multiplication tables were probably recited similarly by the whole class. This method persists to the present times, and is known to have been prevailing in South India in the 17th century A. D.[3]

The writers of this period have some interesting observations to make about the treatment and

---

[1] *A. S. R.*, 1903-4, pp. 246-7, pl. LXVI, 1. The sculptor seems to have intended to show that the first words written by the future Buddha were '[*ata*]*sa paraṇa* [*hi*]*ta*' '[My mission is to bring about] my salvation, as also that of others.'

[2] Cf. तत्र बोधिसत्वाधिष्ठानेन तेषां दारकाणां मातृकां वाचयतां यदा अकारं परिकीर्तयन्ति स्म तदा अनित्यः संस्कारशब्दो निश्चरति स्म ।

Chap. X.

[3] *Travells of Pietra delle Valle,* (Haklyt Society's pub.) II, p 227.

discipline of infant children. They were not subjected to any severe discipline as was the case with the students who had performed the Upanayana. In the matter of food, drink and play the utmost liberty was usually extended to them. It seems to have been recognised that up to the age of eight free bodily and mental development should be allowed untrammelled by any theological or disciplinary considerations.[1]

Who imparted primary education and how it was financed are questions about which very meagre information is available. Manu defines an Upādhyāya as a person who teaches portion of the Veda or the Vedāṅgas in return for a fee.[2] This Upādhyāya was probably the primary teacher also, because a part of the study of the Vedāṅgas was included in the primary curriculum. The education of an Aryan youth, who had no literary ambition, was precisely similar to the education which the Upādhyāya imparted.

Many persons used to take the profession of primary teachers and were employed by the rich to teach their children. In the *Rājataraṅgiṇī* we come across two youths, Suyya and Kāmadeva, who had taken up the profession of the primary teacher, and who were employed by rich persons to teach their

---

1 *SCS.*, p. 63-65.

2 II, 141.

little children[1]. It is quite probable that children of other persons also were permitted to attend these schools by the rich persons who used to engage the teachers. If a village had no single individual rich enough to engage the services of a teacher on his own account, primary schools may have been started by adventurous young men, who were prepared to rely upon the uncertain support of the guardians of the boys studying under them for their maintenance. These teachers were probably the members of the families of the village priest or accountant or the Baniya. Their intellectual calibre was not very high; at least the two teachers in the *Rājataraṅgiṇī*, referred to above, are described as commencing their career after they had learnt their *Aksharas* or alphabet. Of course we cannot perhaps take the statements of the Kashmir chronicle too literally, but it is clear that the literary equipment of both the teachers was very poor in quantity and quality. The case in earlier times and in provinces more settled than Kashmir may perhaps have been different.

Buddhist monasteries at this time used to impart higher education both to monks and laymen. It is quite probable that they may have been also providing primary education, as do the monasteries in Burma even in the present times. The distinction between the primary and the higher education in these days was

---

[1] I, p. 196 and p. 134 (English translation).

not so clear cut as it is in modern times. Secular students, who used to serve their monk teachers as pages giving them water, serving them their food etc., appear from I-tsing's description[1] to have been the students of the primary rather than of the secondary course.

Smritis very often refer to non-Brahmana teachers and lay down that Brahmanas should not learn under them.[2] These teachers could not have been Vedic teachers in the age we are discussing; they were almost certainly primary teachers belonging to the trading classes. Perhaps a few Kshatriyas also may have taken to this line, but their number must have been small.

In the absence of definite evidence, it is difficult and risky to estimate the precise prevalence of literacy during this period. As we shall see in Chap. VIII, a great impetus was given in this age to the foundation of institutions of higher education. This must have in its turn given an impetus to the primary education also. On the other hand it has to be noted that Upanayana practically disappeared from a large section of the Kshatriya and Vaishya population; this must have given a set back to the spread of primary education among the non-Brahmanas. It may be presumed that about 40 per cent of the boys of the school going age were receiving primary education towards the end of

[1] Takakusu, pp. 105-6.

[2] E.g., Manu, II, 242.

this period. As we shall see in the next section, at the advent of the British rule about 15 per cent of the boys of the school going age were attending primary schools in most of the provinces of India. If in spite of the prevailing anarchy of the few immediately preceding decades and of the Muslim rule of the preceding several centuries, which was by no means very favourable to the spread of education among the non-Muslims, the percentage of literacy was so high as 15 per cent towards the beginning of the 19th century, we may fairly conclude that it must have been at least 40% towards the beginning of the 9th century A. D.

## SECTION V.

(From c. 800 A. D. to c. 1200 A. D.)

Vernaculars began to develop in this period and they must have begun to form an important part of the primary curriculum. In 1158 A. D. there existed provision to teach Canarese in the school at Talgund.[1] In the college at Narsipuram in Karnatak arrangements were made for the teaching of three vernaculars, Canarese, Telagu and Marathi in 1290 A. D.[2] It is quite probable that these two schools were typical of the age. Primary education of the vast number of Kshatriya, Vaishya and Śūdra boys could not have laid particular emphasis on Sanskrit language and

---

[1] *E. C.*, VII, Shikarpur No. 185.

[2] *E. C.*, III, Narsipur No. 27.

grammar during this period. Reading, hand-writing, arithmetic, accounts keeping and a fairly good knowledge of vernaculars, with perhaps a smattering of Sanskrit, was all that was taught to the vast majority of the non-Brahmana scholars. If provision was made for the teaching of the vernaculars of the provinces of origin of boys who came to centres of higher education like Narsipur, it is certain that primary education must have laid a greater stress on the cultivation of vernaculars than of Sanskrit, at least in the case of non-Brahmana scholars. Some of the teachers of primary education must have undoubtedly belonged to the non-Brahmana classes as was the case in the last period.

The percentage of the literate population must have gone further down in this period as society prohibited Vedic education to the Vaishyas in direct opposition to the Smriti direction on the point.[1] Among the village servants who were remunerated by the village communities by an assignment of the grain share at the time of the harvest, the village teacher does not figure. Some of the Madras witnesses before the Education Commission of 1882 averred that the village teacher was a member of the village staff maintained by the assignment of a grain share,[2] but their testimony

---

1 Sachau, Alberuni, I, p. 125.

2 *Report of the Madras Provincial Committee*, Evidence, pp. 20; 154, 173.

was contradicted by others.[1] The correct conclusion seems to be that the village teacher as a grain sharing servant of the community was known only to a few districts of Madras presidency. There is no clear evidence so far forthcoming to prove that he was maintained as a community servant in India as a whole. The average farmer of this period was illiterate;[2] he was in need of the services of a smith, carpenter or potter but not of a teacher. He would, therefore, have deemed it a grievance if a share of his produce was snatched away from him for the maintenance of the primary teacher in the village.

Primary education was imparted in this period either by the village priest[3] or some members of the families of the accountant or the sub-accountant of the village. The teacher may have been engaged on definite terms in some localities by the merchants of

---

[1] *Ibid*, p. 20.

[2] This is clear from a simile introduced by Vāchaspatya Miśra in his commentary on *Sāṅkhya-tattva-kaumudī*, Vol. II, p. 158 (Jha's edition):—तत्र व्यक्तं स्वरूपतः पांसुलपादिको हालिकोऽपि प्रत्यक्षतः प्रतिपद्यते ।

[3] In Bengal and Bihar at the beginning of the 19th century village schools (*pāṭha-śālās*) were usually organised by priests in charge of the village temples. They were supported by the temple lands and free-will offerings, and occasionally by fees.

*Report of the Bengal Provincial Committee, Education Commission*, 1882. p. 1.

the place or by the guardians of rich parents, who were anxious to get their children educated. In other places where circumstances were not favourable for any such definite agreement, he may have depended on the fees paid by the guardians in proportion to their means. The latter system was prevailing by the beginning of the 19th century in several villages of Malva[1] and probably goes back to this period. The teacher, when a Brahmana, used to combine the functions of the village priest and astrologer also.[2] Down to the advent of the British rule the teacher was held in high estimation[3]; in several places annual festivals were held in his honour when he used to go through the streets in procession with his students, and a collection was made for his school.

The extent of the literacy at the end of the Hindu period (*c.* 1200 A. D.) is not definitely known, but some conclusions may be drawn from the data

---

[1] Malcolm, *Memoirs of Central India and Malva*, Vol. II, p. 158.

[2] Tarikere inscription No. 21, dated 1655 A. D. grants a piece of land to a Brahmana for the office of the village teacher and astrologer, with the right to receive honorarium at the time of *Śrāddha* and *Sanskāras*. (*E. C.*, Vol. VI). In Malbar the term *Panikkar* denotes both a school master and an astrologer. *Report of the Madras Prov. Com., Educa. Comm.*, 1882, evidence p. 91.

[3] Molcolm, *op. cit*: The Court of Directors' despatch, dated June 3, 1814.

available about the beginning of the British rule. At the beginning of the 19th century, there existed a fairly wide-spread organisation for primary education in most parts of India. In Madras presidency Sir Thomas Monroe found a primary school in every village.[1] In Bengal Ward discovered that almost all villages possessed schools for teaching reading, writing and elementary arithmetic.[2] Even in Malva, which was for more than half a century suffering from continuous anarchy, Malcolm noticed that every village with about a hundred houses had an elementary school at the time of its coming under the British suzerainty.[3] It should be, however, noted that though primary schools were common, only some sections of society like the Brahmanas and merchants were taking their advantage. As a result only about 15 per cent of the children of the school going age were attending schools in Madras presidency.[4] The percentage was probably a little lower in Bombay and Bengal presidencies.

If in spite of the unsettled conditions of the times, about 15 per cent of the children were attending schools at the beginning of the 19th century, the percentage

---

[1] Mill, *History of British India*, Vol. I, p. 526 (4th edition).

[2] Ward, *View of the Hindoos*, Vol. I, pp. 160 ff.

[3] Malcolm, *op. cit.*

[4] *Report of the Madras Provincial Committee*, p. 5.

must have been at least twice that figure at the end of the Hindu period. For, we must remember, that Muslim rule, extending over about seven centuries, had intervened between the advent of the British and the disappearance of the Hindu rule. The Muslim rule no doubt looked after the education of Muslims through the Maktabs and Madrassas but did not take any active steps to foster education among the Hindus. Its educational efforts were confined 'to a very large extent, to that minority of population which embraced the religion of the Islam.'[1] State patronage, both direct and indirect, which had helped considerably the spread of the higher and primary education in the Hindu period, was now withdrawn; openings for educated Hindus in Government employment became very few. All this must have affected the spread of education and the percentage of literacy among the Hindu population. If therefore the percentage of literate population among Indians as a whole was fifteen at the beginning of the 19th century, it may very easily have been about thirty by the end of the 12th century. At the time when the Upanayana ritual was general in the Aryan community, the percentage of literacy may have been about 75. In the Gupta period, when a vast majority of the Kshatriyas and Vaishyas had ceased to perform the Upanayana ritual, it may have been about 50 per cent.

---

[1] Keay, *Ancient India Education*, p. 142.

# CHAPTER VII.

## FEMALE EDUCATION.

The history of the most of the known civilisations shows that the further back we go into antiqity, the more unsatisfactory is found to be the general position of women. Hindu civilisation is unique in this respect, for here we find a surprising exception to the general rule. The further back we go, the more satisfactory is found to be the position of women in more spheres than one. And the field of education is most noteworthy in this respect.

## SECTION I.

### VEDIC AND BRAHMANIC PERIODS.

(down to about 800 B. C.)

The theory of the Smriti period, that women being practically of the same status as the Śūdras, are naturally disqualified for Upanayana, Vedic studies and rituals was altogether unknown in the Vedic age. The observation of the *Satapatha Brāhmaṇa*, that husband and wife are the two halfs of one entity,[1] was not merely a courtly compliment to the fair sex; for an unmarried man was debarred from performing a sacrifice.[2] So, early in this period, women had not

---

[1] अर्धो ह वा एष आत्मनो यज्जाया। V. 1, 6, 10.

[2] अयज्ञियो वा एष योऽपत्नीकः। *Ibid.*

only no religious disabilities for themselves, but could indirectly impose them upon men if they refused to marry.

Wives then must have played an important part in sacrifices. Pāṇini points out that the very derivation of the term *Patnī* refers to her special connection with the sacrifice of her husband.[1] At the commencement of the sacrifice, she used to receive a regular *dīkshā* as was the case with men; this was known as *Vratopanayana* because fresh girdles were supplied on the occassion.[2] One passage in the Rig-veda describes how both the husband and wife used to take a joint part in pressing the Soma juice and supervising over or participating in the various functions going on in the sacrificial pandal.[3] In another place we read that women were entitled to go to and participate in sacrifices.[4]

But participation in sacrifices, in order to be real, required a fairly intelligent aquaintance with Vedic literature and rituals. This was not possible without Upanayana, followed by at least a short period of Vedic studies. Serious lady students passing some period

---

1 पत्युर्नो यज्ञसंयोगे । IV, 1, 33.

2 *Tai. Br.*, III, 3, 3; *Śat. Br.*, 1, 3, 1, 12.

3 या दंपती सुमनसा सुनुत आ च धावतः । देवासो नित्ययाशिरा ॥ VIII, 31, 5.

4 सं होत्रं स्म पुरा नारी समनं वाव गच्छति । X, 85, 10.

of life in regular *brahmacharya* before marriage are referred to in a passage in the *Atharva-veda*,[1] but we have no means to ascertain their percentage in the Vedic period. Some of them seem to have attained fair eminence in the realm of scholarship and literature, for at least two ladies, Ghoshā and Lopāmudrā, enjoy the unique distinction of being included among the authors (*Mantradṛics*) of the Rigvedic Saṁhitā.[2] It is quite probable that there may have existed other lady poets of note; their compositions may not have been included in the final selection made for the Vedic Saṁhitās.

Sometime towards the end of the Vedic period, the wife's participation in sacrifices began to degenerate into a merely formal association with her husband. Sacrificial duties and operations, which formerly none but the wife could perform, began to be gradually transferred to others. One such instance is noted in the *Śatapatha Brāhmaṇa*;[3] formerly in a certain sacrifice, when *Havishkṛid* was called upon to rise and perform the allotted duty, none but the sacrificer's wife could respond to the call and do the needful. In the days of the *Satapatha Brāhmaṇa*, however, some one from among the priests could serve as a substitute. It is

---

1 ब्रह्मचर्येण कन्या युवानं विन्दते पतिम् । XI, 5, 18.

2 X, 39 & 40; I, 179.

3 तद्ध स्मैतत्पुरा । जायैव हविष्कृदुपोत्तिष्ठति । तदिदमप्येतर्हि य एव कश्चनोपतिष्ठति । I, 1, 4, 13.

clear that wives were gradually losing their religious privileges. This may have been partly the cause and partly the consequence of the growing educational backwardness of women.

There are some indications to show that at least in cultured families music and dancing were taught to and appreciated by ladies. A legend in the *Śatapatha Brāhmaṇa* narrates how gods were enabled to win over *Vāk* (goddess of speech) because unlike the Asuras, they sang and played on lyre before her. The author slyly observes that women can be easily won over by one who sings and dances before them.[1] Appreciation of music and dancing presupposes at least an elementary knowledge of these arts on the part of women.

## SECTION II.

### UPANISHADIC AND EPIC TIMES

(*c.* 800 B. C. to *c.* 200 B. C.)

A working knowledge of the daily Vedic and Smārta rituals and of some of their Mantras seems to have been possessed by the ladies of the higher classes during this period. The evidence in this respect is fairly conclusive. The housewife was expected to offer oblations, unaided by her husband, normally in the evening and sometimes in the morning also.[2] In the *Srastarārohaṇa* ritual of the *Āgrahāyaṇī* ceremony

---

[1] *Sat. Br.*, III, 2, 4, 6.

[2] कामं गृह्येऽग्नौ पत्नीजुंहुयात्सायंप्रातर्होमौ । *Go. Gr. S.*, I, 3.

performed in the rainy season, the wife had to recite a number of Mantras along with her husband and *upanīta* sons. Independently of men, women used to perform the harvest sacrifice (*sītā-yajña*), where about a dozen Vedic verses had to be recited, 'because such was the custom of long standing'[1] Actual instances of women performing Vedic rituals on their own account and therefore possessing Vedic and general education are not wanting. At the time when Rāma went to bid adieu to his mother, when about to start for the forest, he found her offering oblations along with the necessary Mantras.[2] Tārā, the wife of Vāli, is described as well grounded in Mantras; at the time when her husband went out to fight with Sugrīva, she was engaged in performing a certain ritual to secure his victory.[3] When Māruti searched Laṅkā in vain for Sītā for a long time, he thought of waiting for her on the bank of a river; the evening was approaching, and he thought

---

1 *Pā. Gr. S.*, III, 2. The commentator Harihara observes:-पुरुषाणां स्त्रीणां सर्वेषां मंत्रपाठः। The direction in the *Garga-paddhati*, पत्नीवर्जं सर्वस्त्रीणां मंत्राभावः shows that for several centuries the wife continued to be regarded as eligible for the recitation of these Mantras.

2 सा क्षौमवसना हृष्टा नित्यं व्रतपरायणा।
अग्निं जुहोति स्म तदा मंत्रवित्कृतमंगला॥

Ayodhyā-Kāṇḍa, 20, 15.

3 ततः स्वस्त्ययनं कृत्वा मंत्रविद्विजयैषिणी। IV, 16, 12.

that Sītā would surely turn up at the bank to perform her Sandhyā.[1]

Grounding in Vedic studies presupposed Upanayana and it was general among girls at this time. A passage in the *Hārīta Dharma Sūtra* shows that girls in this period used to be divided into two classes, *Brahma-vādinīs* and *Sadyodvāhās.*[2] The former continued their education for a long time and used to become experts in religion, philosophy and literature. The latter used to stop their education on coming of age when their marriages were arranged. Many fathers at this time were anxious to give their daughters as high an education as their sons used to receive; there is a ritual in the *Bṛihadāraṇyaka Upanishad* for the benefit of a person anxious for the birth of a daughter, who should become distinguished for her scholarship in due time.[3]

The extent of the learning of the *Brahmavādinīs* of this period can be gagued from the data of a varied

---

[1] संध्याकालमनाः श्यामा ध्रुवमेष्यति जानकी ।
नदीं चेमां शुभजलां संध्यार्थं वरवर्णिनी ॥

Sundara-kāṇḍa, 15, 48.

[2] द्विविधाः स्त्रियो ब्रह्मवादिन्यः सद्योद्वाहाश्च । तत्र ब्रह्मवादिनीनां अग्नीन्धनं वेदाध्ययनं स्वगृहे च भैक्षचर्येति । सद्योवधूनां तूपस्थिते विवाहे कथंचिदुपनयनमात्रं कृत्वा विवाहः कार्यः ।

Quoted in *VMS.*, p. 402; *SCS.*, p. 62.

[3] अथ य इच्छेद्दुहिता मे पंडिता जायेत सर्वमायुरियादिति तिलौदनं पाचयित्वा सर्पिष्मन्तमश्नीयाताम् । *Br. Up.*, VI, 4, 17.

character. Their education was not confined to Vedic learning only; some used to study the deeper problems of philosophy. Yājñavalkya's wife Maitreyī belonged to this class; she was more interested in studying deeper problems of philosophy than in wearing costly jewels and apparels.[1] In the philosophical tournament held during the sacrificial session performed under the auspices of king Janaka, it is interesting to note that the subtlest philosophical question was asked by the lady philosopher Gārgī Vāchaknavī.[2] The question was so subtle and esoteric in character that Yājñavalkya refused to discuss it in public. The keen reasoning and subtle cross-examination of Yājñavalkya by Gārgī shows that she was a dialectician and philosopher of a high order. Ātreyī of the *Uttara-Rāma-charit* was another lady, who was studying Vedānta under Vālmiki and Agastya.[3] Some ladies used to specialise in the dry branch of the Pūrvamīmānsā also. Kāśakṛitsni had composed a work on Mīmānsā known as *Kāśakṛitsnī* and Brahmana lady scholars, who had specialised in it were known as *Kāśakṛitsnā*.[4] If lady specialists in a technical subject like Mīmānsā were so numerous as to necessitate the coining of a new special term, it is

---

[1] *Ibid*, II, 4; IV, 5. Cf.—सा होवाच मैत्रेयी। येनाहं नामृता स्याम् किं तेनाहं कुर्यामिति।

[2] अनतिप्रश्न्यां वै देवतामतिपृच्छसि। *Ibid*, III, 6, 1.

[3] तेभ्योऽधिगन्तुं निगमान्तविद्यां वाल्मीकिपार्श्वादिह संचरामि। Act II.

[4] एवमपि काशकृत्स्निना प्रोक्ता मीमांसा।काशकृत्स्नी। काशकृत्स्नीमधीते काशकृत्स्ना ब्राह्मणी। On IV, 1, 14; 3, 155.

reasonable to conclude that the number of those who used to receive general cultural education must have been considerable.

The eventual permission, which the Buddha accorded to the admission of ladies to his Church, gave an impetus to the spread of education and philosophy among the ladies of the aristocratic and commercial communities. Like Brahmavādinīs, several ladies in Buddhist families also used to lead a life of celebacy, with the aim of understanding and following the eternal truths of religion and philosophy. Among the authoresses of the *Therī-gāthā*, who were believed to have attained salvation, 32 were unmarried women and 18 married ones. Amongst the former, Subhā, Anopamā and Sumedhā belonged to very rich families, and are said to have been wooed by princes and rich merchants.[1] When so large a percentage of girls was leading a life of celibacy in pursuit of religion and philosophy, it is but natural that the general average of intelligence and education among them must have been fairly high.

When there were so many distinguished lady scholars in society, some of whom used to remain unmarried, it is but natural that some may have taken to the teaching profession. We have evidence to this effect in the special meanings attached to the terms Upādhyāyānī and Upādhyāyā in Sanskrit language.

[1] Horner, *Women under Primitive Buddhism*, Chap. III.

Patañjali, who lived in the 2nd century B. C., informs us that the former of the above two terms indicates the wife of a teacher, while the latter denotes a female teacher.[1] That a special term should have been coined to denote lady teachers shows that their number could not have been quite a negligible one in the society. Some of them like Sulabhā, Vaḍavā, Prāthiteyī, Maitreyī, Gārgī and Vāchaknavī seem to have made some real contributions to the advancement of knowledge, for they enjoy the rare privilege of being included among the galaxy of distinguished scholars, to whom a daily tribute of gratitude was to be given by posterity at the time of the *Brahma-yajña.*[2]

The extent of the actual prevalence of higher education among women during this period is difficult to determine. There were no schools for women, nor were they encouraged to leave their parents and go to famous teachers for the completion of their education. Ātreyī's case in the *Uttara-Rāma-charit* was rather exceptional; she seems to be a lady of advanced age going out in search of philosophy. What the *Hārīta Dharma Sūtra* and Yama[3] have to observe seems to be

1 उपत्याधोयत अस्याः सा उपाध्याया। On III, 322

2 *Aś. Gr. S.*, III, 4, 4; *Śa. Gr. S.*, IV, 10, 3; Śaunaka in *SCS.*, p. 519.

3 Cf. पुराकल्पे तु नारीणां मौंजीबन्धनमिष्यते।
अध्यापनं च वेदानां सावित्रीवचनं तथा॥
पिता पितृव्यो भ्राता वा नैनामध्यापयेत्परः।

P. T. O.

applicable to ordinary lady scholars. These authorities lay down that only the father, the brother or the uncle could be entrusted with the teaching of girl students and that they were not to go out for the daily round for alms like the male Brahmachārins. Under these conditions higher education could have been possible only to girls in high and cultured families. Where the near male relatives had not the time or the ability to teach personally to their girl wards, the higher education of the latter must have been an impossibility. Elementary education must have been all that they could have received from their guardians. Their Upanayana could not have been followed by any serious higher or Vedic studies.

Towards the end of this period (c. 250 B. C.) even the formal Upanayana, necessitating some amount of primary and Vedic education, was becoming unpopular. Aitiśāyana was the leader of the movement advocating the cancellation of the religious and educational privileges of women. Bādarāyaṇa and Jaimini opposed the new school vehemently, but their advocacy proved eventually of no avail.[1] The views of the Aitiśāyana school became popular as early as the 3rd century B. C.,

---

(*Continued from the last page*)

स्वगृहे चैव कन्याया भैक्षचर्या विधीयते ॥

Cf also, *ante* p. 225, Footnote No. 2.

[1] See *Pūrvamīmānsā*, VI, 1, 6-16. The whole section is very interesting.

for Megasthenes observes, 'Brahmanas do not communicate a knowledge of their philosophy to their wives.'[1]

It is not necessary to discuss here the causes that led to the popularisation of the view that women are virtually of the same status as the Sūdras, and as such should not be extended the privileges of Upanayana, Vedic studies and sacrifices. The view that barbarian invasions were responsible for the degradation of the status of women does not seem to be a sound one, for the situation had begun to change even before the time of the Mauryas, when there were no barbarian invasions. The Parthians, Scythians and Kushanas came much later. The real cause for the degradation of women seems to have been the practice of selecting non-Aryan wives by the three higher castes. In the Vedic period inter-caste marriages among the first three castes were not unknown, but the marriage with the non-Aryan wife seems to have been rare. In the Punjab, the non-Aryans seem to have been annihilated by the Aryans. When, however, they proceeded to the Gangetic plain, the non-Aryan opposition became stouter and the two civilisations had to live side by side. The recorded instances of the marriages of Arjuna and Bhīma with Uḍupī and Hiḍimbā show that many Aryan chiefs began to take non-Aryan wives. This practice was legalised by early writers, who permit the marriage with a Śūdra woman. Now the Śūdra or the

[1] Fragment XLI.

non-Aryan wife with her ignorance or very imperfect knowledge of Sanskrit language and Hindu religion could obviously not enjoy the same religious privileges as the Aryan wife. Association with her must have tended to lower the standard of education of the Aryan co-wife also. The non-Aryan wives may very often have been the favourites of their husbands, who may have attempted to associate them in their religious sacrifices in preference to the better qualified but less loved Aryan wives. This must have led to grave mistakes and anomalies in the performance of the rituals, which must have shocked orthodoxy. The marriageable age of girls also was being lowered at this time, rendering any education worth the name next to impossible. Thinkers like Aitiśāyana therefore began to think that the only way to put an end to such a state of affairs was to disqualify all wives for sacrifices and to declare that only men could perform them. If the marriageable age of girls had not been lowered by this time, the Aitiśāyana school would probably not have succeeded. But early marriage had already begun to make Upanayana a nominal Sanskāra in the case of the vast majority of girls, which was not followed by any course of education worth the name. It was therefore thought that nothing was to be lost by the discontinuance of the meaningless formality of the Upanayana Sanskāra. This new change profoundly affected the educational prospects of lady students as will be shown in the next section.

## SECTION III.

### THE AGE OF THE SMRITIS AND PURĀṆAS.

### (c. 200 B. C. to 1200 A. D.)

Upanayana of ladies continued as a kind of unmeaning formality for a few centuries during this period. Thus Manu is seen to be in favour of the Upanayana of girls, provided no Vedic Mantras are used for the occasion.[1] Upanayana without Vedic Mantras is a contradiction in terms; Manu takes up this illogical position probably because he regarded Upanayana as a *Śārīra* rather than a *Vaidika* Sanskāra possessing some spiritual and cultural value. *Manu-smṛiti* is definitely against permitting women to recite,—and therefore to study—Vedic stanzas; A Brahmana is advised to boycott a feast given in connection with a sacrifice performed by a woman.[2] By about the 3rd century A. D. even the formality of an Upanayana, un-accompanied by any Vedic Mantras, had gone out of vogue in society; for the *Yājñavalkya-smṛiti* deliberately departs from the *Manu-smṛiti* in laying down that only pre-Upanayana Sanskāras were to be performed in the case of girls.[3] Upanayana having disappeared, even the elementary education that it pre-

---

[1] Cf.— अमंत्रिका तु कार्येयं स्त्रीणामावृदशेषतः । II, 66.
नास्ति स्त्रीणां क्रिया मंत्रैरिति धर्मे व्यवस्थितिः ।
निरिन्द्रिया ह्यमंत्राश्च स्त्रियोऽनृतमिति स्थितिः ॥ IX, 18.

[2] *Ibid*, IV, 205.

[3] I, 13.

suppossed, began to become rarer and rarer among the girls of the poorer classes; very soon brides were found to be unable to recite the few Vedic Mantras that they were expected to recite at the time of marriage. We therefore find the ritual writers of this period laying down that if a bride is unable to recite any Mantras on account of illiteracy, the husband or the priest may do so on her behalf.[1] When the vast majority of women were unable to recite properly the Vedic hymns, it was but natural that they should be regarded as ineligible for Vedic studies.[2] Some of the writers like Yama of this age were aware of the practice of the earlier times, which enjoined Upanayana in the cases of girls also, but they viewed this custom as unsuitable for the changed conditions. Medhātithi, who flourished in the 9th century A. D., is at pains to point out that *Manusmriti*, II, 66, when interpreted along with other passages of the book like V, 155 etc., does not really permit even a non-Vedic Upanayana to girls.[3] The view of Vijñāneśvara[4] and Kullūka[5] is

---

[1] *Go. Gr. Su.*, II, 1, 21; *Jai. Gr. S.*, I, 20.

[2] (i) स्त्रीशूद्रद्विजबन्धूनां त्रयी न श्रुतिगोचरा ।
इति भारतमाख्यानं कृपया मुनिना कृतम् ॥
(ii) वदन्ति मुनयः केचित्स्त्रीणां शूद्रसमानताम् ॥
'पुराणान्तरम्' in *VMS.*, p. 40.
(iii) *Gitā*, IX, 32.

[3] See the commentary on II, 67.

[4] On Yājñavalkya I, 15.

[5] On Manu II, 66.

the same. In practice, therefore, the Upanayana of girls must have disappeared from about the 3rd or the 4th century A. D. at the latest.

The mischief caused by the discontinuance of Upanayana was enhanced by the further lowering of the marriageable age. The writers towards the end of the last period, (400-200 B. C.) had begun to advocate that girls should be married soon *after* coming of age.[1] Manu, though in favour of a marriage at 12 in normal circumstances, was prepared to contemplate the possibility of a girl remaining unmarried to the end of her life if no suitable bridegroom could be found.[2] Later writers, however, of this period like Yājñavalkya,[3] Saṁvarta[4] and Yama,[5] most vehemently condemn the guardian who fails to marry a girl before the attainment of the puberty. This condemnation had the natural effect; from Alberuni we learn that in the 11th century Hindus used to marry at an early age, and that a Brahmana was never allowed to marry a girl above the age of 12.[6] Many

---

[1] E. g., *Va. Dh. S.*, कुमारी ऋतुमती त्रीणि वर्षाण्युपासीत। ऊर्ध्वं त्रिभ्यो वर्षेभ्यः पतिं विंदेत्तुल्यम्। XVII. 59
See also Vishṇu, 24, 41.

[2] काममामरणात्तिष्ठेद्गृहे कन्यर्तुमत्यपि।
न चैवैनां प्रयच्छेत्तु गुणहीनाय कर्हिचित्॥ IX, 89.

[3] अप्रयच्छन्समाप्नोति भ्रूणहत्यां ऋतौ ऋतौ। I, 64.

[4] I, 67.

[5] I, 22.

[6] Sachau, II, 131.

marriages must have taken place much earlier, for the Smritis written at the end of this period begin to glorify the virtue of a girl's marriage at the age of 7, 8, or 9.[1] When it was regarded as an ideal to celebrate a girl's marriage at so young an age, the death knell had been already rung of the female education.

Though Upanayana was prohibited to girls, some provison continued to be made in higher families for the secular and literary education of the fair sex down to about the 10th century A. D. From the *Lalita-vistāra*, it would appear that girls in cultured families could

---

[1] See Aśvalāyana, Saṁvarta, Kāśyapa etc. quoted in *VMS.*, p. 767. It is undoubtedly true that Mādhava, who flourished in the 14th century, observes in his *Nyāya-mālā-vistāra* (p. 335, Bombay edition) that women are entitled to Upanayana. A similar statement is made by Mitramiśra of the 17th century when discussing Manu II, 66. The statements of these authors in these passages do not warrant the view that Upanayana of girls was performed in some families even in the 17th century A. D. The above authors are simply expounding the views of the earlier writers they are commenting upon, and not attesting to the contemporary practice. This would be quite clear from a wrong construction which Mitramiśra elsewhere places upon a passage in the *Pāraskara Gṛihya Sūtra* :—बाह्यतः स्त्री बलिमुपहरति II, 17. Mitramiśra combines the two words स्त्री and बलिम् into स्त्रीबलिम् on the ground that women were incapable of offering any oblations owing to their ignorance. Cf. एतादृशव्याख्याने स्त्रीणां तत्तद्बलिप्रदानानुकूलविद्याकल्पना स्यात्। *VMS.*, p. 903.

read and write, compose poems, and understand Sāstras in the early centuries of the Christian era. At this time there flourished several lady poets in southern India, who have composed poetry in Prakrit. Among the authors from whom selections have been made in the *Gāthā-sapta-śatī* of Hāla, there are seven poetesses, their names being Revā,[1] Rohā,[2] Mādhavī,[3] Anulakshmī,[4] Pāhaī,[5] Vaddhavahī,[6] and Śaśiprabhā.[7] Some of the Sanskrit anthologies also have preserved the memory of a few other poetesses, some of whom seemed to have composed poetry of a very high order. Sīlabhaṭṭārikā was famous for her easy and graceful style, noted for a harmonious combination of sense and sound.[8] Devī was a well known poetess of Gujarat, who continued to enchant her readers on the earth even after her departure to heaven.[9] Vijayāṅkā's fame in Berar was second only to that of Kālidāsa.[10] She seems to

---

[1] I, 87 and 90. [2] II, 63.

[3] I, 91. [4] III, 28, 63, 74, 76.

[5] I, 70. [6] I, 86. [7] IV, 4.

[8] शब्दार्थयोः समो गुंफः पांचालीरीतिरुच्यते ।
शीलभट्टारिकावाचि......................॥

[9] सूक्तीनां स्मरकेलीनां कलानां च विलासभूः ।
प्रभुदवी कवी लाटी गतापि हृदि तिष्ठति ॥

[10] सरस्वतीव कर्णाटी विजयांका जयत्यसौ ।
या वैदर्भगिरां वासः कालिदासादनंतरम् ॥

These verses are attributed to Rājaśekhara in the *Sūktimuktāvali.*

have attained a really high position among Sanskrit poets and poetesses, for the poet Rājaśekhara compares her to Saraswatī.[1] Rājśekhara's own wife, a Kshatriya by caste, was a good literary critic and poetess. The umpire in the controversy between Sankara and Maṇḍanamiśra was the accomplished wife of the latter; she must have been well grounded in Mīmānsā, Vedānta and literature. Some ladies were attracted by medical studies also; the majority of these must be specialising in gynæcology. Some of the lady doctors had also written authoritative works on the medical science. Among the Hindu works on medicine translated into Arabic in the 8th century A. D. was a book on midwifery, written by a lady doctor, whose name appears as Rūsā in the Arabic garb.[2] The number however of lady students taking to medicine must have been very small, as female education had received a general set back in this period.

Unfortunately we do not know anything about the status of the lady poets, philosophers and doctors whose names have been handed down to us. We would have been very glad to learn whether they had finished their studies before their marriages or whether they continued them in their married life. Very probably most of these must have belonged to cultured families of officers,

---

1 नीलोत्पलदलश्यामां विजयांकामजानता ।
वृथैव दण्डिनाप्युक्तं सर्वशुक्ला सरस्वती ॥ Ibid.

2 Nadvi, *Arab aur Bhārat ke Sambandha*, p. 122.

ministers and princes. For, we know from Rājśekhara that girls in such families used to receive higher education which would often enable them to acquire literary fame.[1]

The literary equipment of the average lady in cultured families may not have been very high; she was, however, usually able to read and write and follow non-technical Sanskrit and Prakrit works. This conclusion is confirmed by the fiction and drama of this period, where we often come across heroines writing and receiving love letters.

There are also several stories current in learned circles about clever wives saving their unwary husbands from the reproach of faulty speech by their own cleverness. One such story may be narrated. A scholar, who had invited some friends for a party, said to his wife *'Bhārye, dadhimānaya.'* The educated wife knew the grammatical blunder committed by her husband and in order to save him from the reproach of ungrammatical speech, brought milk, explaining that the order being not clear and specific she had fetched milk.[2] Such stories would not have been

---

[1] पुरुषवद्योषितोऽपि कवीभवेयुः।...। श्रूयन्ते दृश्यन्ते च राजपुत्र्यो महामात्रदुहितरो गणिकाः कौटुंबिकभार्याश्च शास्त्रप्रहितबुद्धयः कवयश्च।

*Kāvyamīmānsā* p. 53.

[2] The husband wanted to order curds and therefore said, *'Dadhimāṇaya'* forgetting that the word *Dadhi* cannot

*P. T. O.*

current if ladies in cultured families were not usually receiving some literary education.

Cultured families are, however, relatively few in society. They could afford to employ for their girls special teachers like Bṛihannaḍā, Gaṇadāsa or Haradatta. Ordinary families, however, were not so well situated, and it is therefore doubtful whether the average woman was receiving anything like education after about the 6th or the 7th century A. D. Asahāya, a commentator on the *Nārada-Smṛiti*, who flourished in the 8th century A. D., justifies the theory of the dependence of women on the ground that their intelligence is not developed like that of men on account of the absence of proper training.[1] It is hazardous to make any statement about the percentage of literate women in society at the end of the 12th century A. D., but it could not have been higher than 10 percent. Literacy among men at this time was probably about 30 percent as has been shown in the last chapter.

Girls in cultured families used to get some training in fine arts also in this period. Vātsyāyana lays down a number of such arts in which cultured ladies in towns

---

(*Continued from the last page*)

have *Dadhim* as its accusative singular. The wife pretends to understand the order as *dadhi mā ānaya*. 'Do not bring curds' and therefore brings milk.

1 शास्त्राध्ययनानधिकारित्वात् शास्त्रमात्रोपजीविधर्माधर्मसंज्ञानाभावात् अस्वातंत्र्यम्। On XIII, 30.

and cities were expected to be well versed. Vocal and instrumental music, dancing, painting, garland making, personal and house decorations were the chief among them.[1] Special tutors were appointed in rich families for the training of girls in these branches. Dancing girls used to attain high proficiency in these arts and some of them could also stage dramas down to the 13th century A. D.[2]

Girls in ruling and aristocratic families were given some administrative and military training also. When the king of the Massagas died at the time of the invasion of Alexander the Great his widow could carry on the government and direct and organise the defence. In the 2nd century B. C., queen Nayanikā of the Sātavāhana dynasty was governing the extensive empire of her husband during her son's minority.[3] In the 4th century A. D. Prabhāvatīguptā of the Vākāṭaka dynasty was directing the administration of her kingdom as the regent of her minor son.[4] In the 7th century A. D. Vijayabhaṭṭārikā, the senior wife of the elder brother of Vikramāditya I of the Badami Chalukya dynasty, was discharging the duties of a governor.[5] Kashmir annals have recorded the reigns

---

1 *Kāma-sūtra*, I, 3, 16.

2 *S. I. E. R.*, No. 557 of 1916.

3 Nānāghat inscription, *A. S. W. I.*, V. p. 60.

4 *E. I.*, XV, p. 41.

5 *I. A.*, VII, p. 163.

of two queens, Sugandhā and Diddā, whose coins also have been discovered. Under the later Chālukyas of Kalyaṇī lady governors were common. Mailādevī, a wife of Someśvara, was governing the extensive province of Banavāsi in 1053 A. D.[1] Akkādevī, an elder sister of Jayasinha III, was governing the Tehsil of Kinsukad 70 in 1022 A. D. Kunkumadevī, an elder sister of Vijayāditya, was in charge of the district of Purigere 300 in 1077 A. D.[2] Lakshmīdevī, the senior queen of Vikramāditya VI was in charge of 18 *agrahāras* in 1095 A. D.

Since the ladies in ruling families were expected to be at the helm of the realm in the case of emergency, provision must have been made to give them a fairly good military and administrative training. They must have been fairly well aquainted with the use of arms. Some of them could ride and swim. The son of queen Vijayamahādevī was called Gangadatta, because the mother used to swim about in the Ganges owing to a strong desire to do so during pregnancy.[3] In ordinary Kshatriya families also some military training seems to have been imparted to the lady folk. Village women are often seen defending their hearths and homes in times of danger. Inscription No. 173 of 1911 records the

---

[1] *I. A.*, IX, p. 274. [2] *I. A.*, XVIII, p. 37.

[3] *E. C.*, VII, Shimoga No. 4, dated 1122 A. D. See also *Rājataraṅgiṇī* VII, 905, 909, 931, VIII, 1137-9 for Kashmir queens fighting on the battle field.

death of a heroine in a village affray in 1041 A. D. at Siddhanhalli in Karnatak.[1] In 1264 A. D. another Karnatak heroine was honoured by government with the reward of a nose-jewel in recognition of her bravery in overpowering Tingu Nadak, who had led an expedition to carry away the cattle from her village.[2] The tradition of military training for ladies in high Kshatriya families continued down to the advent of the British rule. There still exists a commemorative tablet in Shikarpur Taluka immortalising the memory of a spirited lady, Hariyakkā by name, who died fighting in 1446 A. D. while avenging the murder of her father.[3] Maratha and Rajput princesses could usually ply the sword and wield the lance.[4]

In ordinary families, however, literature and fine arts were usually the favourite topics of female education. This education was of course not calculated to make women economically self-sufficient, but we must note that the theory that women ought to be economically independent is of quite recent origin. In the case of emergency, however, the Hindu woman could eke out a humble subsistence for herself and her children by taking to spinning and weaving in her spare time. In Pali literature we find instances of wives imploring their dying husbands to keep composed by

---

1 *S. I. E. R.*, for 1911.

2 *E. C.*, I, No. 75.

3 *E. C.*, VII, Shikarpur No. 2.

4 Malcolm, *Memoirs*, II, pp. 99-100.

pointing out that they could maintain the family by their skill in spinning and weaving.[1] The *Artha-śāstra* of Kauṭilya lays down that the state superintendent of weaving should make special arrangement for sending cotton to, and receiving the yarn from, those women, who were crippled, or whose husbands were dead, or had gone abroad, and who were thus compelled to seek work for their subsistence.[2] From Medhātithi we learn that in the 9th century A. D. widows who were uuprovided for used to have recourse to spinning for their maintenance.[3] This humble but independent means of existence was available to the women in distress in India down to the middle of the last century, when the hand spinning and hand weaving industry was crushed out of existence by the mill competition.

It will be interesting to take here a rapid bird's eye view of the fortunes of female education during the next seven centuries. During the Muslim rule the percentage of literacy among women went down very rapidly. Old rich and cultured families were, as a rule, ruined by the political revolution, and they were no longer in a position to make special arrangements for the education of their girls. There were of course no

---

[1] Cf. कुसलाहं गहपति कप्पासं कंतितुं वेणिमोलिखितुं सक्काहं गहपति तवाच्चयेन दारके पोसेतुम् ।

[2] II, 23; cf. याश्चानिष्कासिन्यः प्रोषितविधवा न्यङ्गाः कन्यका वाऽऽत्मानं बिभृयुः ताः स्वदासीभिरनुसार्य सोपग्रहं कर्म कारयितव्याः ।

[3] मृतपतिकाया अनपत्याया असति भर्तृधनादौ दायिके च कर्तनादिना केनचिदुपायेन जीवन्त्याः…… । On Manu V, 157.

schools for girls. Some new Hindu families may have no doubt risen to importance in the new regime; but their number was very small and they did not generally possess sufficient culture to induce them to appoint teachers for their girls. Daughters of the Rajput chiefs were usually able to read and write down to the 19th century; Jain widows too were sometimes taught reading and writing by the monks with a view to enable them to read their scriptures.[1] These were, however, exceptional cases. The decline in literacy after the 11th century was so rapid that by the beginning of the 19th century hardly one woman in hundred could read. Such was the state of affairs in Malva and also in Madras presidency. In the latter province, in 1826, only 4023 girls were attending schools as against 1,57,664 boys.[2] According to the then population of the presidency, 16 percent of the boys of the school-going age were receiving primary education; the percentage of the girls receiving the same was therefore less than one half. In certain sections of Hindu population as among the Nāyars, literacy was much higher, but such groups were few and exceptional. All the available evidence shows that by the beginning of the 19th century, about 99 per cent of the women population had grown illiterate.

---

1 Malcolm, *Memoirs*, II, 159.

2 *Report of the Madras Prov. Committee*, p. 5.

## CHAPTER VIII.

### SOME EDUCATIONAL CENTRES AND INSTITUTIONS.

For several centuries organised public institutions for education did not exist in ancient India. Education was left entirely to private agency. Teaching was made the religious duty of one section of the society, viz., the Brahmanas; and religion had so strong a hold over public mind that for centuries this class went on discharging its obligations without stipulating for any fees. Brahmanas had no corporate organisation like the Buddhist Church. In early times several Vedic Śākhās and Charaṇas were formed, but these did not develop into schools. In some tribes and localities learned Brahmanas used to form a *Parishad*, which used to be the custodian of traditional law and prescribe punishment for those who violated its rules.[1] We also find young scholars like Śvetaketu approaching their tribal Parishad at the end of their education to get recognition for their scholarship.[2] In later times tribal Parishads split into local bodies of learned men to which scholars, who had finished their education, used to be formally presented by their teachers.[3] But these Parishads in their corporate capacity do not seem to have taken any steps to organise public educational

---

[1] *Bau. Dh. S.*, II, 1, 44.

[2] *Br. Up.*, VI, 2, 1.

[3] *Ante*, p. 41.

institutions. Education was left entirely to individual teachers. Teachers too did not think of combining into public societies for organising educational institutions. Both at Takshaśilā and Benares, which were centres of education of hoary antiquity, there were, as we shall see presently, no public schools or colleges. Education was being given by private teachers entirely on their own account. Corporate educational organisations were first evolved in connection with Buddhist monasteries. The Buddha had emphasised the vital importance of imparting systematic education to novices, who were required to be trained for ten years. Buddhist monasteries became big institutions from the time of Asoka onwards, and they gradually developed into centres of education, at first for the monks and nuns only, but later on for the lay population as well. Hindu educational institutions, so far known, are all later than the time of the Nālandā University. It is probable that the starting of organised public institutions for education may have been suggested to the Hindus by the transformation of Buddhist monasteries into colleges and universities.

Capitals, holy places (*tīrthas*), monasteries, temples, and special colonies of learned Brahmanas (*agrahāra* villages) were the usual centres of education in Ancient India. Kings and feudal chiefs were as a rule patrons of learning. Many of the copper plate grants, that have been published so far, show that capitals of prosperous kingdoms used to attract many men of learning and would thus naturally become centres of education. Takshaśilā, Benares, Kanauj and Mithilā in northern India, Dhārā and Ujjayinī in central India and Paithan, Mālkhed and Kalyāṇī in southern India owe, to a great extent, their educational fame to their being capitals.

The holy places of Hinduism have been from times immemorial centres of pious and learned Brahmanas, who have never shown any unwillingness to impart education free to deserving students. Towns and cities like Benares, Kāñchī, Karhāṭaka, Nasik owe their educational preeminence to their being Tīrthas to a great extent. The causes that led to the development of the Buddhist monasteries into educational centres have been indicated above already. When Hindu temples began to be richly endowed like Buddhist monasteries, a part of the money came to be set apart for the purpose of education, either by the temple trustees or by the donors, as we shall soon see. Temples as a matter of fact were centres for the spread of Hindu religion, culture and civilization. They therefore naturally became centres of education. *Agrahāra* villages used to be given in charity specially to colonies of learned Brahmanas with a view to enable them to discharge their scriptural duties, among which teaching was an important one. They therefore naturally afforded good facilities for higher education, as will be shown in the course of this chapter.

It is proposed to give a short and succinct account of the important centres and institutions of education in Ancient India in the present chapter. The places have been arranged from the point of view of their importance and antiquity.

## TAKSHAŚILĀ.

Takshaśilā is undoubtedly the most important and ancient seat of learning in Ancient India. It was the capital of the important province of Gandhāra and its history goes back into hoary antiquity. The *Rāmāyaṇa*[1] asserts that it was founded by Bharata and named after prince Taksha, who was established there as its ruler. Janamejaya's serpent sacrifice was performed at this very place.[2] Neither the *Rāmāyaṇa* nor the *Mahābhārata* mentions Takshaśilā as a centre of learning, probably because there was no occasion to do so. In the 7th century B. C., however, it was already a famous seat of learning, attracting scholars from distant cities like Rājagriha, Benares and Mithilā. It was famous for its philosophers in the days of Alexander the Great. Unfortunately we know very little about its educational activities from non-Jātaka sources.

Takshaśilā was conquered and occupied by the Persians in the 6th century B. C., by the Indo-Baktrians in the 2nd century B. C., by the Scythians in the 1st century B. C., and by the Kushāṇas in the 1st century A. D. We do not know what effect these political vicissitudes had over the educational activity of

---

[1] VII, 101, 10-16.

[2] *MBH*, I, 3, 20.

the place. The ruins give traces of three different city sites occupied at the beginning of the Baktrian, Scythian and Kushāṇa periods. It is quite possible that these political vicissitudes may have told upon the city's prosperity, which may in turn have affected the cause of education. Every successive power, however, continued to maintain its provincial head-quarters at Takshaśilā, which must have soon obliterated the ravages of war.

The Persian and Greek occupation must have affected the curricula of schools and colleges; we have, however, no direct evidence on the point. Epigraphical testimony shows conclusively that the Persian occupation resulted in the replacement of the national Brāhmī script by the Kharoshṭī, which was an adaptation of the Akhæmenian script, the court script of the Persian emperors, to the needs of Sanskrit language. The Scythian and Kushāṇa conquerors had no culture or civilisation of their own, but the Indo-Baktrian rulers were the inheriters of the rich Greek civilisation. Their rule in Takshaśilā extended over a century and a half, and must have made some impression on the educational system of the place. It is quite possible that some of the 'world renowned' teachers of Takshaśilā may have mastered Greek language and literature and opened classes for the subject to facilitate the appointment of their students in Government services under the Greek administration. Among the '*sippas*' taught at Takshaśilā must have been included the training in Greek processes of coinage and sculpture. There was as yet no prejudice against foreign culture. It is quite possible that Greek dramas may have been performed in the courts of some of the numerous Greek princes and princelings. Some Indians also may have read and appreciated Sophocles and Eurepedes. A working knowledge of Greek language may have been possessed by several classes of Hindu society as it was the language of the conqueror.[1] But Greek orientation in Takshaśilā studies could not have been considerable. Indo-Greek rulers themselves were cut off from their mother country, and many of the conquerors soon succumbed to the culture and religion of the conquered. It is, however, a great pity that the historian of ancient Indian education should still be unable to supply authentic information about the extent of Greek influence on the Takshaśilā system of education.

It may be observed at the outset that Takshaśilā did not possess any college or university in the modern

---

[1] From the romantic history of Apollonius of Tyana by Philostratus we learn that in the 1st century A. D. Indians and Greeks at Takshaśilā knew each other's philosophy, and that the villagers around the Gandhāra capital could understand and speak Greek. There may be some exaggeration in this account, but recent excavations at Takshaśilā have confirmed some of the topographical details given by Philostratus. (*Guide to Taxila*, by Sir John Marshall, pp. 15 & 97). We may therefore conclude that his information about Indians' acquaintance with Greek language and literature may be at least partly true. Greek studies, therefore, must have figured in Takshaśilā curriculum during the Greek rule.

sense of the term. It was simply a centre of education. It had many famous teachers to whom hundreds of students flocked for higher education from all parts of northern India. But these teachers were not members of any institutions like professors in a modern college, nor were they teaching any courses prescribed by any central body like a modern university. Every teacher, assisted by his advanced students, formed an institution by himself. He admitted as many students as he liked. He taught what his students were anxious to learn. Students terminated their courses according to their individual convenience. As shown already, there were no degree examinations and therefore no degrees or diplomas.

Jātakas usually state the 'world renowned' teachers of Takshaśilā used to have 500 students under their charge. This figure seems to be more conventional than real as has been shown already.[1] We get only one instance in the Mahāsutasoma Jātaka[2] of what appears to be a real number of students reading under one teacher. Under the 'world renowned' teacher of this Jātaka we are told that 103 princes from different parts of the country were learning archery. Very probably this teacher may have had many assistants under him. Normally speaking, however, the number of students working under one teacher does not seem to have been more than 20 as has been shown already.[3]

---

[1] *Ante*, p. 151. [2] No. 537. [3] *Ante*, p. 151.

The excavations at Takshaśilā have not so far unearthed any extensive buildings, which can be taken to be big hostels or lecture halls. Students at Takshaśilā used to live ordinarily under their teacher's roof, the richer ones like prince Juṇha having their own separate establishments.[1]

The fame of Takshaśilā as a centre of learning was unrivalled in the 6th century B. C. In these days communications were so difficult and dangerous that when their sons used to return home, parents used to congratulate themselves on having seen them returning during their own life time.[2] And yet we find students flocking to Takashśilā from far off cities like Benares,[3] Rājagṛiha,[4] Mithilā[5] and Ujjayinī.[6] Kuru and Kośala countries sent their own quota of students. One of the archery school at Takshaśilā had on its muster roll, as we have seen already, 103 princes from different parts of India. Heir-apparents of Benares are usually seen being educated at Takshaśilā in the Jātakas. King Prasenajit of Kośala, a contemporary of the Buddha, was educated in the Gandharan capital.[7] Prince Jīvaka, an illegitimate son of Bimbisāra, spent seven years at Takshaśilā in learnlng medicine and

---

1 Jātaka No. 456.

2 Tilamuṭṭhi Jātaka, No. 252.

3 *Ibid.*

4 *Ibid*, No. 378.

5 *Ibid*, No. 489.

6 *Ibid*, No. 336.

7 *Ibid*, No. 498.

surgery.[1] As Pāṇini hailed from Sālātura near Attok, he also must have been an alumnus of Takshaśilā university.

Students, who used to proceed to Takshaśilā for education used to be about 16 or 17. There is no information about the duration of the Arts or Science courses in Takshaśilā. but it has been shown already how they appear to have extended over a period of about six to eight years.[2]

There were no caste restrictions on the choice of subjects. The caste system had not yet become very rigorous; Brahmana and Kshatriya youths were studying together under the same teachers. The case of the Brahmana Purohita of Benares sending his son to Takshaśilā for specialisation in archery would show how it was still possible to have free choice of profession, unfettered by caste considerations.[3] Fees were not compulsory aud teachers could not refuse a student because he was too poor to offer them an honorarium, either at the beginning or at the end of the course. Teachers used to receive manual service from poor students by day and teach them in special classes at night.[4]

---

[1] *Mahā-vagga*, Chap. VIII.

[2] *Ante*, p. 171.

[3] *Jātaka* No. 522; *ante*, pp. 161 ff.

[4] *Ante*, p. 79.

Jātakas represent that the three Vedas and eighteen arts and professions (*sippas*) were taught at Takshaśilā. The precise denotation of the term eighteen *sippas* is not yet definitely known, but it is clear from the data discussed before at pp. 127-8 that these *sippas* included medicine, surgery, archery and allied military arts, astronomy, astrology, accountancy, commerce, agriculture, divination, snake charming and magic.[1] The study of the Vedas included that of the Vedānta as well; the place was well known as a centre of philosophy at the time of Alexander's invasion.

As has been already observed, nothing is known of educational activities of Takshaśilā after the Mauryan period. The place, however, probably continued to flourish as an educational centre down to the end of the Kushāṇa empire (*c.* 250 A. D.). The Little Yueh-chis, who succeeded the Kushāṇas in the government of Takshaśila, were barbarous chiefs as their coins indicate, and the cause of education must have suffered under their unenlightened administration. At the beginning of the 5th century A. D. when Fa Hsien visited the place, there was nothing there of any educational importance.[2] Worse days, however, were

---

[1] See also Bhīma-sena Jātaka, No. 80 : Mahā-suta-soma Jātaka No. 537 ; Kosiya Jātaka, No. 130 ; Anabhirati Jātaka, No. 185 , Parantapa Jātaka, No. 416 ; Sañjīva Jātaka, No. 150.

[2] Legge, Fa Hsien, p 32.

in store for this Queen of Learning. The Hūṇa avalanche came at the end of the 5th century A. D. and ruined whatever was left after the Little Yueh-chi depradations.[1] At the time when Yuan Chwang visited the city in the 7th century A. D., it had lost all its glory and importance. The famous monastery of Kumāralabdha, where that celebrated Sautrāntika scholar had composed his expository works, was in ruins and the condition of the vast majority of the remaining Buddhist establishments was no better.[2] When it is remembered that the inhabitants of Takshaśilā at this time were plucky and devoted adherents of Buddhism, the sad plight of their monasteries will at once convince us that the city was completely wrecked by the Hūṇa invasions. Gone were the days of its former educational glory, never to return.

## BENARES.

Benares has been a very famous centre of Hindu religion and education for the last two thousand years and more. However, we possess very little information about Benares as a centre of learning. Neither epigraphs, nor foreign travellers nor Purāṇas, which contain extensive passages in glorification of the city, supply any information about the educational activity of the place.

---

[1] *M. A. S. I.*, 7, p. 20.

[2] Watters, I, p. 240 ; p. 245.

As a centre of Aryan education, Benares could not have been as old as Takshaśilā. For a long time when Sapta-sindhu (the Punjab) and Kuru-Pañchāla countries were centres of Aryan culture and education, eastern countries like Videha, Kāśī, Anga and Vanga were but imperfectly aryanised and were therefore held in contempt. According to the Pippalāda Śākhā reading, *Atharva-veda*, V, 22, 14 prays that the fever, which is being excorcised, should go to the peoples of Benares and Magadha.[1] This attests to the deep prejudice against the people of Benares in orthodox circles in the late Vedic period, probably due to its non-Aryan predelections. Even when Benares accepted the new Aryan religion, it was not unswerving in its loyalty to it. Dhṛitarāshṭra, one of its early kings, had performed a horse sacrifice, probably soon after his conversion to the Aryan faith. As ill luck would have it, the sacrifice was not successful and the horse was carried away by Śatānīka Satrājit, a Bharata prince. The Benares royal family lost its faith in the new religion and gave up the sacrificial fires, saying 'The Soma has been taken away from us'.[2]

Dhṛitarāsṭra's successors were eventually induced to return to the Vedic religion, and they became zealous patrons of Aryan culture and learning. One of them, Ajātaśatru, was himself a philosopher and was anxious

[1] Cf. गंधारिभ्यो मूजवद्भ्यः काशिभ्यो मगधेभ्यः ।

[2] *Saṭ. Br.*, XIII, 5, 4, 19.

to emulate the example of Janaka, his Videha contemporary, in extending generous patronage to men of light and learning. Down to about the beginning of the Christian era, Takshaśilā, however, was a more famous centre of education than Benares. Jātakas invariably represent kings of Benares as sending their sons to Takshaśilā for the completion of their education. Tilamuṭṭhi Jātaka no doubt informs us that the kings of Benares used to send their sons to Takshaśilā, not because there were no 'world renowned' teachers in their own capital, but because they thought that the pride and haughtiness of the young princes would be broken and they would become better aquainted with the ways of the world if they were sent to distant Takshaśilā.[1] In Kosiya and Tittiri Jātakas we come across famous teachers of Benares teaching the three Vedas and eighteen *sippas* to their students.[2] But some of these teachers were ex-students of Takshaśilā. Many poor students of Benares used to go to the distant Gandhara capital for their education,[3] showing thereby that the 'world famous' teachers at Benares were not so 'world famous' as those at Takshaśilā.

In the days of the Buddha, Benares was probably the most famous centre of learning in eastern India. Buddha's choice of Benares for the promulgation of his gospel may not have been quite accidental. The five

[1] No. 252. [2] Nos. 130 and 438.

[3] Mahā-Dhammapāla Jātaka, No. 447.

disciples to whom the Buddha wanted to preach had probably selected Benares as their place of sojourn, because it was famous as a centre of philosophers and scholars. We have, however, no definite evidence on the point. With the imperial patronage under Asoka, the Sārnāth monastery must have become a famous centre of Buddhist religion and scholarship. It went on prospering continuously; in the 7th century A. D. its tiers of balconies and rows of halls were extremely artistic, and there were 1500 monks in the establishment.[1] Yuan Chwang does not say anything about the educational activity of the place, but we shall not be far wrong in supposing that the monks at Sārnāth must have emulated the example of their brethren at Nālandā, so close to their establishment.

The Purāṇas supply us considerable information about Benares as a place of pilgrimage (*Tīrtha*) but very little about Benares as a centre of learning. They are silent on the point with the solitary exception of the *Bhavishya Purāṇa*, which refers to its literary atmosphere; it prophesies that all the Brahmanas at Benares will be distinguished scholars.[2] Hindu *Tīrthas* were usually crowded with learned Brahmanas, who were religiously devoted to their traditional duty of teaching; most of the Purāṇas may therefore have thought it superfluous to describe the educational activity of the holiest of the

[1] Watters, II, 48.

[2] Brahma-khaṇḍa, Chap. 51, 2-3.

Hindu *Tīrthas.* Inscriptions are also silent on the point; we have not so far discovered any epigraph recording a grant in favour of any educational institution of Benares. In spite of the example of neighbouring Nālandā, Hindu Benares does not seem to have organised any educational institution during the period 500-1200 A.D. Numerous copper plate grants have been unearthed recording the donations of the Gahaḍwāla rulers in favour of Brahmana scholars of Benares; not one of them, however, is in favour of any public college. At this time Benares was of course a recognised centre of Hindu learning and scholarship; scholars and philosophers like Śaṅkarāchārya had to repair to it to get their new theories recognised and published. Alberuni also notes that Benares and Kashmir were the most famous centres of learning in the 11th century A. D.[1] The educational activity of Benares was a natural consequence of the presence of numerous learned Brahmanas in that *Tīrtha,* honestly striving to discharge their traditional and religious duty to teach. Most of the Benares donees of the Gahaḍwāla grants must have been conducting small free schools for higher learning; royal grants were made in order to enable them to discharge this function efficiently and continuously.

---

1 At this time the scholarly population of Benares and Kashmir was considerably increased owing to the exodus of Brahmana scholars from the Punjab and northern parts of U. P., which were being harassed by the Muslims. Sachau, Alberuni, I, p. 173.

The same state of affairs continued down to the Muslim period and exists even today. While describing the state of affairs at Benares during the 17th century, Bernier observes, 'Benares is a kind of University, but it has no college or regular classes as in our Universities, but it resembles rather the schools of the ancients, the masters being spread over the different parts of the town in private houses. ......Some teachers have four and some six disciples; the most eminent may have twelve or fifteen, but this is the largest number.'[1] Throughout its history, Benares seems to have followed this method for the spread of education. There is no evidence of the city having ever possessed public educational institutions like those that flourished in Buddhist centres like Nālandā or Valabhi or Hindu centres like Salotgi, Ennāyiram and Tirumukkudul.

## NĀLANDĀ.

It is indeed strange that the most famous Buddhist centre of education should have been at a relatively obscure and unimportant place like Nālandā, which was neither a royal capital nor in any way connected with the life of the Buddha, and therefore of any particular sanctity to the Buddhist world. Why it should have suddenly risen in importance and become an international centre of learning in the 5th century A. D. is still a mystery. Patronage of Gupta kings was of

---

[1] Bernier, *Travels in India*, p. 341.

course the cause of the rise of Nālandā, but we cannot explain why the Guptas should have selected for their liberal patronage this particular monastery in preference to numerous others that existed in their dominions.

The rise of Nālandā, which is about 40 miles to the south-west of Patna, has to be placed towards the middle of the 5th century A. D.[1] When Fa Hsien visited the place in about 410 A. D., it was only an unimportant village possessing only one Stūpa to commemorate the memory of Sāriputta, the right-hand disciple of the Buddha. Very soon thereafter Nālandā rapidly rose into importance owing to the patronage of a number of Gupta emperors. That the Gupta rulers, who were themselves orthodox Hindus, should have contributed a lion's share to the development, equipment and endowment of the greatest Buddhist monastery and University, speaks volumes for the catholicity of the age. Sakrāditya, who was probably Kumāragupta I (414-454 A. D.), laid the foundation of the greatness of Nālandā by founding and endowing a monastery there. The Buddha temple in this monastery, which he built, was for centuries the central place of worship for the congregation.

---

[1] According to Tārānāth, Āryadeva, a disciple of Nāgārjuna, was a Nālandā scholar. This, if true, would take back the antiquity of Nālandā by about a couple of centuries. The identity of both Nāgārjuna and Āryadeva and their precise time are not yet definitely determined. Bose, *Indian Teachers*, pp. 108-9.

Tathāgatagupta (who cannot yet be definitely identified), Narasiṁhagupta Bālāditya, (468-472 A. D.) and Buddhagupta (*c.* 475-500 A. D.) added one monastery each to the establishment.[1] Vajra, an unidentified successor of Bālāditya, and another unnamed king of Central India added two further monasteries to the establishment.

The history of Nālandā during the 6th century is obscure. Mihirakula, the barbarian Hūṇa ruler, had an intense hatred against Buddhism. He is said to have penetrated right up to the capital of Magadha and driven its ruler Bālāditya to the Bay of Bengal. It is quite possible that Nālandā may have suffered from the Hūṇa conqueror on his way to Pāṭaliputra. The Harsha-Śaśāṅka war of the first quarter of the 7th century may have also affected the fortunes of the place. In his intense hatred of Buddhism, Śaśāṅka is said to have uprooted the Bodhi Tree and burnt the monasteries at Bodha-Gaya. Since Nālandā is so near to this place, it is quite possible that it may have to some extent suffered from Śaśāṅka's attentions. At the time of Yuan Chwang's visit, however, the damages of war and bigotry, if any, were repaired and the establishment was in its full glory. The central college had seven halls attached to it. Monastic buildings were superb, several stories in height. Hwui Li's

1 The sequence of these rulers and their time, given both by Yuan Chwang and his biographer, seem to be wrong. See Watters, II. p. 164 ; *Life*, pp. 110-111.

statement that the topmost storey towered above the clouds and enabled a spectator to see how clouds changed their shape is of course an exaggeration, but it receives an unexpected corroboration from the Nālandā Stone Inscription of Yaśovarman, which also avers that the tops of the Vihāras at Nālandā touched the clouds.[1] We may therefore take it that the towers and turrets of the Nālandā temples and monasteries must have been of impressive height. There were also deep and translucent ponds covered with blue lotuses, which added to the beauty of the place and supplied water and flowers to the establishment. The whole colony was surrounded by an encircling wall with a door in the southern side.[2]

When I-tsing was living at Nālandā (*c.* 675 A.D.), there were more than 3,000 monks residing in the establishment.[3] The biographer of Yuan Chwang states that in the second quarter of the seventh century the number of the monks at Nālandā would always reach 10,000.[4] The biographer had never been to India, and his information therefore was second-hand.

---

1 यस्यामम्बुधरावलेहिशिखरश्रेणी विहारावली ।
मालेवोर्ध्वविराजिनी विरचिता धात्रा मनोज्ञा भुवः ॥ E.I., XX, p. 43

2 Beal, *The Life of Hiuen Tsang* by Shaman Hwui, pp. 109-114. Watters, II, pp. 164-171 and I-tsing, pp. 30, 65, 86 and 154 are the main sources of our information for Nālandā.

3 I-tsing p. 154.

4 *Life*, p. 112.

His figure seems to be a little exaggerated since it is given in round number, and since Yuan Chwang himself simply observes that there were some thousand brethren residing at the place.[1] It would, however, seem certain that the actual number of the monks studying at Nālandā must have been at least about 5,000 towards the middle of the 7th century A. D. Rooms were assigned to the monks according to their seniority, and redistribution took place every year. Excavations have now shown that some of the rooms were single seated and some double seated; each room had one or two stone cots for sleeping, a nitch for the lamp and another for books. *Chullas* (hearths) of huge dimensions have been unearthed in each monastery, showing that the messing arrangements were common.

Nālandā, however, was not a mere monastery; it had become so important a monastery primarily because it was a very famous centre of learning. Yuan Chwang says, 'In the establishment were some thousand brethren, all men of great learning and ability, several hundreds being highly esteemed and famous; the brethren were very strict in observing the precepts and regulations of their order; learning and discussing they found the day too short, day and night they admonished each other, juniors and seniors mutually helping to perfection....*Hence foreign students come to the establishment to put an end to their doubts and then*

[1] Watters, II, p. 165.

*become celebrated, and those, who stole the name (of Nālandā) were all treated with respect wherever they went'.*[1]

The head abbots of Nālandā used to be as much celebrated for piety as for scholarship. Amongst them were 'Dharmapāla and Chandrapāla, who gave a fragrance to the Buddha's teachings, Guṇamati and Sthiramati of excellent reputation among contemporaries, Prabhāmitra of clear argument, Jinamitra of elevated conversation, Jinachandra of model character and perspicacious intellect and Śīlabhadra whose perfect excellence was buried in obscurity.'[2] These scholars were not, however, content merely to teach and expound; they were authors of several treatises widely known and highly valued by their contemporaries. The above seven scholars flourished in the first half of the 7th century; the total number of high class scholars produced at Nālandā during its history of about 700 years must have been very great. At the time of Yuan Chwang's visit the average scholarship of the establishment also was very high. Out of its 5,000 (or 10,000) monks, there were a thousand who could explain twenty collections of Sūtras; 500 who could explain thirty collections, and perhaps ten who could explain fifty collections.[3]

---

[1] Watters, II, p. 165.

[2] *Ibid*

[3] *Life*, p. 112.

Curriculum at Nālandā was not confined to the study of the Buddhist religion, philosophy and literature. The establishment was a Mahāyāna one, but along with the works of the Great Vehicle, not only those of the 18 sects but also 'the Vedas and other books, the *Hetuvidyā* (logic), the *Śabda-vidyā* (grammar), *Chikitsāvidyā* (medicine), the works on magic (*Atharvaveda*), and the Sāṅkhya philosophy' were also expounded to the students. They used to study and investigate miscellaneous works also.[1]

In the monk population of about 5,000 (perhaps 10,000) a thousand could explain, as we have seen already, twenty collections of Sūtras. This means that there were about a thousand competent teachers to look after the education of about 4,000, but in no case more than 9,000, monk students. On the average, therefore, each teacher was in charge of not more than nine students. Personal attention was thus possible to each student and the teaching therefore must have been very efficient. The college had eight big halls and 300 smaller apartments, and every day the authorities used to arrange for about a hundred lectures.[2] Learned monk teachers were held in high veneration and were provided with sedan chairs.[3] They were experts in the art of teaching and ex-

[1] *Life*, p. 112.
[2] *Ibid.*
[3] I-tsing, p. 30.

pounding; I-tsing gratefully observes: 'I have been very glad that I have had an opportunity of acquiring a knowledge personally from them, which I should otherwise have never possessed.'[1]

There was a great rush for admission to the Nālandā University. Students from all parts of India and also from distant foreign countries were anxious to get the benefit of its instructions. Fa Hsien, Yuan Chwang and I-tsing were not the only Chinese scholars that were attracted to Nālandā by its fame as a centre of learning. During the short interval of thirty years between the visits of Yuan Chwang and I-tsing, Thon-mi, Hiuen Chiu, Taou-hi, Hwui-nieh, Āryavarman, Buddhadharma, Taou-sing, Tang and Hwui Lu, hailing from distant countries like China, Korea, Tibet and Tokhara, had visited Nālandā for prosecuting higher studies and procuring rare manuscripts.[2]

The standard of admission was naturally high; 'of those from abroad, who wished to enter the schools of discussions, the majority, beaten by the difficulties of the problems, withdrew; and those who were deeply versed in old and modern learning were admitted, only two or three out of ten succeeding'.[3]

The Nālandā authorities had realised that a monastery without a library was like a castle without

[1] I-tsing, p. 185.

[2] *Life*, Introduction, pp. XXVII-XXXVI.

[3] Watters, II, p. 165.

an armoury. The University was maintaining a splendid library to meet the needs of the hundreds of teachers and thousands of students that were engaged in the study of different sciences. One of the reasons why Chinese scholars used to spend months together at Nālandā was to get true copies of the sacred texts and other works of Buddhism. I-tsing got copied at Nālandā 400 Sanskrit works amounting to 5,00,000 verses.[1] Significantly enough the library quarter was known as *Dharma-gañja*, 'mart of knowledge.' It was located in three splendid buildings appropriately called *Ratnasāgara, Ratnodadhi and Ratnarañjaka.*[2]

Nālandā University was richly endowed by a succession of Gupta and other rulers; it owned a hundred villages yielding rich revenues.[3] Hwui Li informs us that the state favour thus shown enabled the authorities to provide free boarding and lodging, clothing and medicine to its thousands of students.[4] I-tsing states that the usual practice of Indian monasteries was not to offer free boarding to lay students, studying secular subjects unless they agreed to perform

---

[1] I-tsing, p. 1.

[2] Vidyabhushana, *History of Indian Logic*, p. 516.

[3] This is the number given by Hwui Li, (*Life*, p. 113). I-tsing, who had stayed for ten years at Nālandā, gives the number as 200 (p. 65). Villages endowed were obviously not less than 100.

[4] *Life*, p. 113.

some manual service as pages.[1] Whether this rule was enforced at Nālandā we do not know. It is not impossible that the rich endowments received by Nālandā,—in majority of cases from Hindu rulers,—and its international reputation may have induced the authorities to offer free boarding and lodging to all sincere seekers after truth.

Nālandā continued to retain its fame for scholarship till its destruction at the hands of the Muslims in the beginning of the 13th century. From the Nālandā inscription of Yaśovarman[2] we learn that towards the middle of the 8th century the monastery excelled all other towns and cities on account of its scholars, who were well versed in the sacred texts and arts. In the 9th century the University continued to enjoy international reputation; Balaputradeva, a king of Java and Sumatra, being attracted by its fame, built a monastery there, and induced his friend and ally, King Devapāla of Bengal, to grant five villages for the upkeep of his

---

[1] p. 106. The practice in the medieval monasteries of Europe was also somewhat similar. Tuition was generally free and universal for all those who intended to join the Church ; small fees were sometimes voluntarily paid by the laity for the education of their children. Graves, *A History*, II, p. 31

[2] E. I., XX, p. 43.

monastery.[1] Part of this endowment was reserved for the purpose of copying books for the University library (*Dharmaratnasya lekhanārtham*).

From the 8th century onwards, the scholars at Nālandā began to play an active part in the propagation of Buddhist religion and culture in Tibet. Arrangements therefore must have been made for teaching Tibetan at the institution. Chandragomin, a Nālandā monk, who flourished at the beginning of the 8th century A. D., was the pioneer in the field. Scores of his works were translated into Tibetan; many scholars were in fact engaged in the translation work. Śāntarakshita, another Nālandā monk and scholar, was invited to Tibet by its king Khri-sren-deu-tsan in 749 A. D. for the purpose of preaching Buddhism. He was given a royal reception and the first Buddhist monastery in Tibet was built under his instructions. He became its chief abbot and vigorously helped the spread of Buddhism till his death in 762 A. D. He received very valuable cooperation in this work from Padma-sambhava, a Kashmirian monk educated at

---

[1] E. I., XVII, p. 310, Cf. :—

नालंदागुणवृन्दलुब्धमनसा भक्त्या च शौद्धोदनेः ।
नानासद्गुणभिक्षुसंघवसतिस्तस्यां विहारः कृतः ॥
...........................................

सुवर्णद्वीपाधिपमहाराजश्रीबालपुत्रदेवेन वयं विज्ञापिताः ।
यथा मया श्रीनालंदायां विहारः कृतः ।............... ॥

Nālandā.[1] Intellectual and literary activity of Nālandā must have continued in subsequent centuries also, for several manuscripts have been preserved to this time, which were copied at Nālandā during the 10th, 11th and 12th centuries A. D.

Tārānāth informs us that the professors of Vikrama-śilā were often appointed to watch over the affairs of Nālandā by the Pāla rulers.[2] From the 11th century onwards the new university of Vikramaśilā began to receive a greater share of the royal patronage; this circumstance may have led to the decline of Nālandā during the 11th and the 12th centuries. Evidence from the Tibetan sources shows that by this time Tantric religion had acquired a hold over the Buddhist mind and it may have perhaps affected the progress of serious studies. We have, however, no definite evidence on the point.

The ruin of the establishment was brought about by the Muslim invaders towards the end of the 12th century. The buildings were burnt or destroyed and a larger part of the population was put to the sword. According to the Tibetan accounts, the temples and monasteries of Nālandā were repaired after the Turushka invasion had passed off by a sage called Mudita-bhadra, and that the final destruction was brought about by the

---

[1] Bose, *Indian Teachers of Buddhist Universities*, pp. 116-31.

[2] *Ibid*, p. 36.

miraculous living embers thrown into the establishment by two exasperated Tīrthikas, who were insulted by some young novices at Nālandā.[1] Not much reliance can, however, be placed on this semi-legendary account. A similar legend about the destruction of Valabhi due to the curse of an enraged Brahmana exists, which is found to be altogether misleading.[2]

## VALABHI.

Valabhi,—modern Wala in Kathiawar,—was the capital of the Maitrakas from *c.* 475 A. D. to *c.* 775 A. D.[3] It was an important port for export and import, and we learn from Yuan Chwang that in the 7th century its warehouses were full of rarest and costliest merchandise imported from the different quarters of the globe. The city was very rich, there were a hundred, says the Chinese pilgrim, whose wealth amounted to a million.[4]

Curiously enough Yuan Chwang is altogether silent about the educational activity of the place. We would hardly have known much about Valabhi as a centre of education had not I-tsing written on the point. From him we learn that Nālandā and Valabhi

---

1 Vidyabhushana, *History of Indian Logic*, p. 561.

2 Altekar, *A History of Important Ancient Towns and Cities in Gujarat and Kathiawar*, p. 40.

3 For the history of this city, See *Ibid*, p. 39-40.

4 Beal, *A Record of the Western World*, II, p. 260.

were the two most famous centres of education in the 7th century A. D., where scholars used to stay at least for two or three years to complete their higher education. Yuan Chwang notes that there were about a hundred Buddhist monasteries at Valabhi;[1] some of them may have been very small, but at least a few must have been big establishments, conducting regular classes for higher studies. From Yuan Chwang we learn that the famous Buddhist scholars, Sthiramati and Guṇamati, were for some years in charge of the Buddhist establishment at Val.bhi, and his statement is partly confirmed by a grant of Dharasena I, dated 580 A. D., made in favour of a Vihāra, founded by the venerable Āchārya Sthiramati.[2]

Scholars from all parts of India used to assemble at Valabhi to discuss 'possible and impossible doctrines'. They used to become famous for their wisdom when they were assured of the excellence and correctness of their opinions by the doctors at Valabhi.[3] The royal family used to extend its patronage to the educational monasteries; one of them was as a matter of fact founded by princess Duḍḍā, a daughter of the aunt of king Dharasena I.[4] The famous Vihāra, founded by Sthiramati and Guṇamati, was situated at some

---

[1] *Ibid*; Watters, II, p. 246.

[2] *I. A.*, VI., p. 11.

[3] I-tsing, p. 177.

[4] *I. A.*, IV, p. 115.

distance from the city; it was probably the centre of higher studies. It had a library of its own; a fragmentary grant of Guhasena I, dated 559 A. D.,[1] makes provision, *inter alia*, for the purchase of books.

Scholars trained at Valabhi and Nālandā used to proceed to royal courts to try the sharpness of their wits, to present their schemes and to show their political talent with a view to be appointed in practical government[2] It is therefore clear that instructions in higher secular learning like law (Dharmaśāstra), economics (Arthaśāstra), accountancy and literature must have been imparted in Valabhi. Students, who were well versed only in works like the Tripīṭaka and Jātakamālā, could not have been selected for high executive and administrative posts.

Like Takshaśila and Nālandā, Valabhi also used to attract students from far and near. The *Kathā-sarit-sāgara* mentions the case of a Brahmana of the Gangetic plain sending his son to Valabhi for higher education.[3] That a Brahmana should have sent his son to Valabhi shows that it was not a centre only of Buddhist learning; unfortunately we have no data to determine the

[1] *I. A.*, VII., p. 67 ff. Cf :—सद्धर्मस्य पुस्तकोपचयार्थम् ।

[2] I-tsing, p. 177.

[3] अन्तर्वेद्यामभूत्पूर्वं वसुदत्त इति द्विजः ।
विष्णुदत्ताभिधानश्च पुत्रस्तस्योपपद्यत ॥
स विष्णुदत्तो वयसा पूर्णषोडशवत्सरः ।
गंतुं प्रववृते विद्याप्राप्तये वलभीपुरम् ॥ Chap. XXXII, 42-43.

Hindu quota to the fame of Valabhi as a centre of learning. When we remember that parents in the distant Gangetic plain were sending their sons to Valabhi for education in preference to Benares and Nālandā, which were close by, the conclusion becomes irresistible that it must have been really a very famous place of education. It is a great a pity that we should possess no detailed knowledge about so famous a centre of education, about its educational organisation, its method of teaching, its curriculum, and its subjects for specialisation.

## VIKRAMAŚILĀ.[1]

Vikramaśilā monastery, founded by king Dharmapāla in the 8th century, was a famous centre of international learning for more than four centuries. King Dharmapāla is said to have built for the establishment 108 temples and several halls, and surrounded them by a high wall. He richly endowed the monastery and made provision for the maintenance of 108 monks.[2] The monks of the establishment were

---

[1] Tibetan sources inform us that this monastery was situated in Bihar on a hill on the right bank of the Ganges. Mr. De's identification of Vikramaśilā with Patharaghata hill, 24 miles to the east of Bhagalpur, seems to be correct. The place is full of ancient and extensive ruins, and may yield a rich reward to the excavator. See *J. A. S. B., N. S.*, V. p. 7.

[2] Bose, *Indian Teachers*, pp. 30 ff.

usually distinguished scholars and the fame of the monastery soon spread beyond the Himalayas. There was a continuous intercourse going on between Tibet and Vikramaśilā for four centuries. A special guest house was maintained for the use of Tibetan scholars coming to learn at the feet of Indian Pandits.[1] One cannot help admiring the continuous tradition of high scholarship that was maintained at Vikramaśilā throughout its history. Tibetan sources inform us that Buddha, Jnānapāda, Vairochana, Rakshita, Jetārī, Ratnākara-Śānti, Jñāna-śrī-mitra, Ratnavajra, Abhayaṅkaragupta, Tathāgata-rakshita and a host of other Vikramaśilā scholars wrote numerous books in Sanskrit and translated scores of them in Tibetan. The most distinguished in this galary of Vikramaśilā scholars was undoubtedly Dīpaṅkara Śrī-Jñāna, more commonly known as Upādhyāya Atīśa, who flourished in the 11th century A. D. He went to Tibet at the invitation of its king Chan Chūb and played an important part in the reformation of the Buddhism of that country. As many as 200 books, both original and in translation, have been attributed to him by the Tibetan tradition.[2]

When there was such a distinguished galaxy of scholars at Vikramaśilā, it is but natural that the numerical strength of the establishment should have enormously increased by a large number of scholars being attracted to the establishment. In the 12th

[1] Das, *Indian Pandits in the Land of Snow*, p. 58.

[2] Bose, *Indian Teachers*, pp. 32-105.

century there were 3,000 monk scholars residing at the place.[1] The college possessed a rich and extensive library, which excited admiration even of its Muslim destroyers.

The administrative management of the Vikramaśilā establishment was entrusted by the Pāla rulers to a board of six monks presided over by the chief abbot. Different members of the board were assigned different administrative duties like the ordination of the novices, supply and supervision of servants, distribution of food and fuel, assignment of monastic work etc. Monk professors led a simple life, the cost of maintaining one of them being equal to the cost of supporting four ordinary monks.[2]

Educational administration was vested in a council of six *dvārapaṇḍitas* presided over by the chief abbot. The function of the Dvārapaṇḍita was to test the scholarship of those who saught admission to the college. During the reign of King Kanaka, the following were the Dvāra-paṇḍitas of the establishment :—

Eastern Gate : Āchārya Ratnākara-śānti
Western ,, : Vāgīśvara-kīrti of Benares
Northern ,, : Naropa
Southern ,, : Prajñākara-mati
First Central Gate : Ratna-vajra of Kashmir
Second Central Gate : Jñāna-śrī-mitra of Gauḍa[3]

1 Bose, *Indian Teachers*, p. 84.
2 *Ibid*, p. 35.
3 Vidyabhushana, *History of Indian Logic*, p. 520.

Grammar, logic, metaphysics and ritualism were the subjects specialised at the institution.

Unfortunately we have no information of the duration or the gradation of the course at Vikramaśilā, but there is every probablity that it was more systematically organised than was the case at any other centre of Ancient Indian Education. For, unlike at any other college, we find diplomas and titles being given to the Vikramaśilā students at the end of their course by the reigning kings of Bengal. Tibetan authorities inform us that Jetāri and Ratnavajra had received diplomas at the hands of kings Mahīpāla and Kanaka respectively.[1] The memory of the distinguished alumni of the place was kept ever green in the mind of the congregation by their pictures being put on the walls of the college halls. This honour is known to have been shown to Nāgārjuna and Atīśa.

In 1203, the Vikramaśilā monastery was destroyed by the Mahomadens under Bakhtyar Khilji, who seem to have mistaken it for a fort. At that time Śākya-śribhadra was at the helm of the monastic affairs. The account of the destruction of the monastery has been preserved by the author of *Tabākāt-i-nāsiri*. We read : 'The greater number of the inhabitants of the place were Brahmanas (i. e. Buddhist Bhikshus) and the whole of these Brahmanas had their heads shaven, and they were all slain. There were a great number of books

[1] Bose, *Indian Teachers*, pp. 47, 61.

on the religion of the Hindus there, and when all these books came under the observation of the Mussalmans, they summoned a number of Hindus that they might give them information respecting the import of these books; but the whole of the Hindus had been killed. On becoming aquainted (with the contents of these books), it was found that the whole fortress and city was a college'[1]

Śākya-śrī-bhadra and a few others, who escaped the general slaughter, fled to Tibet. Such was the tragic end of this famous college.

## SOME OTHER BUDDHIST MONASTIC CENTRES OF EDUCATION.

Nālandā, Valabhi and Vikramaśilā were not the only monastic colleges promoting the cause of learning and scholarship. The Buddha had laid down that every monk should be trained for ten years after his admission to the Order. The training was to be not only in spiritual practices but also in higher literature, for the novice had to be taught the Tripīṭaka and various other Sūtras and religious works,—which required a thorough grounding in Pali and Sanskrit languages,—as also grammar, logic, and metaphysics. In the beginning the senior monks used to educate only the novices who had entered the Order; but it was soon discovered that

1 Raverty's translation of *Tabākāt-i-Nāsiri*, Vol. I, p. 552; (1881).

the best way of getting a good supply of novices of the right type and of propagating the religion was to mould the pliant minds of young children by taking up the education of the rising generation. From about the 5th century A. D., if not from a little earlier date, the Buddhist monasteries began to take an active interest in fostering the cause of education.[1]

From the Travels and Life of Yuan Chwang we get a fragmentary account of some of those monstic colleges with which India was strewn in the 7th century A. D. Jayendra monastery near the capital of Kashmir was a famous centre of education. The venerable

[1] It is interesting to note that in Europe also from about the 6th to the 11th century A. D. education was centred in monasteries. The causes were somewhat similar. Monks were required to read, so they had to be taught. They must have books and they must in turn teach novices to read and copy manuscripts. Hence arose monastic schools. After the closure of all the pagan schools by Justinian's decree in 529 A. D., monasteries became the sole schools for teaching. "They offered the only professional training, they were the only Universities of research ; they alone served as publishing houses for the multiplication of books ; they were the only libraries for the preservation of learning ; they produced the only scholars. It was not till the 11th century that there was any education to speak of outside monastic schools, and not till the 13th century that there occurred marked changes in the character of education given in any institution ; until then all these schools were taught by monks." Monroe, *A Text Book*, pp. 255-261.

abbot of the place was a scholar of eminent parts; he used to expound the Kośa-śāstra in the forenoon, the Nyāyānusāra śāstra in the afternoon and the Hetu-vidyā at night. On these occasions, says the biographer of Yuan Chwang, all learned men of the province used to assemble without exception to hear his discourses.[1] The fact that Yuan Chwang found it necessary to spend two years in this convent for the purpose of his studies would show that the place must have been a famous centre of learning. It possessed a good library also; Yuan Chwang had employed twenty clerks for two years to copy the books he wanted to take with him.

Chinapati monastery in the Punjab was also a good centre of learning. Its abbot Vinīta-prabha was a distinguished scholar, who had composed commentaries on the *Pañcha-skandha-śāstra* and *Vidyā-mātra-siddhi-tridaśa-śāstra.* Yuan Chwang had to spend fourteen months at this monastry in order to learn what it could teach.[2]

In Jalandar monastery Yuan Chwang stayed for four months for studying *Prakaraṇa-pāda-vibhāshā-śāstra,*[3] in Matipura monastery (Bijnor district) for six months for studying *Tattvasatya-śāstra* and *Abhi-dharma-jñāna-prasthāna-śāstra,*[4] in the Bhadra Vihāra (at Kanauj) for three months for studying *Varma-*

[1] Beal, *Life*, p. 69-70.
[2] *Ibid*, p. 76.
[3] *Ibid*, p. 77.
[4] *Ibid*, p. 81.

*vibhāshā-vyākaraṇa*[1] (?), in a monastery in Hiraṇya (?) country for one year for studying *Vibhāshā*, *Nyāyānuśāsana*, and other *śāstras*,[2] and in the Amaraoti monastery (in Āndhradeśa) for several months for studying the *Mūlābhidharma* and other *śāstras*.[3] All these must have been notable places of learning. Unfortunately we have no information about the Buddhist monasteries of later centuries. Buddism was then on the decline, and so there may have been a set back to the educaticnal activities as well. But there is ample evidence available to show that in provinces like Bihar and Bengal where it was flourishing, its monasteries continued to be centres of learning. The cases of Nālandā and Vikramaśilā have been already discussed. A few others are also known. Jagadalla Vihāra, founded by king Rāmapāla at his capital Rāmāvati towards the end of the 12th century, was a famous centre of Buddhist and Tibetan scholarship for more than a century. The same was the case of the Vihāra at Odantapurī. We may not therefore be wrong in concluding that about ten per cent of the well endowed Buddhist monasteries were respectable centres of education, at least of the status of the modern Intermediate colleges.

## Hindu Temple Colleges.

Hindu temples and Buddhist monasteries expressed the spirit of the age from *c.* 400 A. D. to *c.* 1200 A. D.

---

[1] *Ibid*, p. 84. [2] *Ibid*, p. 127. [3] *Ibid*, p. 137.

as ports, factories and railway stations do of the modern time. It is definitely known that educational activity became a part of the daily monastic life from *c.* 500 A. D.; it is, however, only in the 10th century that we get evidence of Hindu temples becoming centres of higher education. It is quite possible that temples began to undertake the educational duty much earlier, though we have yet no evidence on the point.

## SALOTGI TEMPLE COLLEGE.

The village of Salotgi in Bijapur district was a famous centre of learning in the 10th and 11th centuries A. D. The Sanskrit college that flourished at this place must have existed for a long time, for it has transformed the original name of the place, Pāviṭṭage, into Sāloṭgi, which is an abbreviated and prakritised compound of Śālā and Pāviṭṭage. From one of the inscriptions at this place,[1] we learn that the college was located in a spacious hall, attached to the temple of Trayī-Purusha, which was built by Nārāyaṇa, a minister of the Rāshṭrakūṭa emperor Kṛishṇa III. Owing to its far spread fame for efficiency the colloge could attract students from different parts of the country. The strength of the college is not known, but it seems that 27 houses were necessary for lodging the students. An endowment of 12 Nivartans (probably equal to 60 acres) of land was made for meeting the lighting charges of the boarding houses. The students were

[1] *E. I.*, IV, p. 60.

offered free boarding, an endowment of 500 Nivartanas having been received for that purpose. It would appear that at least 200 students were offered free food, lodging and education at this institution. The salary of the principal was provided for by another endowment of 50 Nivartanas. The inscription is silent about the salaries of the other teachers.

The inhabitants of the village were not slow to appreciate the benefits of the institution; they had agreed to offer to the college a donation of five coins at every marriage, of two and half coins at every Upanayana and of a coin and quarter at every tonsure ceremony. Besides, whenever a feast was given in the village, the host was expected to invite as many teachers and students as possible. A later inscription from the same place informs us that when the college hall built by the minister of Kṛishṇa III in 945 A. D. collapsed in the next century, it was rebuilt by a local magnate.[1]

The inscription does not give us any information about the curriculum of the institution. Very probably it was a Vedic college.[2]

---

[1] *Ibid*, p. 64.

[2] The relevant verses from the inscription are given below:—

नारायणोऽभिधानेन नारायण इवापरः ।<br>
प्रधानः कृष्णराजस्य मन्त्री सन्सन्धिविग्रहे ॥<br>
तेनेयं कारिता शाला श्रीविशाला मनोरमा ।<br>
अत्र विद्यार्थिनः संति नानाजनपदोद्भवाः ।

*P. T. O.*

## ENNĀYIRAM TEMPLE COLLEGE.[1]

At the beginning of the 11th century A. D., there existed a famous and well managed Sanskrit college at Ennāyiram in South Arcot district. The local village community had endowed the institution with 45 Velis (equal to about 300 acres) of land, thus enabling the authorities to offer free tuition, boarding and lodging to 340 students. The admission of students to the college was governed by the principle of reservation of a fixed number of seats for different subjects as shown by the following table :—

| | | | | | |
|---|---|---|---|---|---|
| 75 | seats | for the | students of | the | Ṛigveda |
| 75 | ,, | ,, | ,, | ,, | Kṛishṇa Yajurveda |
| 20 | ,, | ,, | ,, | ,, | Chāndogya Sāmaveda |
| 20 | ,, | ,, | ,, | ,, | Tālavachāra ,, |
| 20 | ,, | ,, | ,, | ,, | Śukla Yajurveda |
| 10 | ,, | ,, | ,, | ,, | Atharvaveda |

---

(*Continued from the last page.*)

शालाविद्यार्थिसंधाय दत्तवान्भूमिमुत्तमाम् ।
मान्यां निवर्तनानां तु पंचभिश्च शतैर्मिताम् ॥
निवर्तनानि दीपार्थं मान्यानि द्वादशैव च ।
पंच पुष्पाणि देयानि विवाहे सति तज्जनैः ।
देयं तथोपनयने विवाहे यत्पुरोदितम् ॥
केनचित्कारणेनेह कर्तव्ये विप्रभोजने ।
भोजयेत्तु यथाशक्ति परिषत्परिषज्जनम् ॥

[1] *S. I. E. R.* for 1918, p. 145; Inscription No. 333 of 1917.

10 seats for the students of the Bauddhāyana Gṛihya-sūtra
40 " " " " Rūpāvatāra (?)
25 " " " " Grammar
35 " " " " Prabhākara Mīmānsā
10 " " " " Vedānta.

For the Ṛigveda and Kṛishṇa Yajurveda there were three teachers each, for the Mīmānsā two, and for the rest of the subjects one each. It will be thus seen that the highest number of students reading under one teacher was 25 and the average number of students per teacher was about 22. Some teachers had only 10 students to look after. Students must have received personal instructions and attention. Big classes, to which we are accustomed at present, were unknown in this institution.

The inscription supplies interesting information about daily rations given to the students. Every Vedic student received six Nālis or ¾th Karuṇi of paddy per day, and half a Kaḷañju of gold (roughly equal to 25 grains costing about Rs. 2) per year. At this time one Karuṇi of paddy was sufficient for one sumptuous feast; so the rations allowed to the Vedic student were sufficient for his daily needs as he was expected to lead a simple and frugal life. Half a Kaḷañju in gold that was given annually to every student was probably intended to meet the cost of clothing. Every student of Mīmānsā, Vedānta and grammar received an allowance which was about 66 percent higher than that sanctioned for the Vedic student. The reason for this preferential treatment is not given in the document. It may be that a higher scholarship was offered for these subjects because they were relatively difficult. It is also not impossible that students of these subjects may have been more advanced in age and may therefore have received a more liberal allowance, perhaps to meet their family responsibilities. At this time child marriages had already come into vogue.

This record gives us detailed and interesting information about the salaries of the various teachers. The normal allowance for the teacher was one Kaḷam or 12 Karuṇi of paddy per diem and half a Kaḷañju of gold per anum. The cost of the ordinary meal was three fourths of a Karuṇi per day; an ordinary Sanskrit teacher was thus getting as his salary just three times the amount necessary for the food expenses of a family of five adults. It will be thus seen that the Brahmana teacher at Ennāyiram was satisfied with a humble salary, just sufficient for his normal family responsibilities. He was neither rolling in riches nor suffering from abject poverty. The Vedānta was regarded as an abstruse subject and its teacher received an extra allowance of 25 percent. The teacher of grammar was curiously enough paid only in cash; he was given one Kaḷañju (equal to about two-fifths of a Tola) of gold per chapter of the *Ashṭādhyāyī*. Why he alone was paid in this way we do not know.

It will be seen that this institution was a regularly organised college of the modern type, where thirteen teachers were working together for carrying out the courses of the different branches included in the eurriculum. Unfortunately the inscription supplies us no information about the school hours, holidays, vacation and the duration of the various courses.

## TIRUMUKKUDAL TEMPLE COLLEGE.

Venkatesh Perumal Temple at Tirumukkudal in Chingleput district was a very interesting institution. From an inscription, dated 1068 A. D.[1], we learn that it had a college, a hostel and a hospital attached to it. This college was a smaller institution than the one at Ennāyiram, for arrangement was here made for the free boarding and lodging of 60 students only. Out of the 60 seats in the hostel, 10 were reserved for the students of the Ṛigveda, 10 for those of the Yajurveda, 20 for those of grammar, 10 for those of the Pañcha-rātra system, 3 for those of Śivāgama and 7 for Vānaprasthas and Sanyāsins. Hostel students were provided with mats and oil for bath every Saturday.

The teachers' salaries in this institution were lower than those in the Ennāyiram college. Vedic teachers used to receive only sixty Kaḷams of paddy and four Kāsus of gold per anum; their salary was thus about one sixth the salary that was paid in the Ennāyiram

---

[1] *E. I.*, XXI; No. 185 of *S. I. E. R.*, 1915.

college. Vedic teachers of this institution were apparently part-time teachers; for their salary is seen to be practically the same as the wages of the servant appointed in the temple hospital for fetching medicinal herbs and preparing medicines. The latter used to receive 60 Kaḷams of paddy and two Kāsus of gold per anum. The grammar teacher used to reccive 120 Kaḷams of paddy and 10 Kāsus of gold per anum. 10 Kāsus were equal to about 35 Kaḷams of paddy; so the salary of the Tirumukkudul grammar teacher was about one half the salary of the Ennāyīram grammarian. It was just sufficient for the ordinary needs of a Brahmana family. As in modern times so in ancient days also, the salaries varied in different institutions probably in accordance with their financial circumstances.

## TIRUVORRIYUR TEMPLE COLLEGE.

Towards the end of the 13th century there was a big grammar college at Tiruvorriyur in Chingleput district. Unfortunately the record, which contains detailed information about this institution, has not yet been published in full; only a brief report has appeared in the Annual Report of Epigraphy for the year 1912.[1] From this summary we learn that the college was located in a big hall adjoining the local Siva temple. There was a local tradition that God Śiva had appeared in this very temple before Pāṇini for fourteen

[1] No. 201 of 1912.

continuous days in order to teach him the first fourteen aphorisms; the village community had therefore organised an efficient grammer college in the Śiva temple. This college was a much bigger institution than the Ennāyiram college. In the latter place an endowment of 45 Velis had enabled the organisers to arrange for the free food and education of 340 students. The Tiruvorriyur college had received an endowment of 60 Velis; we may not be therefore far wrong iu assuming that this grammar college must have had more than 450 students on its rool call. The number of teachers was probably about 20 to 25.

This college went on performing its functions down to the 14th century; for a record, about a century later than the previous one, mentions how certain additional taxes were assigned for the upkeep of the Vyākaraṇa college.[1] Further information about this college cannot be obtained unless the two records, referred to above, are published in extenso.

### MALKAPURAM TEMPLE COLLEGE.

An inscription from Malkapuram in Guntur district, dated 1268 A. D., reveals the existence of another institution which was a temple, college, hostel and hospital combined. Unfortunately only a summary of this important epigraph has so far been published,[2] which hardly gives any adequate idea of the various

---

1 No. 110 of 1912.

2 *S. I. E. R.*, for 1917, pp. 122-24.

institutions centred in the temple. There were eight teachers in the college, three for the Vedic branch and five for the remaining subjects, viz. grammar, literature, logic and Āgamas. There was one doctor in charge of the hospital. In the south Indian colleges we have seen so far, there used to be about 20 students on the average under the charge of each teacher. The Malkapuram college therefore had probably about 150 students. They were, as usual, offered free food, lodging and education.

Each teacher was given an endowment of two *puṭṭis* of land. We do not know anything about the net income of this land endowment. The inscription, however, states that the carpenters and drummers of the temple establishment were assigned one *puṭṭi* of land for their wages. The teacher's income was thus twice the wages of the skilled labourer. The society was offering him just what was necessary for a decent family life. The salary of the principal is given as 100 *nishkas*; it is difficult to assess its real amount as the denotation of the term *nishka* at this period is not definitely known.

## SOME OTHER TEMPLE EDUCATION CENTRES.

We have got somewhat detailed information about the free Sanskrit colleges that were organised in the five temple establishments mentioned above. There are, however, clear indications that there were many more similar temple colleges in the Deccan in the medieval times (*c.* 900—*c.* 1400 A. D.).

At Hebbal in Dharwar district there existed a Maṭha in Bhujabbeśvara temple in the 10th century A. D.; an inscription, dated 975 A. D., records the grant of 50 *mattars* (probably equal to 200 acres) of land for this Maṭha, where students were given education and food free[1]. The Jaṭiga Rāmeśvara temple on a hill in Chitaldurg district had obtained a grant in 1064 A. D. for defraying the expenses of the temple, and for education[2]. In 1075 A. D., a temple at Bijapur received a big endowment of 300 *mattars* (equal to about 1200 acres) of land for providing food and raiments to ascetics and pupils of Yogeśvara Paṇḍita, who was conducting a free Mīmānsā school there[3]. At Tavargere in Karnatak there existed in 1083 A. D. a *sattra* attached to a local temple, where among others, students were offered free food.[4] At Managoli in Belgaum district during the latter half of the 12th century a local temple used to maintain a grammar school where Kaumāra grammar was taught by a teacher who was given an endowment of four *mattars* or 20 acres of land.[5] At about the same time the Dakshiṇeśvara temple authorities at Belgamve in Karnatak used to offer free boarding to students studying in the temple school.[6] In 1158 A. D. there flourished at Talgund in Shikarpur district a small Sanskrit college in the local Prāṇeśvara temple, where free food

[1] *E. I.*, IV, p. 355.
[2] *Ibid*, p. 214.
[3] *I. A.*, X, pp. 129-31.
[4] *Ibid*, V, p. 344.
[5] *E. I.*, V. p, 22.
[6] *E. C.*, I, No. 45.

and education was offered to 48 students, studying the Ṛigveda, the Yajurveda, the Sāmaveda, Prabhākara-Mīmānsā, Vedānta, Bhāshā-śāstra and Canarese.[1] The institution had employed two cooks to manage the kitchen of the boarding house. At Punnavayil in Tanjore District there existed another grammar college, attached to a local temple and endowed with 60 *Velis* of land. As the endowment for the maintenance of this institution was richer than that enjoyed by the Ennāyiram college, it is quite likely that it may have offered free education and food to about 500 students.[2] South Indian Inscriptions Nos. 604, 667, 671, and 695 of 1916 record various grants for the salaries of teachers and boarding of students studying in different temple colleges in Chola country. The last of these records is an interesting one, for it records a donation for a *Sarasvatī-bhavana* or library of a temple college in Tinevelli district.

The above instances of temple authorities organising Sanskrit schools and colleges are typical of the age. Many more existed, whose memory has not been handed down to the present times. For, down to the 18th century every religious centre in south India used to maintain a Sanskrit Pāṭha-śālā. The whole country was in fact studded with them.[3]

1 *E. C.*, VII, Shikarpur, No 185.

2 *S. I. E. R.* for 1913, pp. 109-110.

3 *Report of the Madras Committee, Education Commission*, 1882. P. 1, foot-note.

Instances of temple colleges given above all hail from South India. It is not however correct to suppose that no such institutions existed in North India, because they are not referred to in any north Indian inscriptions. A very large number of north Indian temples have been destroyed, along with their documents of antiquity, during the Muslim invasions and rule. The temple authorities in the north do not seem to have generally followed the excellent method of the south of engraving public donations along with their purposes on the temple walls. If all the documents conveying extensive properties to most of the rich temples in north and south India are recovered, it would be almost certainly found that a considerable portion of the temple property was originally intended for educational purposes.

## AGRAHĀRA VILLAGES AS CENTRES OF EDUCATION.

Among the copper plate grants that have been so far discovered a large number records the settlements of Brahmana colonies in villages exclusively assigned to them for their maintenance. Such villages were known as Agrahāra villages. The donee Brahmanas of these grants are usually described as being zealous in discharging their six-fold traditional duty. One of the most important of these duties was teaching, and it is therefore almost certain that most of these villages were centres of higher education, where the Vedas and various other branches of Sanskrit learning were taught free to those who were anxious to learn them.

The definite information, which we possess about some of the Agrahāra villages, confirms the above conclusion. The village of Kādiyur, modern Kalas, was made an Agrahāra village in the 10th century by the Rāshṭrakūṭa administration, and assigned to 200 Brahmanas. The Kalas inscription describes these donees as well versed in Vedas, grammar, Purāṇa, Nyāya, works on polity, the science of literary composition and the art of writing commentaries.[1] Verse No. 30 of the record says 'Are there not combined in Kādiyur a surrounding sanctuary, an assembly hall, a *sattra* (free feeding house), a fountain and *a brilliant dispensation of lore?*' It seems that an Agrahāra village was expected to be a centre of higher education, and the inhabitants of Kadiyur are recording with satisfaction their compliance with this unwrittten but nevertheless obligatory condition of Agrahāra grants. The main purpose of the Kalas inscription is to record a further endowment, part of which was reserved for the salaries of teachers. It may be pointed out that the educational activity of this Brahmana centre was not confined to the Vedic studies only; poetics, grammar, logic, Purāṇas and the political science were included in the curriculum.

There is no information as to whether the students, who were studying at Kalas, used to receive free lodging and boarding as well. It was beyond the

---

[1] *E. I*, XIII, p. 317.

normal capacity of an Agrahāra Brahmana community to defray the boarding expenses of students. Very probably free boarding arrangements existed only in those Agrahāra villages, where special donations were received for that purpose.

Sarvajñapura (modern Arsikere in Hassan District, Mysore) was another Agrahāra village, which, as its name would indicate, was another Agrahāra centre of learning. An inscription discovered at this place gives us a graphic description of its literary and pedagogic activities. "In some of its streets the Brahmanas were reading the Vedas, Śāstras and six systems of philosophy ; every group of Brahmanas was either reading the Vedas or engaged in listening to the exposition of some higher science, or carrying on ceaseless discussion on logic, or joyously reciting the Purāṇas or settling the meaning of the Smṛitis, drama or poetry. All the Brahmanas of Sarvajñapura were devoted to study, teaching and listening to the dictates of religion and morality."[1]

What we know specifically of these two Agrahāra villages would render it highly probable that the vast majority of such Brahmana village colonies were centres of higher education, where free instructions were given in different branches of Sanskrit learning by the Brahmana donees in return for the generous provision made for their livelihood by the state or society.

[1] *E. C.*, V, p. 144.

Agrahāra villages and endowed temples and monasteries were fairly numerous ; there used to be at least two or three of them in an area equal to a modern district. We may therefore well conclude that centres for higher education were more numerous in medieval times (*c*. 600-1300 A. D.) than they exist today in British India.

Before concluding this chapter, it will be necessary to refer to *Tols* or Sanskrit Pāṭhśālās, which are still fairly numerous in Bengal and Bihar. From early times, some of the Tols have enjoyed grants of land, on which their teachers and pupils subsisted. These grants were augmented in value and new ones were created, when the *Z*amindars felt themselves secure by the Permanent Settlement of Lord Cornwalis.[1] Tols in such cases are a variety of the Agrahāra type of educational institutions.

Where there is no specific endowment, the teacher subsists on voluntary gifts and arranges for the free boarding, lodging and clothing of his students by collecting the necessary funds by raising subscriptions at chief fairs and festivals.

The classes are usually held in a thatched chamber. As a rule each Tol enrolls about 25 students who are accommodated in mud huts built round the lecture room. The teacher manages to procure the funds necessary

---

[1] *Report of the Bengal Provincial Committee, Education Commission*, 1882.

for the maintenance of these tenements. Study courses usually extend over eight or ten years.

It is indeed noteworthy that such tradition of free education should have persisted in spite of foreign rule of several centuries. Learned Brahmanas in India have always been anxious to impart education free to deserving students irrespective of their own financial condition. This tradition exists even today in ancient centres of Sanskrit education like Benares, Nasik and Wai.

The conclusion therefore seems to be irresistible that in the ancient and medieval period of Indian history, every student, howsoever poor he may have been, could get the highest education free, provided he was willing, if necessary, to do some manual or menial work for his teacher or institution. Poor parents had not to worry about the education expenses, their sons could either find admission to free boarding houses or maintain themselves by begging their food daily, which was regarded as the most honorable means of livelihood for the student.

# CHAPTER IX

## SOCIETY, STATE AND EDUCATION.

Since very early times Hindu society has been alive to the vital importance of education. As early as the Ṛigveda, speech and literature were regarded as divine, and men were exhorted to cultivate them both. Gods befriend only those who are learned. Men are equal to one another as far as the number of hands and feet, and ears and eyes is concerned, superiority arises only out of developed intellect. Learning however did not mean merely the capacity to recite from memory, understanding of meaning was most essential. Sarasvatī or the Goddess of Learning reveals her full charm only to him who understands what he recites. Others are merely beasts of burden.[1]

In the later Vedic period, still higher reverence was shown to learning. A hymn in the Atharvaveda asserts that Indra attained preeminence among gods through the training he received during his Brahma-

[1] यज्ञेन वाचः पदवीयमायंस्तामन्वविन्दन् ऋषिषु प्रविष्टाम् ॥ X, 71, 3.
उत त्वं सख्ये स्थिरपीतमाहुर्नैनं हिन्वंत्यपि वाजिनेषु ॥ X, 71, 5.
अक्षण्वंतः कर्णवन्तः सखायो मनोजवेषु असमा बभूवुः ॥ X, 71, 7.
उत त्वः पश्यन्न ददर्श वाचमुत त्वः शृण्वन्न शृणोत्येनाम् ।
उतो त्वस्मै तन्वं विसस्रे जायेव पत्ये उशती सुवासाः ॥ X, 71, 4.
Cf. also स्थाणुरयं भारहारः किलाभूदधीत्य वेदं न विजानाति योऽर्थम् ॥ *Nirukta*, I, 18.

charya.[1] If cosmic functions take place regularly, it is due to the mystic merit of the Brahmacharya of the rising generation. One of the three debts, which a person contracts at the time of the birth, is *ṛishi-ṛiṇa* or the debt to the savants of the bye-gone ages, which can be liquidated only by a study of their contributions to knowledge and literature.[2] The *Kāṭhaka and* the *Mitrāyaṇīya Saṁhitās* assert that it is not parentage but learning that determines Brahmanahood[3]. The *Taittirīya Saṁhitā* concurs and declares that he alone is Brahmana, who is wise and well-read[4]. It was on behalf of such Brahmanas or learned men that it was claimed that they were above temporal jurisdiction, they were to be governed by their own conscience as developed by their liberal and religious education.[5]

Passages in later literature in glorification of learning and education are numerous and well known, and therefore only a few may be referred to here. The parable mentioned in *Manusmṛiti* of God Brahmā

---

1 XI, 5, 19.

2 *T. S.*, VI, 3, 10, 5; Sa. *Br.*, I, 5, 5, 1-5.

3 किं ब्राह्मणस्य पितरं किमु पृच्छसि मातरम्।
श्रुतं चेदस्मिन्वेद्यं स पिता स पितामहः॥
*M. S.*, 48, 1, 107; *K. S.*, 30, 1.

4 एष वै ब्राह्मण ऋषिरार्षेयः यः शुश्रुवान्॥ VI, 6, 1, 4.

5 *Śa. Br.*, V, 4, 2, 3. Soma, whom Brahmanas recognised as their king, was obviously intended to stand for conscience as developed by liberal and religious education.

justifying the conduct of young Aṅgiras in addressing his old pupils as 'my boys' on the ground that he was their senior by learning is very instructive in this respect.[1] Manu emphatically asserts that it is learning, and neither age nor wealth nor descent, which redounds to the glory of a human being.[2] One poet points out how Vidyā (learning) is at the root of human happiness.[3] Another shows how learning is the best variety of wealth; it is most precious, it is increased by giving to others and cannot be stolen by thieves or robbers.[4] Learning is verily a desire-yielding creeper (*kalpa-latā*); there is hardly anything which it cannot accomplish. It protects us like the mother, directs us to the right path like the father, and gives us delight like the wife and makes us wealthy and famous.[5]

In ancient times religion had a great hold over the popular mind; it is therefore but natural that the Hindu society should have enlisted its help for

---

[1] II, 151-2.

[2] न हायनैर्न पलितैर्न वित्तेन न बंधुभिः। ऋषयश्चक्रिरे धर्मं योऽनूचानः स नो महान्॥ II, 154.

[3] विद्या ददाति विनयं विनयाद्याति पात्रताम्। पात्रत्वाद्धनमाप्नोति धनाद्धर्मं ततः सुखम्॥

[4] सर्वद्रव्येषु विद्यैव धनमाहुरनुत्तमम्। अहार्यत्वादनर्घ्यत्वादक्षयत्वाच्च सर्वदा॥

[5] मातेव रक्षति पितेव हिते नियुंक्ते कान्तेव चापि रमयत्यपनीय खेदम्। लक्ष्मीं तनोति वितनोति च दिक्षु कीर्तिं किं किं न साधयति कल्पलतेव विद्या॥

emphasising the vital importance of education. It made Upanayana a compulsory Sanskāra with a view to ensure the universal spread, not of primary, but of higher education. There are as many as 40 Sanskāras referred to in early texts;[1] but significantly enough Upanayana alone amongst them was made a compulsory Sanskāra and raised to the dignity of the spiritual birth. If this Sanskāra is not performed and the child is left uneducated, it falls from its Aryan status. Social thinkers had realised that nothing that can be done in subsequent life will make up the deficiency wrought by the neglect of education at the proper time.

Hindu thinkers have expressed their high appreciation of the achievements of a full-developed youth, who has completed his proper course of education, by prescribing Samāvartana Sanskāra in his honour. It should be noted that this Sanskāra was not intended to be a meaningless ritual to be performed on the morrow of Upanayana or the eve of marriage, as is the case at present. Only those, who had finished their complete course of education and observed Brahmacharya discipline, were entitled to it. It was intended to express the social appreciation of the effort of the rising generation to carry forward the torch of learning. We have seen already how one of the elements in the ritual embodies the belief that even the sun owes his refulgence to the

---

1 *E. g.*, *Gau. Dh S.*, I, 8, 8.

brilliance of the well-trained intellect of the Snātaka.[1] The Snātaka was to be taken to the assembly of the learned in a chariot or on an elephant. The honour of the *Madhuparka* was reserved for a select few, and even these were to expect it only once in the year. A Snātaka, however, was to be offered *Madhuparka* as often as he visited one's household. Only the king shared this privilege with the Snātaka, but he had to give precedence to the latter on the royal road.[2]

Youths may be well educated but they may slip back into ignorance. This tragedy we see every day. Hindu social thinkers attempted to avert this calamity by prescribing *Svādhyāya* as one of the compulsory daily religious duties. Under the scheme of the *Pañcha-mahā-yajñas*, every householder was daily required to spend some time over *Svādhyāya*, when he was required to recapitulate a portion of what he had learnt during his studenthood. A further step was taken with the same end in view by making Upākarma compulsory for all, and thus drawing the attention of society to the necessity of devoting some time of the year for revising and adding to our knowledge gained during our student life.[3]

Hindu society has expressed its high sense of reverence for learning by holding in special veneration

---

1 *Ante*, p. 40.

2 *Manusmriti*, II, 139.

3 *Ante*, pp. 30-2.

those scholars, who, controlling their natural instincts, devote their whole life to the cause of learning and education. Such scholars were known as Naisṭhika Brahmachārins and Hindu religion promises them the highest salvation. How pious was their life, how intense their love of learning and how high the honour that society showed to them must have already become clear to the reader from Yuan Chwang's description of and tribute to these Naishṭhika Brahmachārins which has been already quoted.[1]

Duty to teach, which was imperative on a learned Brahmana, was regarded by the Hindu society so vitally important that the normal rules of *Āśaucha* (ceremonial impurity after a relative's death) were suspended in his case with a view to avoid interruptions in the education of the rising generation. The usual period of impurity on a relative's death is of ten days, but it is contracted to one day only in the case of a learned and pious Brahmana,[2] and abolished altogether in the case of a Brahmachārin.[3] Society obviously felt that no causes, even of a religious nature, should impede a student's progress in education. He must go on continuously with his work. His teacher too was assigned the minimnm period of impurity consistent with the requirements of religion and decency.

---

[1] *Ante*, pp. 114-5.

[2] एकाहाच्छुध्यते विप्रो योऽग्निवेदसमन्वितः । *Parāśara-smriti*, III, 5.

[3] *Manusmriti*, v, 93.

It is well known that perpetuation of the race by the procreation of progeny is enjoined in Hindu religion. What is, however, not equally well known and therefore deserves to be specially pointed out is that Hinduism does not hold that the debt to the manes is discharged merely by bringing forth children. It will continue to remain unliquidated as long as children are not properly educated. The *Bṛihadāraṇyakopanishad* points out that a father ought to train his son properly, for it is only a properly educated son who can be of any spiritual benefit to his father.[1] Mādhavāchārya concurs with this view and holds that the father's duty does not terminate at the birth of the son. It rather commences at that point, for the father has to see to it that his sons are properly educated and become qualified to carry on the torch of learning to the succeeding generation.[2] Howsoever poor a father or guardian may be, he was required to give some elementary training to his son with a view to make him qualified for the study of a portion of the Vedic literature after his Upanayana. A few rich persons may have now and then neglected their sons' education,[3] but the attitude of the average guardian in ancient India was different. Indian

---

1 तस्मात्पुत्रमनुशिष्टं लोक्यमाहुस्तस्मादेनमनुशास्ति । I, 5, 7.

2 न हि पुत्रजननमात्रेण पितुरानृण्यम् । किं तर्हि सम्यगनुशिष्टेन पुत्रेण शास्त्रीयेषु कर्मस्वनुष्ठितेषु पितुरानृण्यं संपद्यते । Vol. I, part ii, p. 107.

3 We get one such case in Ruru Jātaka (No. 482) where we come across a rich merchant not educating his son, thinking that he would find it a weariness of flesh.

society continued to show deep concern for education down to the advent of the British rule. Describing the state of education in the Punjab towards the middle of the 19th century, Dr. Leitner observes, "Respect for learning has always been the redeeming feature of the East. To this the Punjab formed no exception. Torn by invasion and civil war, it ever preserved and added to educational institutions. The most unscrupulous chief, the avaricious money-lender and even the free-booter vied with the small moneylender in making peace with his conscience by founding schools and rewarding the learned. There was not a mosque, a temple or a Dharmaśālā that had not a school attached to it to which the youth flocked chiefly for religious education. There were few wealthy men who did not entertain a Maulavi, a Pandit or a Guru to teach their sons, and along with them the sons of their friends and dependents. There were hundreds of religious men who gratuitously taught their coreligionists, and sometimes all comers, for the sake of God. There was not a single villager who did not take pride in devoting a portion of his produce to a respected teacher."[1] For obvious reasons the reverence for education in other parts of India in the ancient period could not have been less sincere and deep than it was in the Punjab at the advent of the British rule.

---

[1] *A History of Indigenous Education in the Punjab*, p. 1, Indian Education Commission 1882.

Hindu society tried to express its sympathy for the cause of education by a variety of ways. *Vidyādāna* or the gift of knowledge was regarded as the highest variety of gift.[1] Gift of land was no doubt superior to most other types of charity, but its merit was undoubtedly excelled by that arising from the gift of Vidyā. That society accepted this view would become clear from several donations to educational institutions brought to light by inscriptions. An inscription from Kudarkot belonging to the 8th century A. D. records the erection of a building for a Vedic school by a Brahmana in memory of his son Takshadatta. Both the father and the son are described in the record as well versed in the Vedas.[2] Nārāyaṇa, a minister of Kṛishṇa III of the Rāshṭrakūṭa dynasty, built a hall for the Sanskrit college at Salotgi in Bijapur district in 945 A. D. A local magnate of the locality gave 200 *Nivartanas* of land for the maintenance of the college.[3] Chaṅgadeva, a grandson of Bhāskarāchārya the famous astronomer and mathematician, is known to have founded an astronomical college at Pāṭaṇa in Khandesh for the study of astronomy in general and of his grandfather's works in particular.[4] At Metungi in

---

[1] स्वसहस्रंमिता धेनुरनड्वान्दशधेनवः। दशानुडुत्समं यानं दशयानसमं हयः॥ दशवाजिसमा कन्या भूमिदानं च तत्समम्। भूमिदानात्परं नास्ति विद्यादानं ततोऽधिकम्। Bṛihaspati quoted in *SCS.*, p. 145.

[2] *E. I.*, I, p. 180.

[3] *E. I.*, IV, p. 60.

[4] *E. I.*, I, p. 30.

Bijapur district, a college was founded by Perumal, a Hoysal minister, in 1290 A. D. where Sanskrit, Canarese and Marathi were taught along with the Vedas and other Sāstras.[1] The Sanskrit college at Ennāyiram, where 340 students were being educated and fed free, was being financed out of the endowment of the local village community.[2] A divisional officer at Soratur in Belgaum district is known to have made a grant of about 50 acres of land for the purpose of promoting education.[3] A piece of land of similar dimensions was given for the same purpose by the Belur village community in 1022 A. D.[4] A citizen of Hadale in Dharwar district is known to have given 20 acres of land in 1084 A. D. for the purpose of feeding and clothing students.[5] A rich guild was maintaining a Sanskrit college at Dambal in Dharwar district during the 12th century.[6]

Several inscriptions have been discovered granting endowments for the creation of *Veda-vṛittis* and *Adhyayana-vṛittis* in local temples. The donees of these grants were required to recite and expound Vedas and Purāṇas for the benefit of both the students and

---

[1] *E. C.*, III, Tiru-Narsapur No. 27.
[2] *S. I. E. R.*, 1918, p. 145.
[3] *I. A.*, XII, p. 258.
[4] *I. A.*, XVIII, p. 273.
[5] *Ibid*, XIII, p. 94.
[6] *Ibid*, VIII, p. 185.

householders. These endowments thus provided for both ordinary and extension lectures for the spread of Hindu religion, learning and culture. A few instances may be given here. At Kuttalam in Trichanopali district there existed a provision for the recitation of the Vedas and Purāṇas in the local temple in 1411 A. D.; eighteen years later, however, we find another gift being made to twelve Brahmanas for a similar purpose.[1] Inscriptions disclose two other *Adhyayana-vṛittis* created at the same place in 1573 A. D. It will be thus seen that in this village in the course of 150 years at least 16 *Adhyayana-vṛittis* were created by private individuals for the spread of culture and religion among the masses. Grants for the *Veda-vṛittis* and *Adhyayana-vṛittis* are fairly common in south Indian inscriptions. The case of Kuttalam has been cited as a typical one. Inscriptions indeed disclose several instances of private individuals acting upon the theory that the most meritorious charity is the one for the cause of education. How deep was the impression made by this theory on the governments in ancient India will be soon shown.

In ancient times there was no printing press, and therefore it was essential that rich persons should come forward to defray the expenses of copying books, so that colleges and universities should have an adequate stock of valuable books. To help this desideratum,

---

[1] *S. I. E. R.*, Nos. 481 and 487 of 1917.

religious works began to commend gifts of books. Destiny of the world depends upon knowledge, and hence, says the *Nandī Purāṇa*, the pious man should make it a particular point to make gifts of books.[1] This Purana ascribes different degrees of merit to the gifts of different Puranas. The *Bhavishyottara Purāṇa* lays down that copies of certain Purāṇas should be presented to the learned in certain months.[2] That such recommendations did not fall on deaf ears will be clear from the large libraries that existed in many of the Hindu and Buddhist centres of learning, as shown in the last chapter. One of the purposes for which king Devapāla made a gift of five villages to the Nālandā University was to enable it to make additions to its library, significantly designated as *Ratna-sāgara* or 'Ocean of Gems'.[3] A similar grant for a similar purpose was made by a Valabhi princess in favour of a monastic college at Valabhi.[4] One of the purposes for

---

[1] Quoted by Aparārka on Yāj. I, 212. Cf. :—

शास्त्रे यस्माज्जगत्सर्वं संश्रितं च शुभाशुभम् ।
तस्माच्छास्त्रं प्रयत्नेन दातव्यं शुभकर्मणा ॥
लोकान्सर्वान्कामपूर्णान्यान्ति सर्वशुभोदयान् ।
पुराणविद्यादातारस्त्वनंतफलभागिनः ॥
आत्मविद्याप्रदातारो नरा धर्मसमाश्रयाः ।
न पुनर्योनिनिरयं प्रविशंति दुरत्ययम् ॥

[2] Quoted by Aparārka, *Ibid.*

[3] *E. I.*, XVII, p. 310.

[4] *Ante*, p. 274.

which Avighākara, a merchant from Bengal, made a grant to Kanheri monastery in Western India in the 9th century was the purchase of books.[1] It will be thus seen that the recommendation of Smritis and Puranas about donation of books was acted upon by several persons.

Numerous were the ways, direct and indirect, in which society tried to help the cause of education. Gifts were given only to learned men; Manu pointedly observes that oblations are offered in burning fire, and not in cold ashes. Only learned Brahmanas were invited for the Śrāddha. This must have given considerable indirect help to the cause of education, for people in ancient times used to perform Śrāddhas monthly and not annualy as at present. Takshaśilā teachers and students used to be invited for meals by the neighbouring villagers.[2] The citizens of Salotgi also used to do the same on festive occasions.[3] Voluntary contributions, in cash or kind, were given in many places. Inhabitants of Salotgi used to make agreed donations on occasions like marriage and Upanayana for the support of the local college. The merchants of Patan (in Khandesh) used to give contributions in kind for the upkeep of the local astronomical college founded by Chaṅgadeva, the grandson of Bhāskarāchārya.[4]

---

1 *I. A.*, XIII, p. 134.

2 Chitta-sambhūta Jātaka, No. 498.

3 *E. I.*, IV, p. 60.

4 *E. I.*, I, p. 30.

Feeding houses (*sattras*) for the poor in general and stndents in particular are mentioned in several inscriptions. There existed free feeding houses at Kolagalli,[1] Managoli,[2] Nilgund,[3] Nesarge,[4] Bagewadi,[5] Belgamve,[6] Dambal,[7] Gadag,[8] and Behatti[9] in Karnatak and at Kharepatan[10] in Konkan in the 11th, 12th, 13th, and 14th centuries. Bernier saw many of them in the 17th century, meant exclusively for poor students. This custom was ancient and wide spread, for the Losaka Jātaka also discloses the existence of a feeding house at Benares, financed by local merchants and meant exclusively for the poor students.[11]

Naturally only a few could be rich enough to start or organise feeding houses for poor studends. It was however possible for every house-holder to spare a morsel from the daily food of the family, and to offer it to the poor and hungry Brahmachārin, begging his food at noon time. To turn such a student back from one's door has been pronounced by Hindu thinkers to be the greatest crime against humanity. Āpastamba declares that all the charity and sacrifices standing to

---

1 *I. M. P.*, Bellary No. 82. 2 *E. I.*, V, p. 22.
3 *Ibid*, III, p. 208.
4 *J. B. B. R. A. S.*, X, p. 256.
5 *I. A.*, VII, p. 307. 6 *Ibid*, V, p. 49.
7 *Ibid*, X, p. 188. 8 *Ibid*, I, p. 301.
9 *Ibid*, IV, p. 274. 10 *E. I.*, IV, p. 355. 11 No. 41.

the credit of a person will be of no avail, and dire calamities will befall his children and cattle if a student is refused noon time alms at his door.[1] It was an incumbent duty for every house-holder to contribute his little mite to the cause of the education of the rising generation. If he can do nothing more, he should at least spare a morsel from his daily food to feed a needy student. Precautions were of course taken to see that the poor student did not abuse this privilege. Every student had to show his alms to the teacher, who was to see that nothing more than what was necessary for his own need was collected by the student. If the student collected more food or retailed it, he was guilty of theft. It was further laid down that the privilege of begging would come to an end when the student finishes his education and becomes a Snātaka.[2]

There were no compulsory fees for students, but they were expected to offer an adequate honorarium (*gurudakshiṇā*) to the teacher at the end of their course. Poor students, who had no money, were permitted to raise the necessary sum by subscription. To refuse help to such a Snātaka was a great moral crime. We have already seen how king Raghu thought that it would be a great calamity if a report should get

---

[1] स्त्रीणां प्रत्याचक्षाणां समाहितो ब्रह्मचारी इष्टं दत्तं हुतं प्रजां पशून्ब्रह्मवर्चसमन्नाद्यं वृंक्ते । *Āp. Dh. S.*, I, 1, 3, 24-25.

[2] *Bau. Dh. S.*, II, 1, 63.

abroad that a Snātaka came to him for Gurudakshiṇā and returned empty handed. The *Mahābhārata* has a still more interesting story. In the reign of king Poshya, Uttaṅka was reading under a certain teacher. At the end of his education his teacher asked him, obviously at his wife's pressure, to present him the earrings of the crowned queen of Poshya as his fee. We find the pupil going straight to the palace without any misgivings or apprehensions and the king immediately directing the queen to comply with his request.[1] Public opinion was obviously very emphatic that on no account whatsoever, should a student, collecting subscriptions for his Gurudakshiṇā, be turned out.

Governments usually reflect the views of society; we, therefore, find Hindu governments following a very benevolent policy to the cause of education. The king was required to help the spread of knowledge and education in a variety of ways. Bhīshma pointedly draws king Yudhishṭhira's attention to the duty of providing pensions to distinguished scholars, well versed in Śāstras.[2] Manu lays down that the king should honour those scholars who had finished their education, and also provide for them if they were unable to maintain themselves.[3] The view of Yājñavalkya is the same.[4] Śukra lays down that famous artists and

---

1 *MBH.*, I, chap. 3.

2 *Ibid*, XIII, Chaps. 59, 60.

3 VII. 82; IV. 33.

4 I, 130.

scholars should be honoured by the king with a view to encourage art and literature.[1] As a matter of fact there is hardly any Smṛiti which does not recognise patronage of learning as one of the most important duties of the king. The *Artha-śāstra* of Kauṭilya does the same,[2] and further advises the king to set apart plots in forests to be alotted to learned Brahmanas for their educational Āśramas.[3] The king was not to regard the visit of a learned scholar as a visitation ; he was expected to induce him to come to his court and stay in his kingdom, if he was contemplating going elsewhere.[4]

There is overwhelming evidence to show that these injunctions were followed in practice by the kings of ancient India. In Upanishadic times, king Janaka of Videha was well known for his patronage of men of letters ; his contemporary, king Ajātaśatru of Benares, was anxious to outshine him in this respect.[5] Asoka is famous for his patronage of learned Brahmanas and Sramaṇas. Tradition asserts that Charaka and Aśvaghosha were proteges of Kanishka. His successors, Huvishka and Vāsudeva, are known to have patronised Buddhist religion and scholarship. Sātavāhana kings of the Deccan were so generous to the cause of learning that their fame in this respect remained undimmed

[1] I, 369. [2] II, 1. [3] II, 20.

[4] *MBH.*, XII, chap. 89.

[5] *Bṛih. Up.*, II, 1, 1.

down to the days of Rājaśekhara[1] (c. 900 A. D.) Numerous are the stories still current of the patronage of learning of the Gupta emperor Chandragupta Vikrmāditya. One of his ministers, Śāba, was a poet.[2] His successor, Kumāragupta I, was probably the founder of Nālandā University, and Tathāgatagupta, Narasiṁhagupta and Budhagupta among his successors vied with each other in rendering all possible help to that famous centre of learning.[3] Emperor Harsha was not only a patron of learning, but himself a poet and a dramatist. Bhavabhūti and Vākpati were the members of the entourage of king Yaśovarman, ruling at Kanauj by the middle of the 8th century. Kings Jayāpīḍa, Avantivarman and Harsha of Kashmir were famous for their generosity to men of letters.[4] Kings Mahendrapāla and Mahīpāla of the Gurjara-Pratīhāra dynasty were the patrons of Rājaśekhara. (c. 875—c. 925 A. D.) In the 10th and 11th centuries the cause of scholarship received great help from the Paramāra dynasty of Malva. Kings Muñja, Sindhurāja Navasāhasāṅka and Bhoja of Malva are the centres of numerous anecdotes illustrative of their love of learning. Several works on poetics, erotics and medicine have been attributed by tradition to the last mentioned ruler. Poet Bilhaṇa

---

1 *Kāvya-Mīmānsā*, p. 55.

2 *C. I. I.*, III, No. 6.

3 Watters, II, p. 164.

4 *Rājataraṅgiṇī*, IV, 495, 855.

of Kashmir was invited by king Vikrmāditya VI of Kalyāṇi to become his court poet. Vijñānesvara, the famous author of the *Mitāksharā*, also received patronage at the court of the Later Chālukyas. Umāpatideva, Dhoi, Govardhana and Jayadeva were living at the court of king Lakshmaṇasena of Bengal. Hemachandra, the famous Jain author, was the preceptor of king Kumārapāla of the Chālukya dynasty. Srīharsha, the author of the famous epic *Naishadha-Charit*, was the court poet of the Gahadwal kings Vijayachandra and Jayachandra during the third quarter of the 12th century. This traditional policy of patronage of learning was continued by the Hindu feudatories of Muslim rulers in medieval times.

It is not to be, however, suppossed that only distinguished scholars used to receive state patronage. I-tsing has observed that scholars, who had finished their education at Valabhi, Nālandā and other centres of learning used to repair to royal courts with a view to get appointments in practical government. Those who could not be absorbed in the administration were given grants of land.[1] That this statement of the Chinese pilgrim is true will become clear from the numberless copper plate grants in favour of learned Brahmanas that have come to light. Some of these grants were for the purpose of creating new Brahmana colonies, known as Agrahāra villages; we have seen

---

[1] I-tsing p. 177-8.

already how these were usually centres of free higher education. Rāshṭrakūṭa King Govinda IV had given 600 villages to learned Brahmanas at the time of his accession in 918 A. D. Different rulers of Magadha had endowed the Nālandā establishment at least with 100,—if not with 200—villages. Valabhi monastic colleges were equally well patronised. Grants to temples that have been discovered are as numerous as those given to learned Brahmanas, and we have seen already how many of these temples were notable centres of learning.

Besides land grants many learned Brahmanas must have received gifts in cash. This custom of cash gifts (Dakshiṇā) existed even under the Peshwas, who used to spend annually Rs. 5,00,000 for that purpose. 'But' says Elphinstone, 'the Dakshiṇā formed but a small portion of his (Peshwa's) largesses to Brahmanas and the number of persons devoted to Hindu learning and religion who were supported by him exceeded what would be readily suppossed."[1] If such was the case under a Hindu administration in the 19th century, we may well conclude that the number of scholars receiving state help in one form or another and imparting free education must have been indeed very large in ancient and medieval India.

---

[1] Elphinstone's minute, quoted at p. 5 of the *Report of the Bombay Provincial Committee, Education Commission*, 1882.

We get a few indications to show that some states would often give direct and special scholarships to enable students to prosecute their studies. In Śarabhanga Jātaka, we find the king of Benares sending a scholar to Takshaśilā for receiving special military training, because it was predicted that he would be a celebrated archer.[1] Śukra recommends state scholarships for the promotion of fine and useful arts.[2]

Besides giving direct help, the state in Ancient India tried to help the cause of education in some indirect ways also. There is a practical unanimity of views among the Smṛitis that learned Brahmanas should be exempted from taxation.[3] The exemption was not intended to operate in favour of the Brahmanas engaged in money making professions. Epigraphical evidence in favour of the prevalence of this practice is not conclusive. It is true that all the school masters in his kingdom were exempted from the house tax by Rājendra Kulottunga Chola in the last quarter of the 11th century A. D,;[4] but we usually find lands and villages given to Brahmanas and temples paying a certain quit rent to the state. Taxation did exist but

---

[1] No. 522.

[2] सर्वविद्याकलाभ्यासे शिक्षयेद्भृतिपोषितान् ।
समासविद्यं तं दृष्ट्वा तत्कार्ये तं नियोजयेत् ॥ I, 368.

[3] E. g. Manu, VII, 133; Vishṇu, III, 25-6; *Arthaśāstra*, V, 2.

[4] Mulbagal No. 49 A, *E. C.*, X.

the rate was very low. It is however probable that there may have been complete exemption in the case of those learned Brahmanas, who had received no state pension or help.

Treasure trove laws also were made specially favourable to learned Brahmanas. A Śrotriya or learned Brahmana was allowed to retain the whole of the treasure found by him, others had to refund 16 per cent of the find as the state tax. If the king himself were to discover a hoard, he was required to distribute one half of it among learned Brahmanas.[1] The property of learned Brahmanas was never to escheat to the state: the king was required to distribute it among the learned.

Students also were shown some concessions by the Hindu state. *Āpastamba Dharma Sūtra* recommends that serious students should be exempted from direct taxation.[2] They were not to be charged the ferry tax. The Law of Limitation was specially extended to 50 years in the case of students studying with their preceptors.[3]

---

[1] Manu, VIII, 35-39; Yājñavalkya, II, 34-5.

[2] II, 10, 26, 14-17.

[3] Cf:—ब्रह्मचारी चरेत्कश्चिद्व्रतं षट्त्रिंशदाब्दिकम् ।
समावृत्तो व्रती कुर्याद्धनस्यान्वेषणं ततः ।
पंचाशदाब्दिको भोगस्तद्धनस्यापहारकः ॥

Nārada in *SCS*, quote at S. B. E., 33, pp. 243-4.

It is true that governments in ancient India had no Education Minister or Department of Education; the reason for this was that they did not desire to interfere with the educational policy. There were no Directors of Education or Government Inspectors to inspect schools and dictate educational policy.[1] Even when grants were given to learned Brahmanas, or when Agrahāra villages were created, there was no stipulation that the grants would be withdrawn if free education was not given by the donees. It was the king's duty to give such grants. It was the Brahmana's duty to teach, even when there was no prospect of government help or private donations. Each side went on performing its duties fairly satisfactorily, though there were no specific stipulations.

Kings were to patronise learning but they were not to assume a patronising attitude towards men of letters. The utmost reverence was to be shown to them, as is done by the son to the father or the student to the preceptor.[2] Dushyanta left his army behind him at the time of entering the hermitage of Kaṇva. How deferential was expected to be the behaviour of the king even to a mendicant scholar can be judged from the remarkably courteous and dignified reception that emperor Raghu gave to Kautsa. King Narasiṁhagupta Bālāditya, who was perhaps the most generous

[1] This was not an unmixed blessing. See pp. 325-6.

[2] Manu, VII, 38; Śukra, I, 47; *Arthaśāstra*, I, 2.

patron of the Nālandā University, eventually joined the holy order as a novice. His status, however, was lower than that of all other fully ordained monks. The only concession that was shown to him was to give him precedence over other novices, though senior to him in age.[1] It is of course quite probable that some kings may not have treated learned men with courteous consideration, but their number seems to have been small.

It is interesting to note that in the West it was Martin Luther who for the first time emphasised that education must be supported by the state. In India this theory was advanced much earlier and also followed in practice, as is conclusively proved by the numerous grants for schools and colleges, temples and monasteries, learned men and Brahmana colonies that have been brought to light.

Teachers, who were shown great consideration by the State and Society, were required to follow a very high code of conduct. Teaching was an imperative and religious duty imposed upon every learned Brahmana. If the student, seeking knowledge, was earnest, the teacher was bound to accept him though there may be no chance of any honorarium. Stipulation for fees was vehemently condemned. The poorest student was to be admitted and the utmost that the teacher could expect from him was such manual service as the student could perform without interference with his

[1] Watters, II, 164-5.

education. Teaching was not to be delayed and nothing was to be withheld from the student.

At a fairly early stage of its history, the principle of hereditary professions was accepted by Hindu society. Specially gifted children could change their family professions, but in normal cases children followed the professions of their parents, who were required to train them in the technique of their lines. By making Upanayana compulsory and professions hereditary, by showing encouragement to learning by a variety of ways, by securing ample patronage from rulers and landlords, by penalising any stipulation for fees and by laying down a very high code of conduct for the teaching profession, Hindu society tried to make a fairly efficient arrangement for the proper education of the rising generation. The results show that before the decay set in, these measures for the spread of education proved to be fairly successful. We have seen already how literacy was at least as high as 30 percent at the advent of the Muslim rule and about twice as high a millennium earlier.[1] In contemporary times in no other country in the world was there so wide a spread of literacy. Hindu achievements in the realm of medicine, metallurgy, astronomy, chemistry, and spinning and weaving were also of a high order, if judged by contemporary standards. There was undoubtedly a setback after about 800 A. D.; its causes will be discussed in the course of the next chapter.

---

[1] *Ante*, pp. 206-7, 213-4.

# CHAPTER X.

## AIMS AND IDEALS AND ACHIEVEMENTS AND FAILURES.

In the foregoing chapters, a history of the different aspects of education in India has been attempted from the earliest time down to about 1200 A. D. In barbarous times, unconscious imitation is the only form of education, 'the trial and success' method is the only method known and followed. In India even in the earliest Vedic times, society was advanced much beyond this stage. It will be difficult to emphasise the vital importance of education in a more telling manner than has been done in the 71st hymn of the tenth Maṇḍala of the Ṛigveda.[1] Educational institutions were not developed in that early age, but they existed nowhere else in the world at that time. Home was the centre of education. We do not find educational institutions of the modern type existing earlier than the 5th century A. D.; this however does not mean that education was uncared for. By creating a hereditary class in society whose religious duty it was to teach, and to teach without any stipulation for fees, and by making professions hereditary, Hindu society had made remarkable strides in the domain of knowledge before regular educational institutions of the modern type were evolved in the Gupta age.

---

[1] *Ante*, p. 299.

To persons interested in theories of education, the history of ancient Indian education may appear rather disappointing. Our sources are more concerned with describing the main features of the educational system than with discussing its basic principles. The education system also became stereotyped at a fairly early stage; a few changes did take place, but the writers of later times are more anxious to suppress than describe the changed methods and ideals.

It must be however pointed out that in Europe too there was hardly any systematic discussion of the theories of education till recent times. Controversies about the relative importance of literary and useful education started only in the 17th century A. D. Theories about the importance of the child and its inclinations in outlining an educational system were unknown before the time of Rousseau. Whether memory should be trained more than the reasoning faculty, whether reading should be encouraged more than reflection, whether education is expanse of natural powers or an accretion to them from without, what is the relative importance of and proper time for physical, aesthetic, moral and intellectual training are problems that have begun to be systematically discussed even in the west only in the last hundred years or sc. In ancient India, we sometimes come across stray reflections about some of these problems, but there is no regular and systematic discussion. This was perhaps to some extent a natural consequence of the absence of any social or state control over the education system. Both the state and society gave full liberty to the teachers. As they were not subjected to any appreciable external criticism or control, they went on their traditional grooves without giving much time to the discussion of the fundamental problems of education.

We have further to note that the peculiar constitution of Hindu society rendered a discussion of some of these problems out of question. For instance, the controversy about Literary versus Useful education was inconceivable in ancient Indian society. Professions came to be assigned hereditarily to different groups; if any body had started the discussion of this controversy, he would have been told that for certain classes liberal education was more important than useful education, and for certain others the case was just the reverse.

It is proposed to discuss in this concluding chapter the aims and ideals of ancient Indian educational system with a view to ascertain how far they were realised in practice. We shall also dwell upon certain salient features of the system with a view to appreciate its merits and defects.

Formation of character, building up of personality, preservation of ancient culture and the training of the rising generation in the performance of the social and religious duties,—these were the main aims of the Ancient Indian System of Education. Let us see what were the views of Hindu thinkers about these ideals and how far they were realised in practice.

Educationalists of ancient India have attached the greatest importance to the formation of character. The Vedas were regarded as revealed and therefore their preservation was of paramount importance; and yet we find orthodox thinkers like Manu declaring without any hesitation that a person of good character with a mere smattering of Vedic knowledge is to be preferred to another, who though well versed in all the three Vedas, is impure in his life and habits.[1] Vedic study, charity and sacrifices are of no use to men of questionable character.[2] Purity in thought and life is the key-stone of spiritual progress.[3] Manu grows very eloquent in describing the necessity of self-control to the student (*brahmachārin*).

Apart from such direct injunctions, the very atmosphere in which the Brahmachārin lived, was calculated to give a proper turn to his character. He was to be under the direct supervision of his teacher, who was to watch not only his intellectual progress but also his moral behaviour. We have seen already how Upanayana ritual was calculated to impress the fact that

---

[1] सावित्रीमात्रसारोऽपि वरं विप्रः सुयंत्रितः ।
नायंत्रितस्त्रिवेदोऽपि सर्वाशी सर्वविक्रयी ॥ II, 118.

[2] *Ibid*, II, 97.

[3] यस्य वाङ्मनसी शुद्धे सम्यग्गुप्ते च सर्वदा ।
स वै सर्वमवाप्नोति वेदान्तोपगतं फलम् ॥ *Ibid*, II, 160.

the student's life was a consecrated one, how divine cooperation was secured in his favour to ensure a successful journey along the path of knowledge, and how that cooperation would be withdrawn and dire consequences would follow if he was guilty of a moral lapse. The examples of his teachers and of national and epic heroes like Rāma, Bhīshma, Balabhīma and Hariśchandra that were placed before the student were also calculated to give the right turn to his character.

It is difficult to estimate correctly how far this effort to elevate the national character was successful. In all times and countries there exist some persons of high and some of depraved character, and unfortunately history has largely to deal with these abnormal types. We rarely come across the average man. We can however get some idea of the influence of education on national character by the opinions expressed by foreign observers, who appear to be impartial. Amongst them the Greeks are chrnologically the earliest. Politically the Greeks were not the allies but the enemies of the Hindus; they have made many disparaging remarks about some aspects of Hindu culture, but they have candidly noted the high impression that the Hindu character and veracity produced on their mind. 'An Indian has never been convicted of lying. Truth and virtue they (i.e. Indians) hold in high esteem', says the ambassador Megasthenes.[1] This statement could not have

[1] Megasthenes, Fragment 27.

been literally true, but it shows that the cases of cheating and swindling must have been very few in society. Strabo and Megasthenes have further pointed out that law suits among the Indians were rare owing to their frank dealing. "They are not litigous. Witnesses and seals are not necessary when a man makes a deposit; he acts in trust. Their houses are usually unguarded."[1]

Yuan Chwang pays an equally high compliment to the Indian character during the 7th century A. D. He has carefully noted the weak and strong points in the character of the peoples of different localities; but while summing up his impressions of the Indian character as a whole, he says "They (i. e. Indians) are of hasty and irresolute temperament but *of pure moral principles.* They will not take anything wrongfully and they yield more than fairness requires. They fear for retribution for sins in other lives and make light of what conduct produces in this life. *They do not practice deceit and they keep their sworn obligations.*"[2] The vast majority of Indians in Yuan Chwang's time did not share his religious beliefs and practices and are yet paid the above high compliment by the Chinese pilgrim.

Al Idrisi's impressions of the Hindu character in western India are similar to those of Yuan Chwang's. Though a Muslim, he says of the Hindus, '*The Indians are naturally inclined to justice and never depart from it in their actions.* Their good faith, honesty and fidelity

[1] *Ibid.* [2] Watters, I, p. 171.

to engagements are well known and they are so famous for these qualities that people flock to their country from every side; hence the country is flourishing and their condition prosperous."[1]

In the thirteenth century Marco Polo was impressed equally highly by the character of the Brahmanas of Western India. "You must know" says he, "that these Brahmanas are the best merchants in the the world and the most truthful, for they would never tell a lie for anything on the earth. If a foreign merchant, who does not know the ways of the country, applies to them and entrusts his goods to them, they would take charge of these and sell them in the most zealous manner, seeking zealously the profit of the foreigner and asking no commission except what he pleases to give."[2] When the morality of the trading classes is so high, the character of the average man must have been very noble. Ibn Batuta, another Muslim observer, describes the Marathas of Deogiri and Nandurbar of the 14th century as 'upright, religious and trustworthy'.[3]

Travellers and merchants are usually disposed to make sarcastic remarks about the culture and character of the foreigners among whom they have moved; when so many of them belonging to different

---

[1] Elliot, *History of India*, Vol. I, p. 88.

[2] Yule, *Marco Polo*, Vol. II, p. 363 (Third edition).

[3] Gibs, *Ibn Batuta*, p. 228.

times and climes and professing different faiths agree in paying a high tribute to Indian character, we may well conclude that there is no exaggeration, and that the educational system of the country had suceeded remarkably in its ideal of raising the national character to a high level. It is only after the 17th and 18th centuries A. D. that we come across foreign travellers, traders, missonaries and ex-governors passing strictures upon the Hindu character. Many of them were misled by their prejudices, and it is also possible that the Hindu character may have suffered deterioration during the long spell of foreign rule in medieval times. It is however worth observing that not a single foreign observer is found passing hostile remarks about Hindu character and honesty during the ancient period of Indian history.

The second aim of the Education System was the development of personality. It is very often asserted that Hindu education suppressed personality and originality by prescribing a uniform course of education and by enforcing an iron discipline. The course, however, was not rigidly uniform. In early times there was a free choice of professions and careers. In later times when the caste system became rigid, the theory no doubt was that every one should follow his hereditary profession, but the practice permitted considerable freedom to enterprising individuals. We have also shown how it would be wrong to assert that the whole of the Aryan society was engaged for twelve years in cramming the Vedic texts during the Smṛiti period. Only a section of the Brahmana community followed this line; others used to learn only a few Vedic Mantras sufficient for their daily use, and reserve their main energy for the study of a subject of their own choice like logic, philosophy, literature or poetics. The educational currculum of the Smṛitis represents the Utopian idealism of the Brahmana theologian and not the actual reality in society.

The Hindu educational system helped the development of personality by cultivating self-respect, self-reliance and self-restraint. The Brahmachārin was the custodian of the culture and civilisation of the race. The welfare of the race depended upon his proper discharge of his duties. If Indra is prëeminent among the gods, if the king is successful as a governor, it is all due to their proper training and education.[1] To support the poor student was the sacred duty of society, the non-performance of which would lead to dire spiritual calamities. A well-trained youth, who had finished his education, was to be honoured more than the king himself. It is but natural that such an atmosphere should develop the student's self-respect in a remarkable manner.

Self-confidence was also fostered equally well. The Upanayana ritual, as we have seen already, saught to foster self-confidence by pointing out that divine

---

[1] *A. V.*, XI, 5.

powers would co-operate with the student and help him on to the achievement of his goal, if he on his part did his duty well. Poverty need not depress him, he was the ideal student who would subsist by begging his daily food. If he was willing to work in his spare time, he could demand and get education free from any teacher or institution. Self-reliance is the mother of self-confidence, and the Hindu education system seeks to develop it in a variety of ways, as we have seen already. Uncertainty of the future prospect did not damp self-confidence. If the student was following a professional course, his career was already determined. There was no overcrowding or cut-throat competition in professions. If he was taking religious and liberal education, poverty was to be the ideal of his life. His needs ought to be,—and as a matter of fact they were—few and the state and society supplied them well, as we have seen already in the last chapter.

The element of self-restraint, that was emphasised by the educational ideal, further served to enrich the student's personality. Self-restraint that was recommended was distinctly different from self-repression. Simplicity in life and habits was all that was insisted upon. The student was to have a full meal, only it was to be a simple one. The student was to have sufficient clothing, only it was not to be foppish. The student was to have his recreations, only they were not to be frivolous. He may use shoes when going out to the jungles, only he should be able to do without them in villages and towns where roads were better. He was to lead a life of perfect chastity, but that was only to enable him to be an efficient and healthy householder when he married. It will be thus seen that what the educationalists aimed at did not result in self-repression, but only promoted self-restraint that was so essential for the development of a proper personality. Nor was this self-restraint enforced in Spartan ways of correction and punishment. The teacher was required to use persuasion and spare the rod as far as possible. He was liable to be prosecuted if he used excessive force.

It may be further pointed out in this connection that powers of discrimination and judgment, so necessary for the development of proper personality, were well developed in students taking liberal education and specialising in logic, philosophy, poetics or literature. These branches of study bristled with controversies and the student had to understand both the sides, form his own judgment and defend his position in literary debates. It was only with the Vedic students that education became mechanical training of memory. This became inevitable in later times when the literature to be preserved became very extensive and the modern means of its preservation were unavailable. In earlier days even the Vedic students were well trained in exegesis and could explain the meaning of what they could recite.

The data available to determine how far the education system was successful in evolving personality is meagre. We come across several masterful personalities in different walks of life in ancient India, but how far they were typical of their age we do not know. Hindu achievements, however, in different walks of life and branches of knowledge were of a fairly high order in ancient India, and this would hardly have been possible if the products of the Hindu Education System were not masterful personalities. Things changed for the worse in medieval times; Brahmacharya discipline became nominal when a vast majority of students began to marry at a very early age; growth of independent judgment became stunted with the growing veneration for the past and its time-hallowed tradition. Self-confidence and self-respect disappeared in a great measure when society suffered from convulsions of sudden foreign invasions and long alien rule, imposing a hated religion and strange culture with the aid of the sword. We must not judge the success of the Ancient Indian Education System in building up the personalities of students by conclusions based upon its products at the advent of the British rule.

The development of social efficiency and civic responsibility was another aim of the Education System. Education was no aimless training. Society had accepted the theory of the division of work, which was mainly governed by the principle of heredity. Exceptional talent could always select the profession it liked; it was however deemed to be in the interest of the average man that he should follow his family's profesion. The Education System saught to qualify the members of the rising generation for their more or less predetermined spheres of life. Each trade or guild trained its children in its own art. This system may have sacrificed the individual inclinations of a few, but it was undoubtedly in the interest of many. It trained children efficiently in their family professions. Hindu thinkers did not concur with Milton in thinking that an ideal system of education ought to qualify a youth to perform skilfully, justly and magnanimously all the offices, both private and public, of peace and war. They believed in differentiation of functions and trained different classes for different spheres of work.

The Education System laid particular stress upon civic and social duties and responsibilities. The Snātaka or the educated youth was not to lead a self-centred life. He was called upon to perpetuate the race and culture by raising and educating progeny. He was to perform his duties as a son, husband, and father conscientiously and efficiently. His wealth was not to be utilised soley for his own or his family's wants; he must be hospitable and charitable. Particularly emphatic are the words in the convocation address, emphasising these duties.[1] Professions had their own codes of honour, which emphasised the civic responsibilities of their members. The physician was required to relieve disease and distress even at the cost of

---

1 See Appendix B for the whole passage.

his life. The warrior had his own high code of honour.

Social structure in ancient India was to a great extent independent of government. Governments may come and go, but social and village life was not much affected by these changes. It was probably this circumstance that was responsible for the non-inclusion of patriotism among the civic duties inculcated by the Education System.

The preservation of ancient heritage and culture was perhaps the most important aim of the Ancient Indian System of Education. Any one who takes even a cursory view of Hindu writings on the subject is impressed by the deep concern that was felt for the acquisition and preservation of the ancient literary and cultural heritage of the race. Members of the professions were to train their children in their own lines, rendering available to the rising generation at the outset of its career all the skill and processes that were aquired after painful efforts of the bygone generations. The services of the whole Aryan community were conscripted for the purpose of the preservation of the Vedic literature. Every Dvija must learn at least a portion of his sacred literary heritage. It was an incumbent duty on the priestly class to commit the Vedic literature to memory in order to ensure its transmission to future generations. It is true that not all the Brahmanas obeyed this injunction, but that was because they had the commonsense to realise that the services of their entire class were not necessary for the task. Brahmanas were always available in sufficient numbers to sacrifice their life and talents in order to ensure the preservation of the sacred texts. Theirs was a life long and almost a tragic devotion to the cause of learning. For, they consented to spend their life in committing to memory what others, and not they, could interpret. Secular benefits that they could expect were few and not at all commensurate with the labour involved. Other members of the Brahmana community were fostering the studies of the different branches of liberal education like grammar, literature, poetics, law, philosophy and logic. Here the goal was avowedly cultural and not utilitarian. The aim was not to make money or find out lucrative careers, but to cultivate and develop the different branches of liberal studies. As a matter of fact, the Hindu thinkers disapprove of the idea that the value of liberal education should be judged by its pecuniary productivity. Vishṇu warns that no spiritual benefit will accrue to a person in the life to come if he seeks to live by his learning in the present life.[1] Kālidāsa[2] disapproves the conduct of a

[1] यश्च विद्यामासाद्यास्मिल्लोके तया सह जीवेन्न सा तस्य फलप्रदा भवति। Vishṇu is here referring to liberal education. *Vi. Dh. S.*, 30,39.

[2] यस्यागमः केवलजीविकायै तं ज्ञानपण्यं वणिजं वदंति।

*Mālavikāgnimitram*, Act I v. 17.

scholar, who seeks merely to make money by his learning. His main concern ought to be to spread culture and knowledge and to fight for the discovery and establishment of truth.

A natural consequence of this anxiety for the preservation of the ancient heritage was to make education deep and thorough, rather than broad and many-sided. The heritage of the past was divided into different branches, and different groups of study circles began to specialise in them. This made Hindu scholarship deep, but not without a loss in breadth to a certain extent.

Obedience to parents, proper respect to elders and teachers and gratitude to the savants of the bygone ages are natural consequences of society's intense solicitude for the preservation of ancient culture and civilisation. Especially significant in this connection are the rules about the daily *Svādhyāya* and *Ṛishi-tarpaṇa,* the former enjoining the recapitulation of at least a portion of what was learnt in the student life and the latter requiring a daily tribute of gratitude to the literary giants of the bygone ages.

In later times when Sanskrit became a dead language and the philosophy of the Upanishads and its ramifications were found to be too abstruse for the average man and woman, a new type of literature,—the Purāṇas—was evolved with a view to spread and popularise the national culture and civilisation among the masses. A section of the Brahmana community devoted itself to the task of expounding daily the culture and gospel of the Purāṇas to the masses in their own vernaculars. As a consequence, many features of ancient culture came to be well known to and carefully preserved by even the illiterate sections of Hindu society. The aim of the vernacular Bhakti poets of the Middle Ages was also the same, viz, the preservation and popularisation of ancient culture and religion.

The surprising amount of cultural uniformity that is to be seen even now over the length and breadth of India is largely due to the successful preservation of ancient culture and civilisation. If there are several features common to Hindu life all over the country, contributing to Hindu unity, the credit has to be largely given to the Education System, which has produced uniformity in the culture and outlook on life of the Hindu community.

Friends and foes alike have admitted that the Hindu System of Education has been eminently successful in its aim of preservation of the ancient literary heritage. Very few of the Vedic works have been. lost. It is indeed a wonder how so vast a literature could have been preserved without the help of writing for the purpose. Among later works too, the number of valuable books lost is not considerable. And here too the losses would have been practically insignificant if irreparable damages to temples and monasteries had not been caused at the time of the invasions of the Mahomadens and during their subsequent long rule.

We now proceed to consider the limitations and defects of the Ancient Indian System of Education.

Religion had immense hold over the Hindu mind and many of the admirable features of the Education System have to be attributed to this circumstance, as shown already. But it was also the cause of certain defects that crept into the system.

The view that the hold of religion over the Hindu mind was responsible for making the education system predominently other-worldly is not true. Vānaprastha and Sannyāsa ideals were no doubt suggested by the theories about the life to come, but such was not the case with the theory and ideal of Brahmacharya. The education system aimed at producing youths eminently fit to perform their civic and social duties; if any spiritual merit for the life to come were to be achieved through Brahmacharya, it was to be through the proper performance of its duties, which however were principally determined with a view to make the student an efficient and God-fearing citizen.

The majority of teachers for higher education were priests in ancient India, as was the case in contemporary times all over the world. They did not exploit their position for promoting any selfish ends of their own, but they had the natural limitations of their class. Under their supervision religious and semi-religious studies got undue predominence in the educational curriculum. This phenomenon was not, however, confined to India; for in Europe too down to the medieval times teachers were usually priests and the Bible, the sacred poets and the lives of the Saints dominated the curriculum.[1] Luther was the first to emphasise the necessity of giving proper attention to the needs of secular life by pointing out that even if there were neither soul, nor heaven, nor hell, it would still be necessary to have schools for the affairs here below.

The real defect produced by the hold of religion over the Hindu mind was the tendency to hold reason at a discount, which became prominent a few centuries after the Christian Era. Such was not the case in early times, when there was full intellectual freedom. Upanishadic thinkers advocate bold and divergent theories of philosophy and theology without showing the least anxiety to prove that their views were in a line with those of their predecessors of the Vedic and Brahmanic times. There were as many as sixty-three systems of philosophy in the days of the Buddha, and very few of them cared to rely on Vedic authority for their hypotheses or conclusions. Within the fold of the orthodoxy itself there were the Sāṅkhya, Mīmānsā and Nyāya systems, which had hardly any

---

[1] Monroe, *A Text Book of the History of Education*, p. 351.

appropriate place for the Divine Creator in them. Buddhism and Jainism were not summarily dismissed as atheistic; their scriptures were carefully studied in order to prove that their theories were unsound.

Unfortunately for the progress of learning and scholarship certain works came to be canonized some time about 600 B. C. Their authorship was attributed to divine or inspired agency, and it was averred that what they contained could not be false, what they opposed could not be true. An almost equally high reverence came to be paid to the Smṛitis and Purāṇas in course of time. Theories began to be accepted or rejected according as they were in conformity with or opposed to the statements of the sacred books on the point. Intellectual giants like Sankara and Rāmānuja had to spend a disproportionate amount of time and energy to prove that their systms of philosophy were in conformity with and the natural outcomes of the Upanishadic hypotheses. If the hold of the Śrutis and Smṛitis were not so exacting, there would have been freer development of philosophy. At any rate many of the remarkable intellects of the middle ages would have found it possible to write independent works on their own systems of philosophy, instead of being compelled to present it unsystematically, while engaged in the ostensible task of writing commentaries on the revealed literature. Instead of Nibandha compilations, we would have had original Smṛitis of the later times.

Under such circumstances, there was not much scope left for research and originality in those matters where opinions were expressed in sacred texts. A concrete case may be given to illustrate the point. In the infancy of astronomy, the eclipses were explained by the mythological stories about Rāhu and Ketu attacking and temporarily overpowering the moon and the sun. It was an evil day for the advance of astronomy when this mythological version got a canonical sanction by its inclusion in the Purāṇas. Hindu astronomers like Āryabhaṭa, Brahmagupta and Varāhamihira knew the true cause of eclipses but felt powerless to carry vigorous propaganda to explode the popular and mythological explanation canonized by the Purāṇas. Nay, Brahmagupta, with a view to win cheap popularity, went to the extent of advocating that the popular view was correct, when he knew full well that such was not the case. In the first chapter of his *Brahma-siddhānta,* he gives both the popular and scientific theories about the eclipses, but advocates the cause of the former. "Some people think that the eclipse is not caused by the Head of Rāhu or Ketu. This, however, is a foolish idea.......The Veda, which is the word of God from the mouth of Brahman, says that the Head eclipses, likewise *Manusmṛiti* and *Garga-saṁhitā.*[1]" What is, however, most lamentable

[1] As quoted by Alberuni, II, pp. 110—1. The original book has been lost.

is that Brahmagupta, who knew full well the real cause of eclipses, should have proceeded to condemn Āryabhaṭa, Varāhamihira, Śrisheṇa and Vishṇuchandra for expounding the unorthodox but scientific theory that eclipses are caused by the shadow of the earth. It is important to note that Brahmagupta becomes guilty of intellectual and moral dishonesty because he was anxious to win cheap popularity by supporting the popular view that what was stated in the Vedas and Manusmṛiti could not be untrue. It is interesting to note that Varāhamihira combats the Rāhu-Ketu theory in one part of his work,[1] but succumbs to it in another.[2] Āryabhaṭa alone perhaps has the moral courage to be consistent with his intellectual convictions. But he also only hints that the popular theory is wrong and does not dare to attack it openly.[3] If the Rāhu-Ketu theory of eclipses has continued to retain its hold over the popular Hindu mind for the last 1500 years and more, in spite of the scientific discovery of the true

---

[1] यदि मूर्तो भविचारी शिरोऽथवा भवति मंडली राहुः ।
भगणार्धेनान्तरितो गृह्णाति कथं नियतचारः ॥
अथ भुजगेंद्ररूपः पुच्छेन मुखेन वा स गृह्णाति ।
मुखपुच्छांतरसंस्थं स्थगयति कस्मान्न भगणार्धम् ॥ ६ ॥

*Brihat-saṁhitā*, V, 4, 6.

[2] एवमुपरागकारणमुक्तमिदं दिव्यदृग्भिराचार्यैः ।
राहुः कारणमस्मिन्नित्युक्तः शास्त्रसद्भावः ॥ *Ibid*, V, 13.

[3] यदसज्ज्ञानसमुद्रात्समुद्धृतं देवताप्रसादेन ।
सज्ज्ञानोत्तमरत्नं मया निमग्नं स्वमतिनावा ॥ Golabhāga, v, 49.

cause of eclipses, the reason is that Hindu scholarship of later times was too much in the leading strings of religion to carry on any active propaganda against its hypothses. The discontinuance of dissection in the medical training and the abandonment of agriculture by the Brahmanas, Buddhists and Jains are also to be attributed to the hold of the progressively puritanical notions over the popular mind.[1]

It is, however, but fair to observe that in Europe too, reason had to beat a hasty and precipitate retreat when in conflict with the dicta of scriptures down to the beginning of the modern age. Galileo had to suffer for his astronomical discoveries. Throughout the Middle Ages, educationalists were more anxious to impart traditional theories and formulæ than to train minds capable of forming their own conclusions. Medieval philosophers and commentators were utilising reason only to prove that the scriptural hypotheses were correct. It was Luther who first vindicated the cause of reason by declaring that what is contrary to reason must be certainly much more contrary to God. But Luther too became a renegade towards the end of his life and declared, 'The more subtle and accurate is the reason, the more poisonous is the beast, with many Dragon's head is it against God and all his work'. The truth was that the Reformers were unwilling to concede to others the right to interpret scriptures, which

---

[1] I-tsing, p. 62.

they claimed for themselves. If therefore reason was at a discount in India from the beginning of the Middle Ages, (*c.* 500 A. D.) we must also note that the same was the case in Europe down to the beginning of the modern age. We should not further forget that reason was given full scope by the Hindu scholars and thinkers for more than about 1500 years when it was superseded by the exigencies of the religious situation. The historian, however, cannot help regretting that supression of reason should have taken place among a people, who had given full scope to it for several centuries.

Enrichment of the culture of the past along with its preservation continued to be the goal of the Indian education system for several centuries. Intellect and reason were for a long time given full scope, originality was encouraged, and as a result we find remarkable creative activity in the domain of theology, philosophy, philology, grammar, logic, astronomy, mathematics, medicine, etc. down to about 800 A. D. Indian achievements in many of these fields were remarkable, judged either by the contemporary or by the absolute standard. Scholars from China, Korea, Tibet and Arabia used to visit India in order to learn what she had to teach in the realms of religion, philosophy, medicine, mathematics and astronomy.

Towards the beginning of the 9th century A. D., the creative vein in the Indian intellect got fatigued after an intense activity of more than 2000 years.

Probably the heritage of the past became so great that all the ability of scholars was engrossed in preserving it. Probably the habit of looking back to the past for inspiration and guidance became so confirmed that it began to be instinctively felt that not much could be expected from the present. The golden age of inspiration had gone, no new achievements were possible, the best that the age could do was to preserve, expound or comment upon the masterpieces of the past. Hindu education system was unable to create minds powerful enough to rise above the influence of these theories. For the last one thousand years and more, the Hindu intellect has been almost solely engrossed in the task of writing digests and commentaries on the works of earlier periods. Creative activity has practically come to a standstill. Here also we have to add that the spirit of the times was unfavourable for the formation of independent minds and intellects both in the West and in the East. In Europe too the Middle Ages were a period of intellectual repression. Renaissance and Reformation, however, started an era of intellectual independence and originality in Europe in the sixteenth century; in India, on the other hand the foreign rule and its natural consequences continued the spirit and atmosphere of the Middle Ages down to the time of the national re-awakening towards the end of the 19th century.

Owing to its excessive reverence to the past, the Hindu mind ceased to be assimilative from about

800 A.D. Hindu sculptors assimilated some of the Greek methods and enriched Indian art. Early astronomers like Āryabhaṭa and Varāhamihira were keeping themselves in touch with the activities and achievements of the workers in the same field outside India. Varāhamihira pays even a handsome compliment to Greek astronomers and observes, "The Greeks are no doubt Mlechchhas (impure) but they are well grounded in astronomy and are therefore worshipped and honoured like the Ṛishis[1]." A remarkable change for the worse took place in the Hindu attitude towards foreign scholarship within a couple of centuries or so after Varāhamihira's death. Implicit faith in the past and in the correctness of its canonized tradition made the Hindu scholar narrow, bigotted and conceited. Of the Hindu men of letters of the 11th century A. D., Alberuni observes, "They are haughty, foolish, vain, stolid and self-conceited. According to their belief, there is no country on the earth but theirs, no other race of men but theirs, and no created beings besides them that have any knowledge of science whatever. Their haughtiness is such that if you tell them of any science or scholar in Khūrāsān or Persis, they will think you to be both an ignoramus and a liar. If they travelled and mixed with other nations, they would soon change their mind, for their ancestors were not so narrow-minded as the present generation

[1] म्लेच्छा हि यवनास्तेषु सम्यक् शास्त्रमिदं स्थितम् । ऋषिवत्तेऽपि पूज्यन्ते······ ॥ *Bṛihatsaṁhitā*, II, 14.

is."[1] In proof of the last assertion Alberuni quotes the tribute of Varāhamihira to Greek astronomers, quoted on the last page.

Hindus in Alberuni's time had very good reason to feel a deep prejudice against Muslim scholarship; Alberuni's picture may also have been to some extent overdrawn. But the contemporary Hindu attitude towards the Śrutis, Smṛitis and Purāṇas and other works of the past, which has been discussed above, would show that Alberuni's account of the mentality of the contemporary Hindu scholar is substantially true. Hindu education had ceased to remove prejudices, explode superstitions and broaden the mind, so as to keep it capable of receiving instructions from all quarters by the beginning of the 10th century A. D. Hindu colonising activity, necessitating travel abroad, had also come to an end by this time. Some Hindu doctors are no doubt known to have proceeded to Baghdad at the invitation of Khalifa Harun (786 A. D.-808 A. D.) to act as chief physicians in his hospitals;[2] we however do not know whether public opinion approved of their conduct, whether they returned home and were re-admitted to the Hindu society. Foreign travel for the purpose of education and broadening of views became impossible when the sea voyage was prohibited. Whether it was undertaken in earlier

1 Sachau, Alberuni, I, pp. 22-23

2 *Ibid*, Introduction, p. 31.

days also is doubtful. There are no books in Sanskrit literature descriptive of geography, manners and climate of the countries adjacent to India. Nor do the Pauranic geographers seem to have been in touch with the traders and colonisers, who were familiar with Babylon, Arabia, Ceylon, Burma, Java, Sumatra and Borneo.

It has been shown already how the skill in manual training and industrial arts was highly appreciated in early times. Liberal and useful education was usually combined among high class workers. Brahmanas used to be skilled in mining and metallurgy, medical and military sciences. Weavers were often amateur students of literature, folk lore, astronomy and the art of war. This combination of liberal and useful education began to become progressively rare after the Gupta age. The status of the Vaishya became assimilated to that of the Śūdra as early as the 1st century A.D., and talented persons among the intellectual classes began to think it below their dignity to follow useful and industrial arts. The level of intelligence among the industrial classes became lowered down when their education became rigidly confined to the technique and processes of their own professions from about the 9th century A. D. As a natural consequence of such a state of affairs, the growth and development of the fine, useful and industrial arts became arrested in India from about the 9th century A. D. No advance is to be seen after that date in the realms of sculpture, painting, mining, medicine, surgery, etc. The old type of learning became stereotyped and it soon began to degenerate. It is true that India continued to retain her dominating position in the weaving industry down to the middle of the last century; but it is doubtful whether any progress was made in the technique or processes of its manufacture during the last one thousand years.

At the time when India was making rapid strides in the different domains of knowledge, her education was broad based. In ancient Athens one in ten and in ancient Sparta one in twenty five received education, and women's education was altogether neglected.[1] The case was much different in India down to the commencement of the Christian era. The Śūdras were excluded only from the Vedic studies and we have seen already how literacy was probably as high as 60 per cent in the days of Asoka. Anxious thought and care was also bestowed on female education. Things, however, gradually changed for the worse in the first millennium of the Christian era. The education of women began to be neglected. Kshatriyas and Vaishyas began to become progressively illiterate. It is true that in Europe also the masses were little more than barbarous and took more naturally to warfare than to schooling down to the end of the Middle Ages. We can, however, hardly derive any consolation from this comparison, for the prevalent

---

1 Monroe, *A Text Book*, pp. 26, 29.

2 *Ibid*, p. 261.

illiteracy in India was due to degeneration from a more creditable condition, obtaining in earlier centuries.

Hindu education system was unable to stop this deterioration probably because of its concentration on Sanskrit and neglect of the vernaculars. The revival of Sanskrit that took place early in the first millennium was undoubtedly productive of much good; it immensely enriched Sanskrit literature in its various branches. But when the best minds became engaged in expressing their thoughts in Sanskrit, Prakrits were naturally neglected. As long as Sanskrit was intelligible to the ordinary individual, this was not productive of much harm. But from about the 9th or the 10th century A. D. Prakrits and vernaculars became widely differentiated from Sanskrit and those who were using them began to find it difficult to understand the latter language. Hindu education thinkers did not realise the importance of developing Prakrit literatures in the interest of the man on the street. Alberuni observes, "The language in India is divided into a *neglected vernacular one,* only in use among the common people, and a classical one only in use among the upper and educated classes, which is much cultivated."[1] We no doubt come across a few cases from the 13th century onwards where provision was made for the teaching of Telagu, Canarese and Marathi in some of the schools and colleges of South India, but the general impression produced by a survey of educational system and

[1] Sachau, I, p. 18.

23

institutions is that educationists were not alive to the importance of the teaching and development of vernaculars in the interest of the spread of education among the masses. Things in India were however quite on a par with what they were in contemporary Europe, where Latin continued to be the medium of instruction down to the 17th century A. D. India however could have been much in advance of the world ideas in this matter if the impetus that was given to the cultivation of vernaculars by the two gifted Seers, Mahāvīra and the Buddha, had not died down owing to the revival of Sanskrit.

Hindu education was thorough, but it was not sufficiently broad. Each branch was thinking of its own problems. Educationalists do not seem to have bestowed much thought on the relative utility of the study of the different branches like grammar, literature, logic, philosophy, mathematics and fine arts for the development of the intellect. Specialisation was started too early. A broad-based secondary course embracing a study of grammar, literature, mathematics, astronomy and history did not exist. An undue emphasis was laid on grammar, literature and logic at the cost of history, mathematics and astronomy. Here again the impartial historian has to point out that this defect of the Hindu Education System was not peculiar to India, but was to be seen all over the contemporary civilised world. In Europe all the energies of teachers and students were concentrated on grammar, rhetoric and dialectics down to the 13th century; only that much knowledge of arithmetic was given which was necessary to calculate the church festivals. Natural sciences were introduced very reluctantly only by the middle of the last century.[1]

Some of the defects noted above like the neglect of the education of women and the masses crept into the Hindu Education System only in later times; others like the non-existence of a broad-based secondary course and the neglect of the vernaculars were common to all the contemporary systems. The twentieth century critic often forgets that the West has gone on progressing rapidly during the last 300 years owing to the impetus it has received from the Renaissance, Reformation and the Scientific Movement, while India has gone on deteriorating ever since 1000 A. D. owing to the almost continuous foreign rule and its inevitable consequences. Our Muslim brethren no doubt became domiciled in India, but they were unable to appreciate and encourage Hindu culture and education. The effects of the Muslim rule on the learning and scholar-

---

[1] In Germany, science was introduced in secondary education in 1816 A. D. When the Royal Commission on Education apologetically pleaded for the inclusion of science in the secondary course in 1856, 10 or 12 lectures began to be given annually in some of the Public Schools of England. Faculty of Science was established in London University only in 1860.

ship of Hindus can be described in the words of a Muslim himself. While describing the state of Hindu learning after the invasions of Mahmud of Ghazni, Alberuni observes, 'The present times are not of this kind; they are the very opposite, (because there is no royal support or encouragement to learning) and therefore it is quite impossible that a new science or any new kind of research should arise in our days. *What we have of sciences is but the scanty remains of bygone better times.*'[1] Bernier, while describing the state of Hindu education in Benares towards the middle of the 17th century, observes: "Students stay for ten or twelve years during which the work of instruction proceeds but slowly. ... Feeling no spirit of emulation and entertaining no hope that honour or emoluments may be the reward of extraordinary attainments as with us, the scholars pursue the studies slowly, without much to distract their attention."[2] The Report of Bengal Provincial Committee, Education Commission, 1882, observes: "The Mahomaden conquest proved disastrous to all indigenous educational institutions. ... The proprietory rights in land changed hands ........ The language of the court was changed. Indigenous learning lost most of its support; and after the classes had settled down the well-to-do classes of the Hindus took gradually to the cultivation of foreign language, literature and manners. The *tols* were more and more

---

[1] Sachau, I, p. 252.

[2] Bernier, *Travels in the Mogul Empire*, p. 334.

deserted and left to those only who wanted to learn the Hindu rituals. ........ In course of time the Mussalman teachers and schools drew off the largest portion of the upper and the middle classes of the community and the *tols* and the *pāṭhaśālās* either died or barely managed to survive."[1]

It is therefore hardly fair to compare 'the scanty remains of by-gone better times' with the tremendous advance the West has made during the last century and half under very favourable circumstances.[2] The impartial historian will have to note that in the heyday of her glory, education in India was broad-based, women and a large section of the masses being admitted to its privileges and advantages. It was able to develop character and personality, inculcate civic virtues, and turn out citizens well qualified to follow their professions and discharge their duties in life. It was not only able to preserve the heritage of the past but also to enrich it from generation to generation. It produced a galaxy of able scholars and thinkers from age to age, who made important contributions to the

---

[1] p. 2.

[2] The historically correct procedure would be to compare Hindu Sanskrit learning at the advent of the British rule with the scholarship of the Christian monks who kept the lamp of learning burning during the Dark Ages. If such a comparison is instituted, India will have nothing to be afraid of.

advancement of knowledge in the spheres of philosophy, logic, mathematics, astronomy, medicine and chemistry. It enabled India to achieve high material prosperity by the excellent arrangements it made for training young men in commerce, industry and fine and useful arts. The general principles, which underlay the system,—like intellectual freedom, individual attention to students, the monitorial system, the *gurukula* ideal, plain living and high thinking, mass education, combination of useful and liberal education, etc.—are inherently sound and capable of yielding excellent results even in modern times, if applied with due regard to changed circumstances.

## APPENDIX A.

### YAJÑOPAVITA OR THE SO-CALLED SACRED THREAD.

Yajñopavīta is at present understood as the Sacred Thread, that is to be worn by the twice-born classes from the time of the Upanayana ceremony onwards. The popular belief is that the Upanayana ceremony is primarily intended for investing the boy with this mysterious thread, and the Śrāvaṇī ritual for the purpose of renewing it annuallv we have already shown how both these conceptions are wrong. (*Ante*, pp. 21, 34) Here we propose to trace briefly the history of Yajñopavīta.

Later writers explain Yajñopavīta thread as symbolical of the Guṇamayī Māyā as it was visualised by the Creator at the time of creation;[1] but its original significance was entirely different. Grammatically, Yajñopavīta is an adjective and refers to something that was worn at the time of the sacrifice.

Hindu notion of decency required that the upper part of the body should be properly covered when one

---

[1] सिसृक्षुरेक एवाग्रे समासीनः शिवः स्वयम् ।
दृष्ट्वा गुणमयीं मायां सूत्ररूपामिवाकरोत् ॥
तया तदात्मकं विष्णुं स्पृष्ट्वा पाले दिवौकसाम् ।
स्वयं ब्रह्माऽभवद्रुद्रो रुद्रश्चास्य जयाय सः ॥
ज्ञानात्मकेन हरिणा ब्रह्मात्मनि शिवेऽव्यये ।
तत्सूत्रमुपवीतत्वाद्ब्रह्मसूत्रमिदं कृतम् ॥

Aśvalāyana quoted in *VMS*, p. 419.

was engaged in sacred functions like sacrifices, charity or *svādhyāya.*[1] Yajñopavīta denoted the upper garment when it was worn in the proper manner prescribed for sacred occasions. *Taittirīya Saṁhitā* is explicit on the point; it says that Yajñopavīta means wearing the garment in a particular manner; when the garment is passed under the right and over the left shoulder, it becomes Yajñopavīta according to the authority of Brāhmaṇa works.[2] The same garment was called Prāchīnā...ta when it was worn exactly in the reverse way, and Nivīta wh... it was allowed to hang down like a garland.

The upper garment that was thus used was normally a piece of cloth. But in prehistoric times when the art of spinning and weaving was not known, it was a piece of deer-skin. *Taittirīya Āraṇyaka* states that it should be a piece of deer-skin, rather than a piece of cloth.[3] In course of time when clothes became common, the upper garment also became a cotton product, but earlier tradition of the deer-skin was in a way preserved by continuing the use of a small deer-skin patch on such occasions. In later times when Yajñopavīta as a piece of cloth was replaced by Yajñopavīta in the

---

1 उत्तरं वासः कर्तव्यं पञ्चस्वेतेषु कर्मसु ।
स्वाध्यायोत्सर्गदानेषु भुक्ताचमनयोस्तथा ॥

Baudhāyana in *SCS*, p. 299.

2 वासो विन्यासविशेषो यज्ञोपवीतम् ।
दक्षिणं बाहुमुद्धरतेऽवधत्ते सव्यमिति यज्ञोपवीतमिति ब्राह्मणम् ।

3 अजिनं वासो वा दक्षिणत उपवीय । II.

form of the thread, this piece of deer-skin was strung into it. This custom still obtains at the time of Upanayana.

In the early period, Yajñopavīta was normally in the form of a full upper garment like the *Dupaṭṭā* of northern India or the *uparaṇe* of Maharashtra. *Āpastamba Dharma Sūtra* states distinctly that Yajñopavīta should be normally in the form of the upper garment; wearing a thread instead is only the second alternative.[1] Jātukarṇya quoted in the *Smritichandrikā* distinctly declares that Yajñopavīta in the form of the thread is permissible only when the upper garment of the normal size is not available.[2] The view of Ṛishyaśriṅga is the same.[3]

Yajñopavīta was to be worn on sacred occasions like the sacrifice or the prayer. In course of time the conception of the sacrifice changed; the whole life came to be viewed as a kind of sacrifice when everything that one does should be dedicated to the Creator. If then the Yajñopavīta was to be continuously used during the time one is engaged in sacred duties, it must be used all the twenty-four hours. This could be feasible only if the Yajñopavīta assumed a more

---

1 नित्यमुत्तरं वासः कार्यम् । अपि वा सूत्रमेवोपवीतार्थे । II, 2,4,21-22.

2 वस्त्रोत्तरीयाभावे द्व्यंगुलं त्र्यंगुलं चतुरंगुलं वा सूत्रैस्त्राकृति परिमण्डलं तदुत्तरीयं कुर्यात् । p. 84.

3 अपि वा वाससा यज्ञोपवीतार्थं कुर्यात्तदभावे त्रिवृता सूत्रेण । *Ibid*, quoted in *SCS.*, p. 84.

manageable form. It was probably on this account that Yajñopavīta was allowed to dwindle in form into the modern Sacred Thread. The alternatives placed before society were many. Some were in favour of the continuance of the old custom; they held that it was sufficient if the Yajñopavīta was worn as long as practicable; it need not be worn continuously for 24 hours.[1] Others were in favour of substituting a Kuśa rope for the unmanageable upper garment.[2] But Kuśa rope was not pleasant in touch and so some others advocated that cotton thread should be preferred for the purpose.[3] The reason in recommending the new substitutes was convenience and nothing else. For a long time they were not popular; hence we find that in the Upanayana ceremony, as it is described in most of the *Gṛihya-sutras*, there is no mention of the boy being invested with the Sacred Thread. In stead, we have the description of the boy being offered the *dupaṭṭā* or *uparaṇe* i. e. the upper garment at one stage of the ritual.

In course of time, however, owing to its obvious convenience, the innovation of the Sacred Thread became popular and its original significance was

---

[1] कार्पासक्षौमगोबालशणवल्कतृणोद्भवम् ।
सदा संभवतो धार्यमुपवीतं द्विजातिभिः ॥

*Nigamapariśishṭa in SCS*, p. 84.

[2] यज्ञोपवीतं कुरुते सूत्रं वस्त्रं वापि कुशरज्जुमेव वा ।

*Go. Gr. S.*, I. 2. 1.

[3] अपि वा सूत्रमेवोपवीतार्थे । *Āp. Dh. S.*, II. 2. 4. 22.

gradually forgotten. Brahmachāri was to wear only one Sacred Thread, but Snātaka was to wear two, one for the inner and the other for the upper garment.[1] It was clearly forgotten by this time that Yajñopavīta was intended to be the upper garment. If Snātaka was to wear two Yajñopavītas, the Gṛihastha must wear three, for he was one stage higher. The *Gṛihyā-saṅgraha* however thinks that this third Sacred Thread was in lieu of the upper garment.[2] Devala also holds the same view; an upper garment, he says, is not always at hand, hence the recommendation to wear the third Sacred Thread.[3]

In course of time Yajñopavīta came to be invested with mysterious efficacy. The *Āditya Purāṇa* declares that it has the power of destroying demons. When such notions began to prevail in society, it is no wonder that the view began to be advocated that the greater the number of the Sacred Threads, the better would be our spiritual and material welfare. Kāśyapa would recommend 2, 3, 5, or 10 Sacred Threads for the house-holder;[4] an anonymous text quoted by Mitramiśra is in favour of as many Sacred Threads as possible.[5]

---

[1] स्नातकानां द्वितीयं स्यादन्तर्वासस्तथोत्तरम् ।
Vasishṭha in *VMS.*, p. 421.

[2] तृतीयमुत्तरीयार्थे वस्त्राभावे तदिष्यते । *Ibid*, p. 91.

[3] तृतीयमुत्तरीयार्थे वस्त्रालाभे तदिष्यते । *SCS.*, p. 301.

[4] त्रीणि चत्वारि पञ्चाष्ट गृहिणः स्युर्दशापि वा ॥ *VMS.*, p. 421.

[5] आयुष्कामैः सदा धार्यं बहुयज्ञोपवीतकम् ॥ 'अन्यत्रापि' in *Ibid*.

All this vividly shows how the original significance of the Yajñopavīta was completely forgotten by this time.

When Yajñopavīta assumed the form of the thread, the custom gained ground of making each of its thread a constituent product of nine smaller threads. Oṅkāra, Agni, Bhaga, Soma, Pitṛis, Prajāpati, Vasu, Dharma, and Sarva-devas were taken to be the presiding deities of the nine threads of the Sacred Thread.

Even when the Yajñopavīta dwindled into the Sacred Thread, it could be occasionally removed in the course of the day. The Taittirīya, Kaṭha, Kaṇva, and Vājasaneya schools were in favour of permitting the removal of the Sacred Thread at the time of the daily bath;[1] the Ṛigvedins and the Sāmavedins, however, advocated the doctrine that the Sacred Thread should never be separated from one's person. The latter view eventually prevailed and still obtains in Hindu society.

---

[1] तैत्तिरीयाः कठाः काण्वाश्चरका वाजसेयिनः ।
कण्ठादुत्तार्य सूत्रं तु कुर्युर्वै क्षालनं द्विजाः ॥
बह्वृचाः सामगाश्चैव ये चान्ये यजुःशाखिनः ।
कण्ठादुत्तार्य सूत्रं तु पुनरर्हन्ति संस्क्रियाम् ॥ भृगु in *V.M.S.*, 421.

# APPENDIX B.

## CONVOCATION ADDRESSES.

### *Convocation address to Arts Graduates.*

A specimen of what may be described as a convocation address to Arts Graduates is to be found in the *Taittirīya Upanishad*, I, 11. As the passage is very interesting from several points of view, it is given below along with its translation.

वेदमनूच्याचार्योऽन्तेवासिनमनुशास्ति । "सत्यं वद । धर्म्मं चर । स्वाध्यायान्मा प्रमदः । आचार्याय प्रियं धनमाहृत्य प्रजातन्तुं मा व्यवच्छेत्सीः । सत्यान्न प्रमदितव्यम् । धर्म्मान्न प्रमदितव्यम् । कुशलान्न प्रमदितव्यम् । भूत्यै न प्रमदितव्यम् । स्वाध्यायप्रवचनाभ्यां न प्रमदितव्यम् । देवपितृकार्य्याभ्यां न प्रमदितव्यम् । मातृदेवो भव । पितृदेवो भव । आचार्य्यदेवो भव । अतिथिदेवो भव । यान्यनवद्यानि कर्म्माणि तानि सेवितव्यानि नो इतराणि । यान्यस्माकं सुचरितानि तानि त्वयोपास्यानि नो इतराणि । ये के चास्मच्छ्रेयांसो ब्राह्मणाः तेषां त्वयाऽऽसनेन प्रश्वसितव्यम् । श्रद्धया देयम् । अश्रद्धयाऽदेयम् । श्रिया देयम् । ह्रिया देयम् । भिया देयम् । संविदा देयम् । अथ यदि ते कर्मविचिकित्सा वा वृत्तविचिकित्सा वा स्यात् ये तत्र ब्राह्मणाः संमर्शिनः युक्ता आयुक्ता अलूक्षा धर्म्मकामाः स्युः यथा ते तत्र वर्तेरन् तथा तत्र वर्तेथाः । अथाभ्याख्यातेषु ये तत्र ब्राह्मणाः संमर्शिनः युक्ता आयुक्ता अलूक्षा धर्म्मकामाः स्युः यथा ते तेषु वर्तेरन् तथा तेषु वर्तेथाः । एष आदेशः । एष उपदेशः । एषा वेदोपनिषत् । एतदनुशासनम् । एवमुपासितव्यम् । एवमु चैतदुपास्यम् ।

## TRANSLATION.

After the teaching of the Veda is over, the preceptor exhorts the student:

"Speak the truth. Do your duty. Neglect not the daily study (of the Veda). After having brought to your teacher his proper reward, do not cut off the line of progeny. Do not swerve from the truth. Do not swerve from duty. Do not neglect what is useful. Do not miss opportunities to become great. Do not neglect the daily duties of learning and teaching (the Veda). Do not neglect the (sacrificial) works due to the Gods and Fathers.

Let your mother be to you like unto a god. Let your father be to you like unto a god. Let your teacher be to you like unto a god. Let your guest be to you like unto a god.

Whatever actions are blameless, those should be followed, not others. Whatever good works have been performed by us, those should be emulated by you, not others. And there are some Brahmanas better than we. They should be comforted by you by giving them a seat.

Whatever is given should be given with faith, not without faith,—with joy, with modesty, with fear, with kindness.

If there should be any doubt in your mind with regard to any duty or with regard to conduct,—in that case conduct yourself as Brahmanas, who possess good judgment, conduct themselves therein, whether they be appointed or not, as long as they are not too severe, but devoted to duty. And with regard to things that have been spoken against, conduct yourself as Brahmanas, who possess good judgment, conduct themselves therein, whether they be appointed or not, as long as they are not too severe, but devoted to duty.

Thus conduct yourself. This is the rule. This is the teaching. This is the true purport (Upanishad) of the Veda. This is the command. Thus should you observe. Thus should this be observed."

### *Convocation Address to Medical Graduates.*

We get a very good specimen of the convocation address to medical students in *Charakasaṁhitā*, Vimānasthāna, 8, 6-8. Important passages from it are given below, along with an English rendering.

अनुज्ञातेन प्रविचरता [त्वया] पूर्वं गुर्वर्थोपान्वाहरणे यथाशक्ति प्रयतितव्यम्। कर्मसिद्धिमर्थसिद्धिं यशोलाभं प्रेत्य च स्वर्गमिच्छता त्वया गोब्राह्मणमादौ कृत्वा सर्वप्राणभृतां शर्माशासितव्यम्। अहरहरुत्तिष्ठता चोपविशता च सर्वात्मना चातुराणामारोग्ये प्रयतितव्यम्। जीवहेतोरपि चातुरेभ्यो नाभिद्रोग्धव्यम्। मनसापि च परस्त्रियो नाभिगमनीयास्तथा च सर्वमेव परस्वम्। निभृतवेशपरिच्छदेन भवितव्यम्। अशौण्डेनापापेनापापसहायेन च श्लक्ष्णशुक्लधर्म्यशर्म्यधन्यसत्यहितमितवचसा देशकालविचारिणा स्मृतिमता ज्ञानोत्थापनकरणसंपत्सु नित्यं यत्नवता न च कदाचित्.........अनपवादप्रतिकाराणां मुमूर्षूणां च तथैवासन्नि-

हितेश्वराणां स्त्रीणामनध्यक्षाणां वौषधमनुविधातव्यम् । न च कदाचित्स्त्रीदत्तमामिषमादातव्यमननुज्ञातं भर्त्राथवाऽध्यक्षेण । आतुरकुलं.................. चानुप्रविश्य वाङ्मनोबुद्धीन्द्रियाणि न क्वचित्प्रणिधातव्यानि अन्यत्रातुरादातुरोपकारार्थादातुरगतेष्वन्येषु वा भावेषु । न चातुरकुलप्रवृत्तयो बहिर्निश्चारयितव्याः । ह्रसितं चायुःप्रमाणमातुरस्य न वर्णयितव्यम् जानतापि तत्र यत्रोच्यमानमातुरस्यान्यस्य वाप्युपघाताय संपद्यते ।

विज्ञानवतापि च नात्यर्थमात्मनो ज्ञाने विकत्थितव्यम् । आप्तादपि हि विकत्थ्यमानादत्यर्थमुद्विजन्त्येके । न चैव ह्यस्ति सुतरामायुर्वेदस्य पारम् । तस्मादप्रमत्तः शश्वदभियोगमिच्छन् गच्छेत् ।....। कृत्स्नो हि लोको बुद्धिमतामाचार्यः । शत्रुश्चाबुद्धिमतामेव । अतश्चाभिसमीक्ष्य बुद्धिमताऽमित्रस्यापि यशस्यं...पौष्टिकं....लौक्यमुपदिशता वचः श्रोतव्यमनुविधातव्यं चेति ।

## ENGLISH RENDERING.

"When, on getting permission, you begin to practise, you ought to make an effort to offer an adequate honorarium to your teacher. You should aim at the welfare of Brahmanas, cows and all other beings with a view to win practice, prosperity and fame here and heaven hereafter. Every day you should continuously and whole-heartedly try to promote the health of patients. Even if your own life is in danger, you should not neglect your patients. You should not entertain an evil thought about the wealth or wives of others. Your dress should be modest, not foppish. Avoid drinking, do not commit a sin, nor help one who is committing it. Your speech should be smooth, polished, truthful and to the point. Taking all facts into consideration, you should make a deliberate endeavour to increase the stock of your knowledge and instruments. Do not give medicine to those whose disease is definitely ascertained to be incurable, or to those who are about to die, or to women, if their husbands or guardians are not present. Do not accept any fees from ladies without the assent of their husbands or guardians. When you enter a patient's room, all your attention should be centred on the patient, his expression, movements and medicines, to the exclusion of everything else. You must treat as strictly confidential all information about the patient and his family. Where there is a danger of the patient or any of his relatives receiving a shock, you should not divulge the impending death of the patient even when you are aware of it.

Though well grounded in your line, you should not praise your knowledge much; for some people get disgusted even with their friends and relatives if they are given to boasting. One can never get a mastery of the entire medical science; unelated, one should therefore pass one's time in making a constant effort to learn something more. A wise man will indeed gather something from every quarter; a fool only thinks otherwise, and shows jealousy. Taking all things into consideration, a wise physician should listen to and derive benefit from the discoveries or observations even of an enemy, if they are calculated to promote one's fame and prosperity in this world.

# BIBLIOGRAPHY

## Original sources

### (1) Religious books

Ṛigveda, Atharvaveda, and Yajurveda Saṁhitās

Śatapatha, Gopatha, Aitareya and Jaimini Upanishad Brāhmaṇas.

Bṛihadāraṇyaka, Chhāndogya, Taittirīya, Praśna, Muṇḍaka and Kaṭha Upanishads.

Taittirīya Prātiśakhya

Mānava, Āpastamba, Aśvalāyana, Pāraskara, Gobhila, Bhāradvāja, Drāhyāyaṇa, Jaimini, Hiraṇyakeśi, Baudhāyana and Vārāha Gṛihyasūtras.

Āpastamba, Hārīta, Baudhāyana, Vaśishṭha, Gautama and Vishṇu Dharmasūtras.

Nirukta

Pātañjala Mahābhāshya

The Rāmāyaṇa and the Mahābhārata

Manusmṛiti and Medhātithi's commentary on it.

Yājñavalkyasmṛiti and the commentaries of Aparārka and Vijñāneśvara on it.

Parāśarasmṛiti and Mādhava's commentary on it. (Bombay Sanskrit Series Edition)

Nāradasmṛiti

Yama, Bṛihaspati, Kātyāyana, Hārīta, Atri, Śankha, Vyāsa, Saṁvarta, Kāśyapa and Aśvalāyana Smṛitis as quoted by digest writers.

Bṛihatparāśarasmṛiti. (Bombay Sanskrit Series)

Vīramitrodaya of Mitramiśra (Jivānand's edition)
Smṛitichandrikā of Devaṇabhaṭṭa, (Mysore University edition)
Sanskāraratnamālā of Gopīnathabhaṭṭa.
Ādi, Kūrma, Padma and Bhavishya Purāṇas.

(2) Buddhist works

Diggha, Majjhima and Anguttara Nikāyas
Mahāvagga. Therīgāthā. Milinda Pañha (S. B. E. edition)
Jātakas. (Fausboll's edition). Lalitavistāra
Chalmers, Further Dialogues of the Buddha, Vols. I & II. London, 1926.

(3) Literary works.

Mālavikāgnimitram. Uttararāmacharit. Harshacharit. Kāvyamīmānsā. Kathāsaritsāgara.

(4) Technical works.

Charaka and Suśruta Saṁhitās. Dhanurvedasaṁhitā of Vaśiṣhṭha (edited by Hardayalu Swami, Sanskrit Pustakālaya, Meerut, 1899.)
Vāstuvidyā (Trivendrum Sanskrit Series)
Āryabhaṭīya of Āryabhaṭa
Bṛihatsaṁhitā of Varāhamihira.

(5) Archæological sources.

Ancient Indian Inscriptions as published in various journals like Epigraphia Indica, Indian Antiquary, Epigraphia Carnatica, South India Inscriptions, Corpus Inscriptionum Indicarum, etc.

Annual Reports of the Archæological Survey
" " " South Indian Epigraphy.

(6) Foreign sources

M'crindle, Ancient India as described by Magasthenes and Arrian, Calcutta, 1926

M'crindle, The Invasion of India by Alexander the Great. Westminister, 1896.

Legge, Record of Buddhist Kingdoms, by Fa Hsien, Oxford, 1886.

Watters, On Yuan Chwang's Travells in India, Vols. I and II. London, 1904-5.

Beal, Life of Hiuen Tsiang by Shaman Hwui Li, London, 1911 (New edition).

Takakusu, A Record of the Buddist Religion by Itsing. Oxford, 1896.

Sachau, Alberuni's India, Vols. I and II, London 1888.

Nadvi, Arab aur Bharat ke sambandha, Hindi translation. Hindustani Academy, Allahabad.

Cordier, Yule's Travells of Marco Polo, London, 1926

Bernier, Travells in the Mogul Empire, Oxford, 1914.

## MODERN WORKS.

(1) General.

Winternitz, Geschichte der indischen Littertur. Leipzic, 1920

Macdonel and Keith, Vedic Index of Names and Subjects, London, 1912

Bloomfield, Rig-Veda Repititions. Harvard Oriental Series, 1916

V. A. Smith, Asoka, 3rd edition. Oxford, 1909

Vidyabhushana, A History of Indian Logic. Calcutta, 1921

Altekar, The Rāshṭrakūṭas and their Times. Poona, 1934

Altekar, A History of the Village Communities in Western India. Bombay, 1927

(2) Books on Education.

Keay, Ancient Indian Education. Oxford, 1918

Das, The Educationl System of the Ancient Hindus. Calcutta, 1930

Bokil, A History of Education in India, Vol. I. Bombay, 1925

Venkatesvaram, Indian Culture through the Ages, Vol. I. Education and the Propagation of Culture, Mysore University, 1928

Bose, Indian Teachers of the Buddhist Universities. Madras, 1923

S. C. Das, Indian Pandits in the Land of Snow. Calcutta, 1893

Report of the Education Commission, 1882, along with the reports of its provincial committees.

Munroe, A Text-book of the History of Education.

Graves, A History of Education.

# INDEX

## A



## B.

D



E

H



I

J



K



L



M

## S

T

U

W



Y



Z